Business Process Change Management

Springer

Berlin
Heidelberg
New York
Hong Kong
London
Milan
Paris
Tokyo

August-Wilhelm Scheer
Ferri Abolhassan · Wolfram Jost
Mathias Kirchmer
Editors

Business Process Change Management

ARIS in Practice

Foreword by Michael Hammer

With 123 Figures
and 11 Tables

 Springer

Professor Dr. Dr. h.c. mult. August-Wilhelm Scheer
e-Mail aw.scheer@ids-scheer.de

Dr. Ferri Abolhassan
e-Mail f.abolhassan@ids-scheer.de

Dr. Wolfram Jost
e-Mail w.jost@ids-scheer.de

IDS Scheer AG
Postfach 101534
66015 Saarbrücken
Germany

Dr. Mathias Kirchmer
e-Mail m.kirchmer@ids-scheer.com

IDS Scheer, Inc.
1205 Westlakes Drive, Suite 270
Berwyn, PA 19312
USA

ISBN 3-540-00243-X   Springer-Verlag Berlin Heidelberg New York

Bibliographic information published by Die Deutsche Bibliothek
Die Deutsche Bibliothek lists this publication in the Deutsche Nationalbibliografie;
detailed bibliographic data available in the internet at *http.//dnb.ddb.de*

Springer-Verlag Berlin Heidelberg New York
a member of BertelsmannSpringer Science + Business Media GmbH

http://www.springer.de
© Springer-Verlag Berlin Heidelberg 2003
Printed in Germany

Cover design: Erich Kirchner, Heidelberg

SPIN 10904602   43/3130 – 5 4 3 2 1 0 – Gedruckt auf säurefreiem Papier

Foreword I

Today's business environment is constantly changing: New customer require-ments or products, an evolving competition, new IT solutions like EAI or web services, outsourcing opportunities, mergers & acquisitions or changing legal re-quirements are just a few reasons for this change. Intra and inter-enterprise proc-esses of enterprises have to change accordingly. Therefore organizations have to ensure an efficient and effective business process change management in order to stay competitive and survive on the long term. This is a precondition to achieve and maintain business process excellence.

However, the execution of successful change management has been extremely dif-ficult. Many initiatives failed because of an unclear scooping and a missing defi-nition of deliverables. Only the comprehensive design of the business processes to be improved creates a basis for a focused management of change. Change man-agement can then be handled as a process by itself. It becomes measurable and can be controlled. It is an integral part of business process lifecycle management.

Key-enabler is the ARIS Toolset which supports all activities of the process and change management: Business strategies, the resulting process specifications and execution as well as the process controlling are executed by using ARIS tools – in the phase of change as well as during the daily operation.

This book defines business process change management as information, commu-nication, and training, executed based on the ARIS framework. Case studies from organizations like American Meter, the US Navy, or Amway show, how this change management is applied in practice using ARIS and the three-tier architec-ture of Business Process Excellence.

Finally it is demonstrated that Jazz and management have quite some communali-ties. Information, communication, and training are as important for a Jazz musi-cian as they are for business executives.

We would like to thank all authors who contributed to this book. Their willingness to share their lessons learned will help many other organizations. Special thanks to Michael Hammer for the contribution of the preface. Thanks also to the entire team who supported this book project from an administrative point of view.

Saarbrücken, Germany / Berwyn, USA, January 2003

Prof. Dr. Dr. h.c. mult. August-Wilhelm Scheer   Dr. Ferri Abolhassan

Dr. Wolfram Jost   Dr. Mathias Kirchmer

Foreword II

Few business innovations lead to as much and as deep organizational change as do business process reengineering and the shift to process management. Processes represent a fundamentally new way of thinking about, operating, and managing a business. The impacts of the shift to process begin at the front lines of the organization. Employees' jobs inevitably become broader and more complex, as their responsibilities move from performing individual tasks to working on larger segments of a process. Measurement systems, and the compensation and reward systems to which they are linked, are realigned around processes and their objectives, in order to focus people's attention appropriately. Skills are broadened, a deeper understanding of the business is developed, and more decision-making responsibility is vested at the individual level, all in response to focus on processes. Management is affected at least as much. To succeed in process environment, managers must shift their perspective from narrow functional or geographical units to cross-functional, end-to-end work. New managerial roles, especially that of the process owner, must be created and staffed, while traditional supervisors must move from a command-and-control orientation to being resource managers, supporting and enabling the people who perform the process. Above all, a new culture must permeate the organization, one based on teamwork, individual responsibility, and putting the customer first. Front-line workers can no longer pass the buck and escape blame by claiming that "it's not my job;" managers must move beyond protecting their turf to cooperating in pursuit of optimized enterprise performance and achieving corporate strategic goals. And underlying all of this is a new way of thinking – about work, about business, about one's own role. It is fortunate that the need for process management is so grave and the benefits that it brings are so dramatic, because otherwise the prospect of the amount of change it entails would intimidate all but the most adventurous organizations.

The problem with change is that people resist it – and the bigger the change, the more they resist it. Some managers seem to feel that resistance to change is some kind of Machiavellian plot, concocted by those whose positions and authority will be diminished by the impending change. Would that it were so limited and rational. In fact, resistance to change is a natural and universal human response. People inevitably become attached to, and invested in, whatever they are most familiar with; most people will respond negatively even to change that promises to be good for them. The problem is not the prospective new state itself; it is the pain of the transition from the old to the new. The Bible, in the Books of Exodus and Numbers, offers a remarkable case study of change and resistance to it. On the one hand, the Children of Israel are being asked to experience a change that is on the surface completely advantageous for them: from slavery to freedom, from Egypt to the Promised Land. But desert and wilderness – i.e., transition – lie between the bad old situation and the good new one. And so the Children of Israel continually raise objections to the path on which they are led, uttering frequent complaints and even longing to return to Egypt, the bad situation they know, rather than continuing on to the good one that they do not. The tension between the advantages that a change will yield and the pain inevitably associated with going through it causes mixed emotions even among those leading the charge. And it is just such mixed emotions that manifest themselves as resistance.

Resistance to change is simply any behavior that impedes the successful implementation of that change; such behavior can take innumerable forms. The one that most people not familiar with the realities of change assume will be most common – in fact, the one that they take as practically synonymous with resistance -- is sabotage. In fact, sabotage is both relatively rare and relatively easy to deal with, because it is so explicit. Far more common are such phenomena as passive resistance, in which people superficially support the change program while not taking any of the steps that such support would actually entail, and malicious compliance, where people ostensibly work in accord with the needs of the change program but do so in a way that undermines it. Probably the most common form of resistance, and certainly the most difficult to recognize and deal with, is arguing. Individuals profess absolute commitment to the goals of the enterprise and even to the need for change, but then raise endless objections to the specifics of the change program, requiring those conducting it to waste precious time and resource overcoming these objections. On the surface, these individuals seem on board; in fact, they are sapping the lifeblood out of a program that must either proceed quickly and with vigor or not at all.

In other words, resistance to change is inevitable, universal, and multi-faceted. It is therefore no surprise that it is now the leading cause of failure among organizations seeking to transform their performance by capitalizing on the power of their business processes. This was not always the case. In the early days of the reengineering movement, the lack of effective methodologies and tools was the major impediment to success; many companies (and the consultants advising them) simply did not know how to proceed. No longer. With more than a decade of experience under our collective belt, and the development of such systems as ARIS, the technical side of process management and redesign is relatively well under control. It is the soft side that now confounds us.

Unfortunately, companies do not yet have access to a similarly well-developed body of techniques for preventing and overcoming the many forms of resistance to process-based change. The field known as change management does not offer very much that managers can put to work. There is very little that is agreed-upon or standard in that field; each author has his or her own conception of the discipline. Grand new theories of change management appear and vanish with disturbing regularity. Moreover, too much of the literature on the topic is abstract and ethereal; managers seeking to apply it have little to go on. Even worse, virtually nothing in the change management field is directly applicable to the extraordinarily challenging context of the shift to process management; much of what has been written about change management was developed in situations far less complex and exigent. What much of change management considers change is introducing a new technology without transforming work methods, or conducting an organizational redesign without redefining jobs; in other words, changes that are far less extensive and multi-dimensional than those associated with the process transition.

For these reasons, the appearance of Business Process Change Management: ARIS in Practice is to be welcomed. This book offers concrete case studies and specific methodologies instead of abstract theories. It focuses explicitly on managing the changes associated with business process reengineering and the introduction of process management, instead of on other narrower kinds of organizational change. And it does not treat change management as a separate isolated field of endeavor, but rather one that is integrated organizationally and methodologically with the overall management of the process program. Both organizations contemplating process implementation, and those already in the midst of it, will profit from studying this book.

Boston, January 2003

Michael Hammer

Table of Content

Wolfgang Kraemer, imc information multimedia communication AG
Peter Sprenger, imc information multimedia communication AG

Wolfgang Kraemer, imc information multimedia communication AG
Peter Sprenger, imc information multimedia communication AG

August-Wilhelm Scheer, IDS Scheer AG

Change Management –
Key for Business Process Excellence

Mathias Kirchmer
President and CEO, IDS Scheer, Inc.
CEO, IDS Scheer Japan
Member of the Extended Executive Board, IDS Scheer AG

August-Wilhelm Scheer
Founder and Chairman of the Supervisory Board, IDS Scheer AG

Summary

In order to be successful in a changing and challenging business environment enterprises have to be organized in a business process oriented way. The ARIS-Three-Tier Architecture of Business Process Excellence is an example for the needed enterprise architecture.

Key tasks of change management are information, communication, and training – focusing on the effected people. The business process to be changed can be identified using reference models such as the Y-model. The change management content can be structured based on the ARIS framework.

The audience of change management activities has to be segmented carefully so that various groups of people can be addressed appropriately. Training has to be organized in a process oriented way. Enterprises must establish a common language of change. Modeling methods are efficient and effective for this task. Tools like the ARIS Toolset can be used to build a change management infrastructure to increase efficiency and effectiveness of change management initiatives.

Key Words

ARIS, ARIS Toolset, Three-Tier Architecture of Business Process Excellence, e-Business, Enterprise Architecture, BPM, Change Management, Communication, Continuous Process Improvement (CPI), M-Business, Information, EAI, Real Time Enterprise, Outsourcing, Reference Models, Training, Web Services, Y-Model

1. Change Management – What it Really is

In today's business environment enterprises have to act in a flexible and customer oriented way in order to meet economic challenges and ensure a long term survival of the organization. Therefore organizations move towards business process oriented architectures like defined with the Three-tier Architecture of Business Process Excellence" (cf. Jost & Scheer 2002): On a strategy level aspects like the general business process structure and strategy, the planned innovation and the underlying application system architecture are defined. The information is forwarded to the process specification layer, where the blueprint for the resulting business processes is specified, using techniques like simulation, best practice reference models or ABC costing. This process specification is used as the guideline for the implementation of all physical and information handling processes on the execution layer, within and across enterprises. All information systems, based on standard application software packages, individual developments, EAI components, web services, or business process execution engines are based on the business process specification. The actually executed processes are measured and controlled on the so-called controlling level. If there are differences observed between planned key performance indicators and the actual values, either a continuous improvement process (CPI) is started through the process specification layer or the situation is resolved on a strategic level. The Three-tier Architecture of Business Process Excellence is shown in Fig. 1:

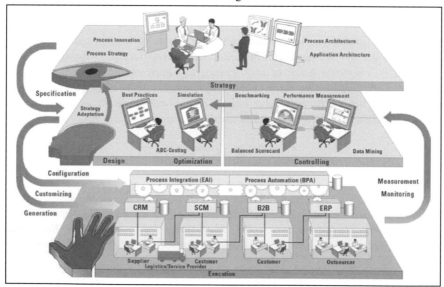

Fig. 1. Three-Tier Architecture of Business Process Excellence

Key advantage of such process-centered organizations is that it enables a fast and flexible reaction to changes. Changes that influence business processes may be caused by

- New or changing customers, suppliers or other market partners

- New or changed market offerings (goods, services, information, others)

- Mergers and Acquisitions

- Changing legal regulations

- Availability of new or modified technologies like application systems

- Outsourcing of specific activities

- New business models

- Cultural differences in various enterprise locations

- Others

The business driven use of new technologies like m-business create a tremendous change of business processes (cf. Kalakota & Robinson 2002). Fig. 2: "M-Business – Technology drives business process changes" shows on the left hand side a traditional process. A truck with office supplies arrives at an office supply store. Then the truck driver checks with the store clerk who consults his IT system to find out which supplies are needed. The truck driver books the necessary inventory changes and fills up the store shelves. Then the store clerk books the inventory adjustments. The M-business process on the right hand side of Fig. 2 shows how this procedure can be improved. The truck driver accesses with his mobile device, which contains a "process portal", his own and the store application systems so that he can do all bookings by himself. How cultural differences can influence business processes is shown in Fig. 3: "Business processes can reflect cultural differences".

4

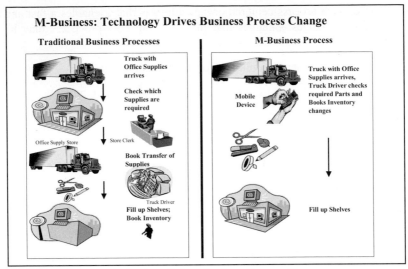

Fig. 2. M-Business – Technology Drives Business Process Changes

On the left hand side you see a process typical for Japanese environments. The quality assurance activities are carried out twice: on the customer and on the supplier side. The redundancy ensures highest quality standards and expresses the typical Japanese attention to details, although the process is not 100% efficient, as the one shown on the right hand side of Fig. 3. Depending on business goals and cultural environment one of the processes may be changed to the other.

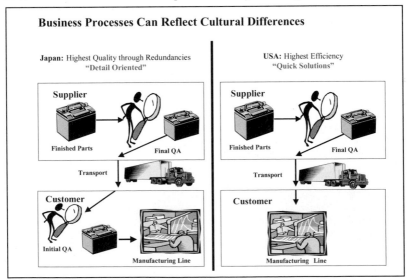

Fig. 3. Business Processes Can Reflect Cultural Differences

All the described business changes require according modifications or creations of business processes. Goal of change management is to ensure that the necessary changes of a business process fulfill the following conditions (cf. Spath et al 04/2001):

- Necessary actions are initiated with an acceptable delay after the change has happened (or has been decided to happen, if pro-active change management is needed)

- Necessary actions are executed in a fast and effective way

- All reactions and actions are initiated and executed in a controlled manner

An effective management of the permanent change becomes a key success-factor for an enterprise (cf. Collins 2001). It is of fundamental importance that the people involved in changing processes are able to understand and accept those changes and make them finally happen. Therefore the most appropriate definition of change management is (cf. Hammer & Stanton 1995):

- Information

- Communication

- Training

People have to be informed about the changes. Then their feedback is required. An intense communication starts. And finally people have to be trained to be success-ful in the new business process environment. Fig. 4: "Change Management – The Activities" shows this basic definition of change management.

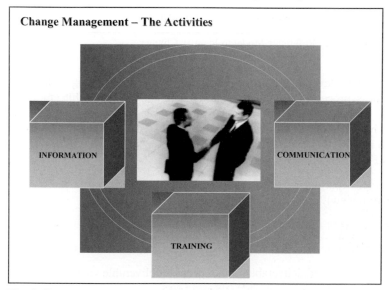

Fig. 4. Change Management – The Activities

6

Change management activities are always related to specific processes. The business processes involved in change management activities can be identified by using process reference models (cf. Kirchmer et al 2002, cf. Kirchmer 1999 Business...). Very well suited to accomplish this task on an enterprise level is the Y-Model as shown in Fig. 5: "Y-Model – Industry Reference Model to Identify Change" (cf. Scheer 1994 Computer..., cf. Scheer 1994 Business...). It shows on the left hand side all the order related processes, on the right hand side all produced focused processes. Horizontally it structures the processes in execution and planning processes. In addition to the shown "Y" the core support processes can be mentioned.

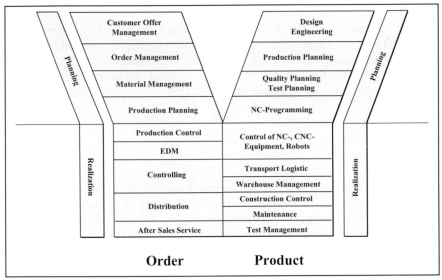

Fig. 5. Y-Model – Industry Reference Model to Identify Change

The content of the relevant information, communication, and training concerning specific business processes can be structured using the ARIS Architecture (cf. Scheer 1998 Business Process Frameworks, cf. Scheer 1998 Business Process Modeling). The major questions that have to be addressed in change management activities can be directly deducted from ARIS as shown in Fig. 6: "ARIS – Business Process Framework... for Change Management":

- Who (people, departments, different enterprises...) is involved in the change (Organization view)?

- What are the new or modified activities (function view)?

- What new or modified information is needed or produced (data view)?

- Which new or modified deliverables are expected (deliverable view)?

- How do the changes fit together and how do they influence the process logic (control view)?

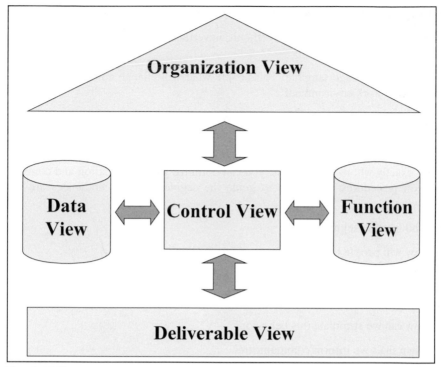

Fig. 6. ARIS – Business Process Framework… for Change Management

2. Preparing Information, Communication, and Training

Starting point of all change management activities are information and communication. Both have to be adapted to the cultural environment of the enterprise. Here some general guidelines (cf. Hammer & Stanton 1995):

- Segment the audience: Different groups of people have to be addresses differently

- Use multiple channels: People have personal preference from where they like to get their news

- Use multiple voices: Switch between various "messengers" who may each address people in another style which facilitates a high level of acceptance

- Be clear: Set clear expectations to avoid later disappointments

- Honesty is the only policy: Sooner or later people will find out the truth anyway

- Use emotions, not just logic: You are dealing with human beings...

- Encourage: Change is always difficult; nevertheless people have to feel good to be successful

- Make the message tangible: Tell people what will change concretely for them and their work environment

- Listen, listen, listen: Your people may know more about their processes than you

Basis to apply all these guidelines is the segmentation of the audience. Once you know exactly whom you address, you can optimize your information and communication procedures. Questions to guide the segmentation of audiences are the following:

- Who is in the segment?

- How will people be affected?

- What reaction will they have to it?

- What behavior will we need from them?

- How can we stimulate this behavior?

- When shall we inform/communicate?

- What medium should we use for each message?

- Who should communicate the message?

Challenges for successful change management activities result from disbelief, false familiarity, fear, the "rumor mill", incomprehensibility, abstraction, complexity, and the use of clichés.

Information and communication prepare the way for training activities. Those have also to be organized in a business process oriented way and address the relevant changes of today's processes. Business process oriented training can be divided up into four major phases (cf. Kirchmer 1999 Business...):

- Basic training – business

- Basic training – enabler

- Process training

- Kick-off training

In the basic business training the changing business background is explained. This allows people to understand the motivation for the change and ensures that they have the required general business know how. The basic "enabler" training is an introduction into new technologies or other enablers to be used in the changed processes. This training phase includes topics like the handling of application software products or the use of new process performance tools. The core-training phase is the process training. These training activities explain how to use the process enablers in the changed business environment. It basically trains all aspects concerning the execution of the new business processes. Shortly before executing the planned change a kick-off training is recommended. It ensures that people recall the key aspects of the change and know what to do in case of problems. The structure of the business process oriented training is shown in Fig. 7: "Business Process Oriented Training".

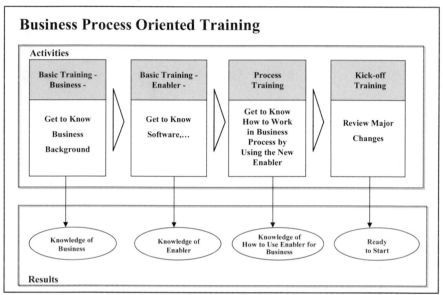

Fig. 7. Business Process Oriented Training

3.   Methods and Tools for the Realization

A key success factor for change management is the establishment of a "common language" to address the business process change and to set up an infrastructure for an efficient and effective application of this language. The language to describe the change of business processes must on one hand easy to use because every employee of a company has to deal with it. On the other hand it must be very precise to avoid misunderstandings. Therefore the use of graphical description methods, of modeling techniques, is recommended. Since the ARIS framework can be used to structure the content of all change management aspects, it can also be used to structure the required description methods, the language of change (cf. Scheer 1998 Business Process Modeling). Fig. 8: "ARIS – Basis of a common language for change" shows various modeling methods, structured based on the ARIS framework.

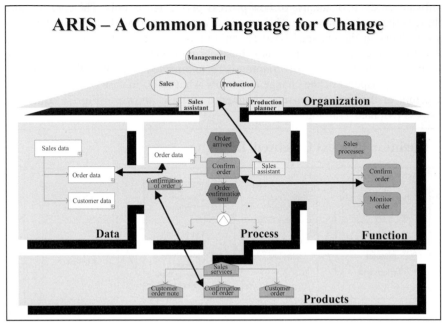

Fig. 8. ARIS – Basis of a Common Language for Change

Organizational changes can be described using org-charts, new activities can be explained by means of function trees, information needed or produced in a process can be described using entity relationship models (ERM), changing deliverables may be presented using hierarchy diagrams, finally the entire process including all relations between the different views on the business process can be described using methods like event-driven process chains (EPC). Especially the definition of new process deliverables in form of new market offerings should be done using appropriate graphical methods in order to understand the structure of those changes fully (cf. Kirchmer 1999 Market...).

The used modeling methods can vary depending on the target audience. Engineers may appreciate the use of very strict symbols like squares or diamonds, whereas manufacturing employees may prefer more "tangible" and concrete symbols in the modeling language. During the enterprise specific definition of the language of change the move from one modeling technique to another has to be defined carefully.

The effective use of such modeling methods as a language for change depends heavily on the tools put in place in order to apply the methods. Those tools have to be very user-friendly and ensure and efficient distribution of information across the organization. The use of Internet based technologies is therefore of high importance. However, it is not sufficient just to publish information through the intranet or Internet. The tools infrastructure must also encourage a communication concerning possible change. Consequently an active modeling via the web is a requirement. Fig. 9: "ARIS Toolset – Example for active web based modeling" shows the user-interface of a possible modeling environment that fulfills the described requirements (cf. IDS Scheer AG 02/2000).

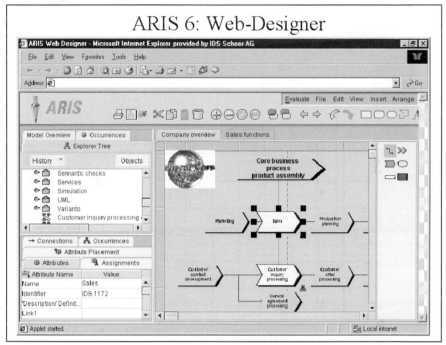

Fig. 9. ARIS Toolset – Example for Active Web Based Modeling

The execution of the necessary training activities is in many cases the largest change management challenge for an enterprise. Very often thousands of people have to be trained in new business processes and new enablers such as application systems. Therefore concepts of distance learning using the Internet as enabler become more and more important (cf. Kraemer & Mueller 1999, cf. Kirchmer 2002, cf. Kraemer et al 04/2001). This concept reduces the logistical challenges tremendously and ensures a constant and consistent training quality. Fig. 10: "Distance Learning via Internet" shows an example of such remote learning environments.

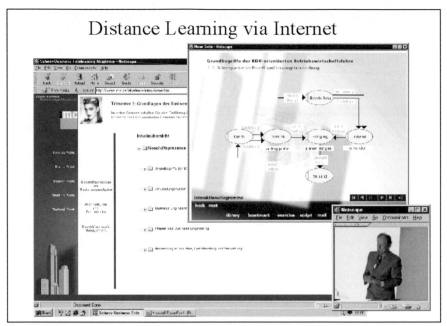

Fig. 10. Distance Learning via Internet

A business process centered enterprise, as described in Fig. 1, is run based on a process management infrastructure that can be easily extended to the described change management environment. With the controlling level it also includes an instance that discovers necessary changes on an operative level, e.g. using the ARIS Process Performance Manager (PPM) (cf. IDS 2000, Process…). The "Three-tier Architecture of Business Process Excellence" includes the necessary change management infrastructure, across all enterprise levels. Change management and continuous process improvement are integrated components of a business process oriented enterprise architecture. Therefore tools for business process lifecycle management, like ARIS or ARIS PPM, become key applications for organizations that manage change successfully.

4. References

Callaos, N., Loutfi, M., Justan, M. (editors): Proceedings of the 6th World Multiconference on Systemics, Cybernetics and Informatics. Orlando 2002.

Collins, J.: Good to Great – Why some companies make the leap…and others don't. New York 2001.

Elzina, D.J., Gulledge, T.R., Lee, C.-Y.: Business Engineering. Norwell 1999.

Hammer, M., Stanton, S.: The Reengineering Revolution. Glasgow 1995.

IDS Scheer AG (editor): Business Process Management – ARIS Toolset Products. White Paper, Saarbruecken 02/2000.

IDS Scheer AG (editor): Process Performance Manager. White Paper, Saarbruecken 02/2000.

Jost, W., Scheer, A.-W.: Business Process Management: A Core Task for any Company Organization. In: Scheer, A.-W., Abolhassan, F., Jost, W., Kirchmer, M.: Business Process Excellence – ARIS in Practice. Berlin, New York, and others 2002, p. 33-43.

Kalakota, R., Robinson, M.: M-Business – The race to mobility. New York e.a. 2002.

Kirchmer, M.: Business Process Oriented Implementation of Standard Software – How to Achieve Competitive Advantage Efficiently and Effectively. 2nd edition, Berlin, New York and others 1999.

Kirchmer, M.: e-Business Processes Improvement (eBPI) – Building and Managing Collaborative e-Business Scenarios. In: Callaos, N., Loutfi, M., Justan, M. (editors): Proceedings of the 6th World Multiconference on Systemics, Cybernetics and Informatics. Orlando 2002, Volume VIII, pp. 387-396.

Kirchmer, M.: Market- and Product-Oriented Definition of Business Processes. In: Elzina, D.J., Gulledge, T.R., Lee, C.-Y.: Business Engineering. Norwell 1999, p. 131-144.

Kirchmer, M., Brown, G., Heinzel, H.: Using SCOR and Other Reference Models for E-Business Process Networks. In: Scheer, A.-W., Abolhassan, F., Jost, W., Kirchmer, M.: Business Process Excellence – ARIS in Practice. Berlin, New York, and others 2002, p. 45-64.

Kraemer, W., Gallenstein, C., Sprendger, P.: Learning Management fuer Fuehrungskraefte. In: Industrie Management – Zeitschrift fuer industrielle Geschaeftsprozesse, 4/2001, pp. 55-59.

Kraemer, W., Mueller, M.: Virtuelle Corporate University – Executive Education Architecture and Knowledge Management. In: Scheer, A.-W. (Editor): Electronic Business und Knowledge Management – Neue Dimensionen fuer den Unternehmenserfolg. Heidelberg 1999, pp. 491-525.

Scheer, A.-W.: Business Process Engineering. 2nd edition, Berlin, New York, and others 1994.

Scheer, A.-W., Abolhassan, F., Jost, W., Kirchmer, M.: Business Process Excellence – ARIS in Practice. Berlin, New York, and others 2002.

Scheer, A.-W.: ARIS – Business Process Frameworks. 2nd edition, Berlin, New York and others 1998.

Scheer, A.-W.: ARIS – Business Process Modeling. 2nd edition, Berlin, New York and others 1998.

Scheer, A.-W.: CIM – Computer Integrated Manufacturing. 3rd edition, Berlin, New York, and others 1994.

Scheer, A.-W. (Editor): Electronic Business und Knowledge Management – Neue Dimensionen fuer den Unternehmenserfolg. Heidelberg 1999.

Spath, D., Baumeister, M., Barrho, T., Dill, C.: Change Management im Wandel. In: Industrie Management – Zeitschrift fuer industrielle Geschaeftsprozesse, 4/2001, pp. 9-13.

The Change Management Process Implemented at IDS Scheer

Ferri Abolhassan
CEO, IDS Scheer AG

Summary

Change Management is often associated with so-called soft factors and is considered difficult to manage. This article intends to show that Change Management is no different from any other business process; that it can, in fact, be measured and controlled, and what methodology is required to achieve this goal.

Additionally, this article will use a case study to show how a Change Management process was carried out within IDS Scheer's Field Management Team and to demonstrate the benefits derived from this process of change.

Key Words

Change Management Process, Business Process, ARIS – Business Process Framework for Change Management, Change Team, Information, Communication, Training, Measurement, Control, Change Roadmap, Internationalization, Information Interface, Country Coaching, Roll-in Process, Roll-out Process, Integration

16

1. Change Management as a Managerial Issue

Nothing is as certain as change! A company's ability to adapt to external changes in its environment is becoming more and more important in order to stay competitive in today's globalized world. Change Management can help ensure your success in daily business life.

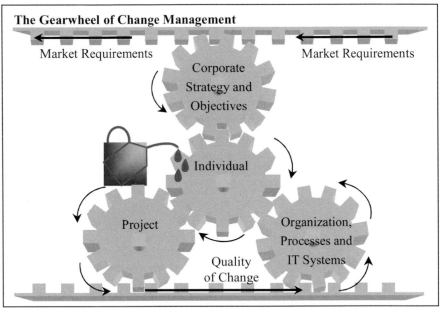

Fig. 1. The Gearwheel of Change Management

But what do we mean by Change Management? Change Management is an organized and systematic application of the knowledge, tools and resources for change. Change Management provides an organization with a core process for achieving its business strategy and staying competitive and responsive in an environment that is constantly changing.

The main idea that made Change Management so popular can be traced back to books such as Tom Peters' "In Search of Excellence" or Rosabeth Moss Kanter's "The Change Masters". Born out of the concept of "management by objectives", it emphasized the ability to respond to changes during a project. Put another way, the philosophy was that you should be prepared before embarking upon a journey: Change Management was the key to coping with changes encountered along the way.

The fact that Change Management deals with so-called soft factors sometimes makes it difficult for companies to manage change effectively. This situation can be improved if Change Management is defined according to a set framework of processes.

2. The Change Management Process

Change Management is business process like any other that a company carries out. This means that clearly defined targets and a strategy are required to achieve a particular goal for change. A business process is based upon a specific organizational structure, a clear definition of relevant functions and data; it can be controlled and can be illustrated clearly. All of these necessary factors are combined in the ARIS – Business Process Framework for Change Management (cf. Kirchmer & Scheer 2003). Treating Change Management as a process also allows you to measure the result.

The organization needs to clearly define the aims and strategy of the change to be made. This definition must be supported by the promoters and stakeholders of the company to lead to the desired change. The aims and strategy for the change should be managed by a specific functional entity, or Change Team. The Change Team must establish a clear, transparent and bi-directional information flow that is mandatory for the entire company and team. The newly changed and improved process must then be implemented and actively carried out within the company. In order to do this, the relevant target group also needs to be trained.

This process requires a clear communication plan including key messages, relevant communication channels, appropriate media types, e.g. newsletter, Intranet platforms, frequent contact, binding time schedules and the possibility for feedback. This allows for the involvement of all employees, ensures a high quality of change and increases the level of acceptance. Thus, the three main activities of Change Management are information, training and communication (cf. Kirchmer & Scheer 2003). These may all be monitored in various ways. The activities can be summed up in a Change Roadmap and be monitored and controlled.

Additional requests for change must be transferred into the existing process and will result in a continuous process of improvement for the entire organization.

3. Case Study: Change Management and Internationalization at IDS Scheer

IDS Scheer AG has seven subsidiaries in Germany and eighteen worldwide, all offering the complete IDS Scheer AG product and service portfolio. The company's international expansion began in 1995 with the establishment of a US subsidiary.

In addition to the subsidiaries owned by IDS Scheer AG, the company is also present in 50 countries worldwide through an extensive partner network. Until recently, the subsidiaries were part of the IDS Scheer Group, but the group did not function as a global company.

In 2001, the internationalization of the company was organized by means of a well developed and structured Change Management process based on the ARIS framework, (cf. Kirchmer & Scheer 2003). This process reflected the basic structure of Change Management and met the requirements of the international subsidiaries while using resources that already existed at IDS Scheer headquarters in Germany. These resources were bundled within the Field Management Team.

3.1 The Field Management Team as Information Interface and Functional Multiplier

The aim of the Field Management team is to enable international growth. To achieve this goal, it needs to function as an interface for information and a multiplier of knowledge.

The communication tools employed vary in form depending on the country in question. Along with standard communication devices such as telephone, fax and e-mail for long-distance communication, direct visits to the subsidiaries and regular meetings of all Managing Directors at the German headquarters are used to establish fixed and clearly defined routes and processes of communication.

In addition to direct forms of communication, an international newsletter informs all employees of IDS Scheer about the firm's international activities and provides news from the subsidiaries. This newsletter has no strict focus as far as what information is included. The usual content deals with new international customers and their projects, new product information or marketing materials that are of importance to employees of IDS Scheer and that might support cross-selling potential. The content is coordinated though an international lead and pipeline management structure. The design of the process allows the entire IDS Scheer Group to improve planning, selling and staffing of projects all over the world.

The Field Management Team has intensive knowledge of the national and international activities of the IDS Scheer Group. This is one of its biggest advantages, since the Team can function as a multiplier, interface and catalyst for information. The process works by assigning specific members of the Field Management Team to a certain country and task. They thus develop a deep knowledge of the specific needs and cultural differences present in the country for which they are providing information.

3.2 The Organization of the Field Management Team

The Field Management Team was implemented and introduced into the entire IDS Scheer organization as an independent body that reports to a relevant board member.

Nevertheless, the information flow into the Field Management Team comes from all parts of the company.

The Field Management Team consists of 5 members. Each member is responsible for a country or region, and, additionally, for a special field such as Sales, Marketing or Financial Controlling.

This form of international Country Coaching ensures that no discussions of competencies arise and disturb the flow of communication and information.

All of the team members are required to have very strong communication skills, be able to speak more than two languages and have an international corporate perspective. Additionally they should be familiar with the corporate culture of the IDS Scheer Group and have knowledge of the cultural features specific to the countries they support.

Due to the necessity for specific knowledge about IDS Scheer AG and its corporate culture, all of the team members were selected from within the company structure of IDS Scheer AG.

3.3 Exchange of Data Through the Field Management Team

Normally, information about the sales pipeline, new customers, requests for resources or financial figures are communicated between the international subsidiaries, headquarters and the Field Management Team. Additionally, this data may include products, services, special knowledge and skills, the availability of resources, market requirements and country-specific needs. The data is communicated by either a push or a pull concept. Again, this allows countries to accept the Field Management Team as an interface between the specific departments and their country.

To achieve a consistent standard of data transfer, all IDS Scheer subsidiaries use identical software platforms and applications. This ensures a high standard of data quality and therefore reduces the costs associated with time-consuming formatting activities.

3.4 Controlling Through the Field Management Team

The monthly report of the data delivered from the international subsidiaries allows the IDS Scheer management to control and coordinate new issues related to change or to the demands of customers and stakeholders within IDS Scheer. Resource planning can be optimized, sales activities can be coordinated and sales figures can improve planning and forecasting for the company as well as the shareholders. The Field Management Team is able to deliver the relevant data for the international subsidiaries. The fact that there is one dedicated team involved – or in some instances, one team member – makes it easier to condense relevant information and communicate changes.

3.5   The Roll-in and Roll-out Process at IDS Scheer AG

The Change Management process that resulted from the activities outlined in the above sections can be described in a consolidated form using the example of the Field Management Team's Roll-in and Roll-out process. This process is based upon a dedicated communication plan that includes clearly defined milestones and activities (e.g. publishing date for the newsletter) but is also open to ad hoc requests for information. The primary factors and deliverables are based on the change requested by the customer or defined by information that will benefit the customer. In either case, a continuous improvement process results from all the demands that have to be fulfilled in order to meet the expectations of the customer or the stakeholders.

Now that a great degree of integration has been achieved, the Field Management Team can identify changes in the environment on a much larger and faster scale and adapt the organization as a whole accordingly. This leads to a continuous improvement process consisting of a series of measurable steps.

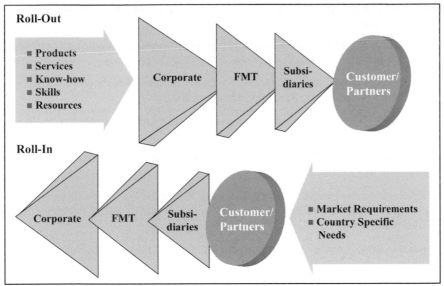

Fig. 2. Roll-in/Roll-out Process – FMT

4. References

Buchholz, S. and Sommer C. (2001). Globale Berater – Lässt sich Wissen globalisieren?. brand eins, June 2001.

Eichstädt, B. (2003). Mit Field-Management zur globalen Familie. Personalwirtschaft 1/2003.

Hindle, T. (2001). Guide to Management Ideas. Profile Books Limited, London.

Hofstede, G. (1980). Culture's Consequences. Sage, Beverly Hills, California.

Kirchmer, M.: Business Process Oriented Implementation of Standard Software – How to Achieve Competitive Advantage Efficiently and Effectively. 2nd edition, Berlin, New York and others 1999.

Kirchmer, M.: e-Business Processes Improvement (eBPI) – Building and Managing Collaborative e-Business Scenarios. In: Callaos, N., Loutfi, M., Justan, M. (editors): Proceedings of the 6th World Multiconference on Systemics, Cybernetics and Informatics. Orlando 2002, Volume VIII, pp. 387-396.

Kirchmer, M., Scheer, A.-W.: Change Management – Key for Business Process Excellence. In: Scheer, A.-W., Abolhassan, F., Jost, W., Kirchmer, M.: Business Process Change Management – ARIS in Practice. Berlin, New York, and others 2003, p. 2-14.

Krober, A and Kluckhohn C. (1952). Culture: A Critical Review of Concepts and Definitions. Harvard University Press, Mass.

Nickols, F. (2000). Change Management 101: A Primer. Article published on homepage: http://home.att.net/~nickols/change.htm. (01-15-03)

Scheer, A.-W., Abolhassan, F., Jost, W., Kirchmer, M.: Business Process Excellence – ARIS in Practice. Berlin, New York, and others 2002.

Scheer, A.-W., "Vom Geschäftsprozess zum Anwendungssystem", Springer Verlag 1998.

Slobodnik, A. and Slobodnik D. (1998). Change Management in Human Systems Model: Four System Types. Presented at the HR Strategies in the M&A Process Conference, Toronto, April, 1998.

Trompenaars, F. and Hampden Turner, C. (1998). Riding the Waves of Culture – Understanding Cultural Diversity in Business, 2nd edition. Nicolas Brealy Publishing, London, Santa Rosa.

Woods, M (2001). International Business: An Introduction. Palgrave, Basingstoke, Hampshire.

Change Management with ARIS

Steffen Exeler
Senior Consultant, IDS Scheer AG

Sven Wilms
Member of the Extended Executive Board, IDS Scheer AG

Summary

In future, increases in efficiency will be achieved primarily on a cross-company basis. Such "collaborative business" can only be implemented successfully if an appropriate change management structure has been implemented both within the company and on a cross-company basis. ARIS Version 6 supports the setup, implementation and continuous execution of successful change management. The procedures and experience of a change management life cycle can been seen from the example of the international implementation of risk management for a bank.

Key Words

Business Process Management, Change Management, ARIS, Risk Management, Change Processes, Increasing Efficiency, Collaborative Business, Corporate Culture, Cooperative Culture, Agile Organization

24

1. Reason for Change Management

Get used to the fact that, in five years' time, you will be working differently from the way you are today! You will be working in a changed company using changed procedures; the customers and vendors with whom you work will have changed, too.

One reason behind this statement lies in the continuing contraction of time and space. Technical advances and globalization have led to a dramatic reduction in product cycles. The ability of technological progress and innovative product to "calm" the populace is on a sustained downslide. The half-life of competitive advantages is constantly decreasing. This makes products more and more similar to, and substitutable for, one another ("commodities"), and the barriers to market entry by new market participants are being lowered. This heralds further pressure on margins.

This phenomenon, known as "margin pressure", is not new, but it is affecting some industries with hitherto unknown force, and responses to it are currently varied. Over the short-term, certainly the effects of margin pressure need to be countered with savings on the costs side. The range of short-term measures available to decision-makers in this regard is limited (reducing the marketing budget, halting or scaling back IT projects, ...). Over the medium- and long-term, however, the only kind of available response to this sustained margin pressure is to enhance efficiency levels in all areas of a company.

For company decision-makers, this thesis is for the most part already an accepted truth. This is illustrated in the continuing increase in the numbers of business-process optimization projects in the areas of vendor and purchasing management, in-house procedures and business-client relations. Studies have found that this potential, far from exhausted, will instead, grow even further over the next few years. (cf. IDS Scheer AG 2002)

Likewise in this connection, the question is being heard increasingly frequently: "Make or buy?" I.e. which links in a company's value chain should or must a company provide on its own, or are there other external service-providers and producers capable of furnishing this piece better (with better quality or greater efficiency, more innovatively...)? The current trend toward focusing on a company's own core competencies is an expression of these strategic considerations. Advances in internet technology also tend to favor this kind of outsourcing of internal functions to external providers. Entire value chains are being disassembled and reconfigured across business boundaries. This reduction in companies' own "depth of production" now affects the finance industry, for example, which in a period of extreme margin decay now outsources all or part of its own IT to out-of-house service providers, or farms out the processing of high-volume yet low-margin transactions to external "transaction factories", known as transaction banks.

Gartner describes these trends as the "end of work in business architectures". Rising up in their place are architectures permitting process co-operation across business boundaries. Gartner predicts that companies which transform themselves into such a virtual-oriented, agile business model will experience substantially faster growth than those hewing to more traditional patterns (cf. Gartner).

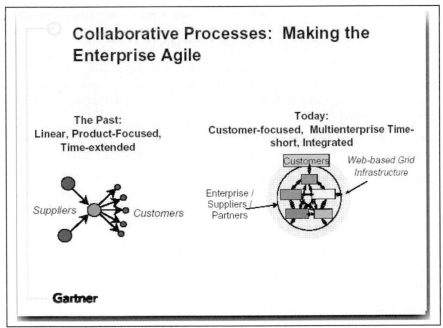

Fig. 1. Gartner

It is growing more and more apparent all the time that the original adoption of e-business as the engine of innovative new business concepts has failed for the most part, but that it is now successfully being enlisted as an enabler for redesigning and optimizing multi-enterprise business processes. The goal here is to reduce transaction costs, not to establish new business ideas. Furthermore, the decisive factor in this collaborative business is not technology but mastery of the organizational dimensions of this collaborative-business approach across business boundaries.

2. The Effects of Change Management

Usually, changes are launched only once they have become inevitable. By that point, however, initiating changes often means carrying out "2nd round" changes. Because by this (too?) late stage, financial, human and legal restrictions frequently only leave room for reaction rather than for planned action. One must also take into account that it takes time before changes can begin yielding positive results. This time is, as described in the introduction, growing increasingly scarce.

The objective must be to create a business culture which questions the status quo and sets changes in motion before routine in times of success and action – according to old patterns – conceal a creeping crisis and let the time required for planned action pass by unused. Modern organization theory describes approaches enlisting emerging processes to enable a dynamic balance between stability and flexibility at the verge of chaos (cf. Scheer 2002, Jazz...).

An essential factor for success in creating such a dynamic in companies, and for creating an agile organization, is the establishment of a corresponding business culture. A key component of this business culture must be the principle of open communication and trust.

As used here, open communication and trust exist where top management clearly and unambiguously formulates and communicates the following questions:

- What is to be changed, and how?
- Why are these changes necessary?
- What are the consequences of this?

In this connection, open communication and trust mean that staff members affected by the changes also have the opportunity to discuss these changes with one another and with the management. Above all, however, a business culture of open communication and trust satisfies the prerequisites for a timely initiation of changes. For what is sought are staff members who point up potential improvements, in a timely manner and on their own initiative. They will only do this, however, if on the one hand they have the technical or organizational "mouthpieces" for the purpose; and if, on the other hand, they have no need to fear being placed at a loss for acting in such a way.

If open communication and trust are important to change management of in-house business changes, this holds true all the more so for change processes across business boundaries. In this case, additional problems arise:

- As a rule, companies having co-operative arrangements with one another also have different business cultures
- These differences in business culture can be compounded through differences of sociocultural membership
- The complexity of processes of collaboration increases and with it the complexity of the change itself
- Businesses having co-operative arrangements with one another are legally independent entities with objectives of their own

It becomes clear from this that what is needed is not just a new kind of in-house business culture, but a new kind of business co-operation culture as well.

Here, too, the first factors to come in for consideration are the "secondary" factors, such as mutual understanding, for instance. Due to increasing electronic exchange of information across company boundaries, staff must accustom themselves to new demands placed upon their "output". Today, information once sent manually is entered and passed along electronically. They may need to be adapted to new data formats at the receiving end. Here, inter-company understanding must be enhanced along the entire value chain, and above all with regard to one's own role and the consequences of one's own actions for the rest of this chain.

Greater attention is also to be given to handling of sensitive data. Given the close and concentrated integrated data exchange between companies legally independent of one another, proper provision must be made for legal aspects, and for aspects bearing on the law regarding data protection. Here, the notion of trust takes on new dimensions.

The fact that understanding and trust are not always enough, and that instead solid financial arrangements are required, becomes clear if we recall the main motivation for collaborative business, which is to reduce costs. Let us take the case of supply chain management. To achieve greater efficiency, several companies in a value chain collaborate with one another with the objective of optimizing their processes holistically and across business boundaries. The different companies involved in the arrangement may well achieve cost-reduction potentials of differing magnitudes. It may even turn out that one company achieves no overall cost reduction at all, but instead must bear cost increases due to particularly high IT expenditure in the SCM infrastructure area. For these multi-enterprise processes, a costs balance sheet covering all processes should be drawn up, and fair financial compensation agreed upon (Horvath 2002).

Understanding and trust, but also clear objectives and statements, are likewise key concepts in the following figure (Fig. 2) representing the steps which should be passed through in a change management process:

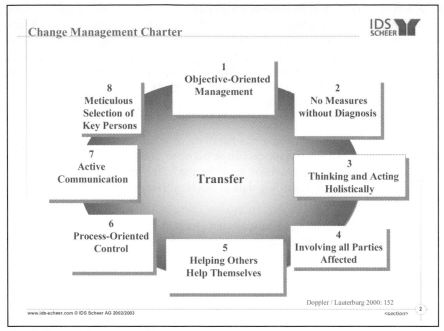

Fig. 2. Change Management Charter

Step 1: Objective-oriented Management

The principal prerequisite to acceptance of change is awareness of what the change is intended to achieve. These objectives must be formulated clearly and unambiguously so that there can be no mistake as to how they should be interpreted. Involved here are both "primary" specifications such as turnover increase, cost reduction, etc.; as well as "secondary" objectives such as increasing customer satisfaction. Secondary factors should be buttressed with the aid of quantitative measurements (customer satisfaction analyses, ...). This statement of the company's objectives must be broken down for the individual areas with which the staff identify themselves.

Step 2: No Measures without Diagnosis

Just as important for acceptance of change is an understanding *why* the change has to take place. Thus, the reasons for this change are to be openly and clearly stated. Staff will understand the reasons for the change from a logical/thematic standpoint before they also lend their emotional support as well. Here, too, it cannot suffice to communicate the reasons for change at the company level; instead, a clear explanation should be made as to why a particular staff member's area must be changed, and in which direction.

Step 3: Thinking and Acting Holistically

A staff member will find it easier to support changes made in his own work environment once he understands the role which his own area – and he personally – plays in the value chain. Most important here is an awareness and understanding for upstream positions ("Why do I receive input from this or that department in such and such a fashion?") and downstream positions ("How does the quality of my output affect units where further processing occurs?").

Step 4: Involving all Parties Affected

Steps 1-3, listed above, lead to greater acceptance on the part of staff. It is only once there has also been acceptance at the emotional level of the need for change and of the shared objectives that an employee can be in a position to participate actively in this change process. On the other hand, the very participation of staff, their enlistment in shaping the changes to take place, also promotes acceptance.

Step 5: Helping Others Help Themselves

Since the change process never comes to a full close, it is important to put staff in a position to carry out the change process themselves. This applies all the more so if our express wish is for staff to identify optimization potentials on their own and to initiate and execute the appropriate processes for change. In this connection, it is the business culture of openness and trust which warrants mentioning.

Step 6: Process-oriented Control

The potentials for change lie within a company's own processes. Yet the implementation of change is also a process unto itself. Here, a determination should be made, among other things, as to the objectives to be pursued and who is involved when and how. Accordingly, to this end a change management system should be set up as described in Chapter 3.

Step 7: Active Communication

A key factor for the success of change management is the manner in which communication takes place. An important factor is open and credible communication by top management, by means of media support (corporate TV, staff periodicals, etc.), as to the What, How and Why. Yet it just equally important for staff to be able to enter into an exchange, with management and with one another, regarding the changes and their consequences. A solid grasp of one's own role in the value and change processes adds to the quality of this communication.

Step 8: Meticulous Selection of Key Persons

Resistance and resisters can be found in every change process. Likewise, every change process also has its promoters. The majority of staff will be skeptical and guarded. The object is to locate those promoters who, based on the steps as set forth, are capable of persuading and motivating their fearful and guarded majority of fellow staff. Here it is important to locate promoters at all levels: top management, middle management and in the individual departments.

3. Organizing a Change Management System

Carrying out changes in a company is no easy task. This is all the more so where change processes need to be designed and implemented across company boundaries. The positive effects unleashed by the changes in one area of a company may involve negative effects in other areas of the same company or in co-operating companies. This is why it is important to establish a comprehensive and holistic approach describing a very wide array of viewpoints and analyzing their interoperation. Fig. 3 offers a depiction of this holistic approach.

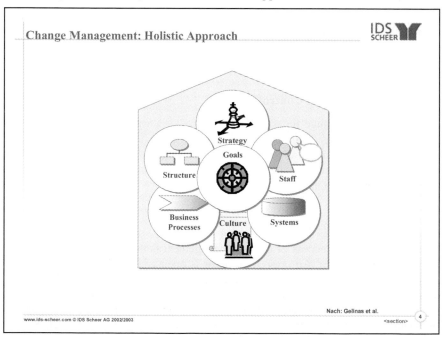

Fig. 3. Change Management: Holistic Approach

Such a holistic description of the very wide array of viewpoints shown in Fig. 3 along with an analysis of their interoperation can only be achieved with the aid of a system suited to the purpose.

The ARIS methodology and the corresponding ARIS product family offer the necessary support:

- With the ARIS Balanced Scorecard, the objectives and strategies of the company and of the change processes are described and linked with operational activities. Described here are the various dimensions of the final financial success to be achieved (customers, innovations, processes and human resources). Using cause-and-effect diagrams, relationships and dependencies among objectives are listed beneath one another. This Balanced Scorecard can thus serve as a basis for incentives systems to support the processes of change.

- The ARIS Toolset, ARIS Easy Design and ARIS WebDesigner products enable description of actual and target processes. Here, the ARIS methodology supports the points referred to in Fig. 3 in various views (cf. Scheer 1998):

  - Who (organizations, departments, roles...) is involved in the actual or target process?

  - Which functions are or should be carried out?

  - Which data from which systems are required for, or produced as a result of, this step?

  - Which services are or should be produced?

  - How do the views mentioned above interoperate in a process?

Existing industry or topic-oriented reference models and best-practice models can accelerate the description of target processes specific to the individual company involved. Describing the organizational units and roles in the value process earmarked for change enables the staff member to identify in the process his own mission along with the consequences of his actions.

E-business scenarios included in ARIS support, above all, the description of processes which go beyond company boundaries, along with the exchange of the data and interface formats concerned (cf. Kirchmer 2002).

Integration of IT systems in the process descriptions enables analysis what consequences the changes envisaged will have for the IT systems involved in the process. The integrated description of the process view and the IT view make it easier to carry out on the IT systems themselves any changes making allowance for the new processes. This can even go so far as to include the generation of applications based on the process description.

Change management processes are being implemented more and more frequently internationally. The three tier architecture ("thin client" architecture) with a central ARIS Repository and decentralized ARIS WebDesigners enables world-wide modeling of actual and target processes with a simple user interface, even via the internet. The multi-lingual capabilities possessed by the tool and repository meet the needs of many international companies regarding multiple language support in project teams or at the subsequent rollout stage.

- ARIS WebPublisher publishes the process description for staff in the various departments on the Intranet/extranet. Role-based access makes it possible to provide the individual staff member with precisely the information he requires to understand his role and its consequences. This promotes holistic thinking and action, along with acceptance of pending changes. The option of incorporating the WebPublishers into existing company portals with the accustomed corporate identity look and feel can further accelerate acceptance. This is also possible across company boundaries.

This publication of process knowledge ("Who does what when in the process, and with which IT systems?") is an important part of establishing an open business culture.

- ARIS Process Performance Manager
Understanding for and acceptance of the needs for change grow if the underlying reasons for change can be plausibly explained. The ARIS Process Performance Manager plays an important role in this. The ARIS Process Performance Manager extracts process-oriented key figures from on-going operational systems (ERP, workflow, CRM applications, ...) such as:

  - How long does the overall process, or how long do individual process steps take?

  - How many and which organizational units were involved, and when?

  - How often were which process sub-steps actually run through in reality (possibly discrepancy with plan probabilities in system implementation)?

Based on these key performance indicators for processes, benchmarks can be derived for a variety of dimensions (products, regions, times, ...).

This analysis using real process key figures makes clear to the individual member of staff what the consequences of his actions are (understood as a role) in the overall process, thereby strengthening the understanding of processes in general and acceptance of any necessary process improvements.

- ARIS Simulation
With the help of the simulation, the consequences of process changes – the combination of hitherto separate departments, for instance – can be simulated in advance. Here, the consequences for process times, throughput, resource requirements, etc., are analyzed and any bottlenecks or improvements in the process made clear. This, too, is a key component in the change-management

area, enabling as it does identification in advance, and avoidance, of potential complications involved in (organizational) changes.

4. Change Management with ARIS V 6.1

On the one hand, a change management project is to be carried out as any other project in phases of design, implementation and control. On the other hand, a change management project, of all projects, is not a closed project unto itself but rather an ongoing process. For, as already indicated above, we would like to structure agile, dynamic companies which continuously adapt to the need for change. Ideally, the changes involved here should not be implemented in radical fashion but should instead integrate themselves in an evolutionary process of continuing development. For this is the best way of winning over and promoting acceptance and self-help on the part of staff. This is further proof of the truth of the realization that companies are "natural" organizations which, like other "living beings", must adapt to changes in their environment, carrying out this task in evolutionary fashion in a constant cycle. For the reasons mentioned above, this organizational change management cycle is presented in Fig. 4 as the well-known ARIS Process Life Cycle.

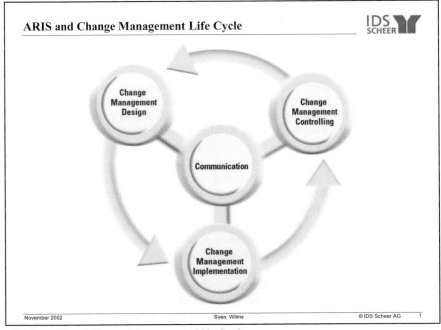

Fig. 4. ARIS and Change Management Life Cycle

As already indicated, the ARIS methodology represents the basis and the comprehensive framework for the establishment of an effective change-management approach. The ARIS product family supports implementation and ongoing execution. In this regard, ARIS Version 6.1 in particular contains several new functionalities which further improve the ongoing change management process. What follows is a description of these functionalities.

4.1 Design Stage

In a project team, the actual processes are documented in ARIS and analyzed for weak points. At this point it is essential to integrate the affected organizational units in the project team for this review of actual processes, and especially for the subsequent modeling of target processes. For one, this makes the "affected parties" into participants; moreover, it is the men and women working on location in the individual departments who know their processes and improvement potentials best of all. As indicated above, the web/internet capability of ARIS supports world-wide modeling on a central repository.

Conceivably, the resulting target processes ("master processes") may be generically correct, and yet require adaptation to the local legal circumstances before being implemented in specific areas or countries. This can be done in ARIS by means of variant modeling. Through appropriate reports, audit-standard proof and analysis can be carried out as to why and how which area has deviated from predetermined specifications. Building upon this analysis, benchmarks can then be carried out as well.

The design stage is also where organizational decisions specific to the "change management project" are made: what characterizes process changes is precisely the fact that they are implemented across departmental or area boundaries. This is why a so-called "process owner" is to be identified for this affected overall process. This should be (and as a rule is) a member of top management. Along with his operational (rather function-oriented) tasks, he also has the task of overall optimization of this process. One issue involved here is the question of his decision-making authority as concerns process optimization. For instance: The process owner discovers that overall optimization of the process requires carrying out changes in a business unit reporting e.g. to his colleague on the Executive Board. Now does the process owner have authority to issue directives to his operationally responsible colleague with regard to this process change or not? As a rule, he will have authority not to issue directives but to escalate the matter, i.e. these problems will be addressed in the joint committee and resolved collectively. As a rule, the process owner will not carry out these process tasks him- or herself but will designate a process manager or a process manager team for these tasks instead. Where very decentrally distributed change management projects are involved, process managers should be designated in the decentralized departmental units as well.

4.2 Implementation Stage

If the target processes have been decided upon in the project team and at the decision-making level, implementation is carried out. Here, among other things, the ARIS "test database" is started up as a "system in production" as during implementation of other software systems and the results, which can encompass target processes, new organizational structures, etc., are made available to affected staff. Today, these results are no longer communicated by means of text and paper but rather in graphic and electronic form by means of electronic standard operating procedures or, as is the convention in banks, by means of electronic organizational manuals. Technical realization is carried out through the ARIS WebPublisher, which automatically converts the models from the ARIS Repository to Java or HTML formats and publishes them using a conventional webserver on the Intranet. The ARIS WebPublisher can be adapted to suit business-specific corporate design approaches or be integrated in existing company portals.

The role-based approach enables communication of information, world-wide, in a manner corresponding precisely to the informational needs of staff having particular roles.

As a rule, at least two different web portals are created. One web portal describes the target business processes for the decentralized end user. The other web portal is intended for the project team, itself likewise potentially distributed world-wide. This project team can also use the "project process web" as a communications center and exchange with one another information such as objectives, documentation, status updates, areas of responsibility, etc.

The following practical example suggests possible uses for portals of this type.

4.3 Feedback/Controlling Stage

The staff member in the decentralized departmental unit sees in the process web, or in the business portal regularly used by him, the processes associated with his role. Since he knows the processes and process improvements in his area better than anyone else, he must be placed in a position where he is able to easily comment to the appropriate persons in charge regarding these processes. For he will be prepared to do so only if this is easy and quick to do. In the corresponding process model, he can go to the model properties area and select the "Change Management" area for this purpose. He will then see a simple script editor indicating the suggestions and comments already made by fellow staff regarding this process along with a listing of when these comments were made; here he can add comments of his own. He can also select the language in which he would like to make these comments. What makes this important is the fact that many internationally active companies have defined English as their corporate standard. But it is entirely possible that staff would rather provide feedback in their mother tongue, where they are on "a more firm footing".

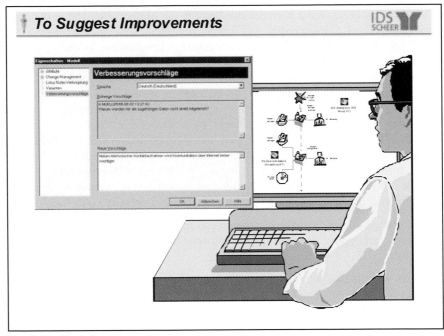

Fig. 5. Feedback Stage

These comments by decentralized staff are saved via the internet to the central ARIS Repository. This makes them an integral part of the ARIS models.

Since they are an integral part of the ARIS Repository, these comments are made accessible to the process manager in charge immediately after they have been saved decentrally. He will collect, analyze and process comments and suggestions made by a very wide array of staff. In so doing, in keeping with his authorizations and area of responsibility, he can carry out the following activities:

- Reject or accept
- In case of acceptance: define and automatically assign measures, to-do lists and areas of responsibility
- Prioritize and schedule

In the Change Management Workbench (Fig. 6) contained in ARIS version 6.1, the process manager has an overview of the status of relevant recommended improvements and can trace project progress accordingly. The staff person originally initiating the improvement suggestion is automatically kept apprised of project progress.

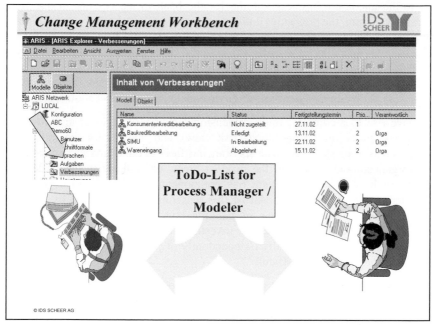

Fig. 6. Change Management Workbench

Once the change has been completed in the process model, and following subsequent release by the process owner, the modified model is in turn transferred to the ARIS "Productions Database" and using ARIS WebPublishing made available once again to decentralized staff as a new target process.

In this way, this database-supported "workflow" ensures an ongoing improvement management cycle. This will now be made concrete in an anonymous practical example.

5. Example: Support for Change Management in Country-Specific Risk Monitoring of a Major International Bank

5.1 The Problem as Identified by the Customer

For its increasing international activities in the area of credit-risk and trade, this major bank had defined an increasingly complex system for control of country-specific risk limits over the course of the years. Country-specific risk limits here refer to the maximum business volume for the bank in the country in question. Within this system, the provisions and procedures were laid down for determining, fixing responsibility, reporting, monitoring and escalating limit overruns for all business units operating in a particular country. This guide was supported by a multitude of standardized and individually developed IT systems, some of which were parked in the mainframe computer environment of the bank, and others of which were parked in the client-server environment at the bank headquarters.

This gave rise to a complex, multi-dimensional matrix of regional and country-related risk limits, on the one hand (risk view), and budgets for the individual business areas at headquarters with its branch offices in the countries and subsidiaries (organizational view) and the product areas, particularly in the trade area with its products and their relevant risk components (product view) as an additional main control component. All of this was further complicated by the fact that, based on various provisions of banking law, portions of the commercial banking business and of the so-called investment banking operated for the most part organizationally and spatially independently of one another, making communication considerably more difficult.

As a result, it came to pass that dealings were proceeding simultaneously within the same product segment (e.g. "company credit") between headquarters to the branch office of a bank customer, on the one hand, while the foreign subsidiary, on the other, used this limit latitude for a local deal of its own. Or, an available country-specific limit reserved for a credit authorization only became apparent in operational systems after approximately 14 days' processing time, during which time the investment-banking dealers made use of this apparent limit leeway to purchase trading items (e.g. state bonds) of their own.

In this weave of limits, IT systems, responsibilities and day trades, it came to light again and again that the objective of controlling business volume under the pre-determined country-specific risk policy was not producing the desired results. The main culprits were quickly identified:

- Complex, at times unclear approvals process for country-specific risk in individual transactions

- Badly arranged and non-co-ordinated support by IT systems in the individual countries and business areas

- Differences among local product versions and, tied in with this, differences in the business processes involved in creating or dealing with bank products involving risk

- Lack of definition as to the methods, pathways and tools of communication in case of business query and the reporting and submission of limit overruns as well as in reporting to business areas and countries of the target and plan values from the central country-specific risk management unit

- Error-prone multitude of IT systems which were not compatible with one another and at times were the creation of headquarters itself

Given the complexity of these issues, it became clear that a solution, particularly one taking the manifold local specificities into account, had to be drawn up, yet not a solution issuing purely from headquarters in "top down" fashion but rather one developed in consultation with the users of the limit system. In light of ongoing business activity and the associated reporting to the Executive Board, a "big bang" style restructuring seemed too risky. The objective, moreover, was to restructure existing structures in an evolutionary fashion, i.e. reshaping them in a continuous process of analysis, modification and control, in consultation with the organizational units affected.

What was needed here was a methodology and a tool for a professional process analysis and an integrated change management approach.

5.2 Paving the Way for the Change Management Project

Following the findings as described above, a project was launched to document existing processes, methods and systems and examine them for weak points. This process-based analysis was then to provide the foundation for development of a new, technically integrated new country-specific risk limit system based on a uniform world-wide process model. Migration from the status quo to the newly designed model, however, was to take place in evolutionary fashion, taking into account the multitude of participating organizational units, countries and IT systems. The objective was to actively incorporate the business units involved in the change process while at the same time establishing ongoing communication with participating units, by means of which any future reporting lines and approvals for individual transactions could even be communicated. Within the framework of the refocusing of bank organizational structures towards a business model described as process-oriented, the plan was for this methodology to be a recognizable dominant factor in the new guidelines and tools as well.

Based on this, it turned out that the central instrument needed to be a professional process-management tool integrating not only the demands of global change management but, along with this, standardized creation of communications platforms and links to the operational product systems or monitoring systems at headquarters. At the same time, demands were issued by the central risk-management unit for incorporation and analysis of operational risks contained in the business processes; these, too, were to be taken into account within the newly created methodology.

Following in-depth analysis of instruments on the market, the choice was made for the ARIS Toolset with its components for process documentation, weak-point analysis, change-management support and the supplemental Process Risk Scout module for integration of operational risks in the process model. Once a survey was made of processes, systems and responsibilities, on the one hand, and of existing shortcomings and operational risks on the other, Intranet portals were created – for the most part automatically – designed to provide support for the change process and analysis and evaluation of operational risks.

5.3 Defining the Country-Specific Risk Policy and Lines of Responsibility

Following installation of necessary software and a short training program for staff of the central project team, first the methodical basis was laid down for new structures under development in the form of definitions of policy and purpose for country-specific risk control, along with the lines of responsibility for those involved in this area.

Under this arrangement, there should be a centrally managed risk framework defined by the bank's own equity capital outlining the greatest possible business volume for all countries but the bank's own home country. These country-specific risk frameworks are then to be defined on a quarterly basis in the form of budgets for the individual regions and countries, for the business areas and subsidiaries and for the various products, in keeping with the business expectations and feasible rates of risk return in the countries. A country-specific risk secretariat was created for this purpose, responsible for creation and communication in the matter. This limits system was designed to be available at all times to all affected staff, providing the latest figures on capacity utilization. In particular the fact that access was also to be provided for those staff who spend the bulk of their time beyond the bank's premises – e.g. when closing a transaction at the client's premises – entailed new and unprecedented requirements for the communications tool.

Within the bank's operational business processes world-wide, an examination now had to be carried out as to the offices for which approval of individual transactions needed to be subject to review, and who would or should issue this approval. Due account needed to be taken, here, to see to it that although the business processes in the individual countries were oriented around a centralized process model, as a practical matter their details would naturally be permitted to depart from this model in significant ways.

Following this, the approval and reporting process as such was defined which would then subsequently be adapted to the various organizational structures in the business areas and subsidiaries.

5.4 Inventorying Processes for Limit Assignment, Notification of Capacity-Utilization Levels and Limit Reporting

All information available was recorded in process-oriented fashion in an ARIS model. To begin with, the essential main processes along with their value chains reappeared here, in like fashion as the model of the IT systems, and links to the relevant documents in standard Excel or Word format with links to the operational (messaging) systems involved.

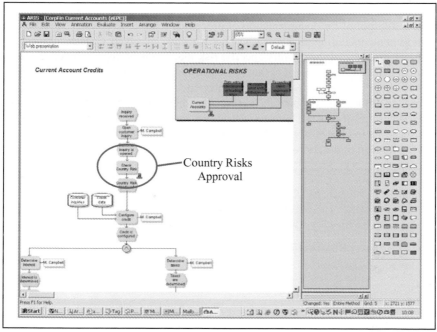

Fig. 7. ARIS

This process model was initially defined by the central project team, based on existing knowledge. At the same time, the change management approach itself was defined as a process model, in order to make the overall project easy to grasp, susceptible of analysis and basically capable of adaptation to any changes of circumstance.

As an auxiliary team for the change-management project, a group was charged with inventorying and evaluating of operational risks in the processes under consideration. This team was also to report its findings to the central operational risk management unit.

5.5 Setting up the Integrated Communication Platforms

To enable worldwide communication with persons in charge for these three project and process worlds (the bank's country-specific risk management, the change management project itself and the drawing-up of operational risks), three Intranet-based portals were created from the existing process model in ARIS:

5.5.1 "Country Risk Portal"

First, a web portal for documentation of processes relating to country-specific risk management, including all known process variants, involved systems, the organizational structure of the country-specific risk management approach and the links to documents and operational systems. Access to this portal was granted to all persons working on the change project, country-specific risk management or the procedure for requests and approvals. Essentially, then, this covers the central change management project team, the central country-specific risk management team, the local persons in charge in the countries themselves and staff in business areas involving foreign transactions and the subsidiaries.

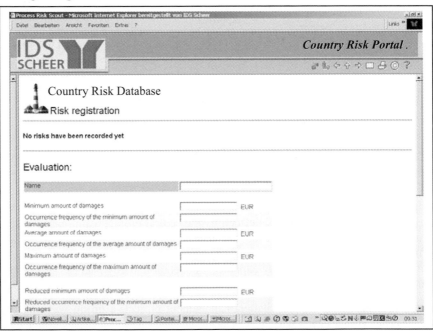

Fig. 8. Country Risk Portal

Within this portal, the staff involved were able to track the current status of the processes, process "released" processes (i.e. those already wrapped up and documented in the portal) in accordance with the conditions of the portal and, within the portal, access those documents (country risk policy, country limit reports, approval guidelines for overruns of country risk limits, etc.) and systems (operational posting and information system, e-mail programs with forms for requesting limit utilization or overrun, etc.) which were of significance within the process itself.

5.5.2 "Change Management Project Portal"

Alongside this, the project portal as such with the objective, documentation and definition of the project as a process model. Since all local country staff in charge of the respective foreign countries were also affected over the short-term, the portal contained a communications feature with which risks, changes, delays or simply news of success could be communicated within the project process. This gave project members, encompassing local country staff in charge for foreign countries ("CM officers") along with the central change management managers ("CM managers"), an integrated communications platform with which they could observe and comment upon the project as such as it progressed.

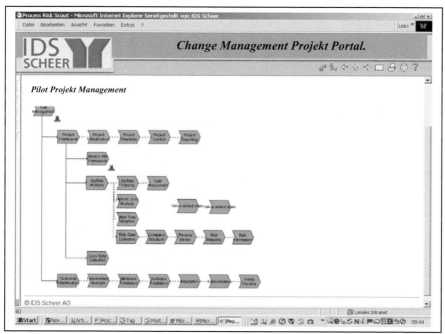

Fig. 9. Change Management Portal

Aside from the above-mentioned CM managers and CM officers, access was limited to both the central project steering committee which had overall responsibility for projects taking place in the bank, and the Executive Board secretariats responsible for country-specific risk, as these were responsible for the costs of this project.

5.5.3 "Operational Risk Portal"

Finally, out of information processed in the process models and pertaining to risks of an operational nature, a portal was created in such a fashion as should be established in future for all other metaprocesses within the bank as well. Here, the process model as such, along with all information pertaining to operational risks (loss potential, loss frequency data, lines of responsibility, key risk indicators, emergency processes, etc.) was made available to the process owners involved, to the risk officers (usually established in the business areas or in the subsidiaries) and to the central operational risk management staff. Risk information was derived from the documentation and analysis of the processes and then communicated, analyzed and updated via the Operational Risk Portal.

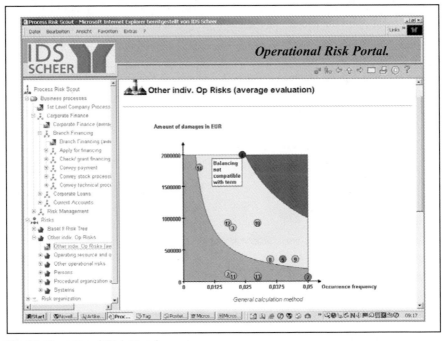

Fig. 10. Operational Risk Portal

The risk officers had the opportunity (again within the portal) to communicate with the risk managers in charge when they discovered new risks in the processes, needed to fill out their so-called OpeRating Self-Assessment forms, or possibly wanted to enter emerging loss events in the central loss database. Information from the communications process within the portal flowed back, for the most part automatically, into the supporting systems (e.g. ARIS models, loss databases or OpeRating databases).

5.5.4 The Variants of the Process Model

Initially, the basic central processes (creation of the country-specific risk budget, approval procedures, report and escalation processed, etc.) were published in the Country Risk Portal, as were the model processes for the business areas and subsidiaries in which the country-specific risk approval sub-process was described on a model basis for a very wide variety of products, and the key documents and reports. This resulted in creation of a centrally maintained, uniform and easy-to-use communications platform, available world-wide, for all staff working in the country-specific risk area.

The next task thus became one of adapting centrally specified model processes for country-specific risk approval to local conditions and, in turn, to announce to bank headquarters these variants upon the model process. Project staff in the individual foreign subsidiaries and foreign departments were now called upon to analyze the model process in detail, to integrate it into their own business processes to the maximum extent possible in the manner specified by headquarters, and only where modifications could be established as necessary (e.g. due to local legislation or IT specifications which could not be changed without substantial expense), to integrate these into a local variant upon the "country-specific risk approval" subprocess and to make this available to bank headquarters as an ARIS model.

In this way, over the course of the next two months the central project team collected all of the local variants upon the sub-process mentioned above, thereby providing themselves with a picture as to how, in certain regions, and for what reasons, deviations from their own process model were warranted. To this end, project staff received special instruction in the use of the ARIS Web Designer. The data were compiled to create a compendium of current processes for country-specific risk approval processes world-wide. The result was a detailed snapshot of the actual situation, based on reports from nearly 80 countries.

5.6 The Ongoing Process of Change

Once this Country Risk Portal had been updated, the basic central processes and local detailed processes for the business areas published anew, and a corresponding message communicated to all persons involved, the actual process of change management could begin: compiling suggestions for improvement; evaluating these, prioritizing them and assigning them to the CM managers, who in turn had to revise the underlying process model accordingly. Following this, work could begin on implementing the revised process models within the operational systems. Since the entire cycle of this change process occurred on the basis of an integrated process database organization, and as a result the models were kept up do date at all times and accompanied by personal comments by project staff, communication and analysis and implementation of recommended improvements proceeded much more smoothly than in previous, similar attempts to standardize and integrate this complex system of country-specific risk control.

During the course of business-case processing and without major interruption to their local process model, staff in affected areas across the globe now had the opportunity to navigate to places within the process where they wanted to recommend improvements. Thanks to the portal's user-friendly interface, and web browser functionality familiar to all, this avenue met with quite a high level of acceptance. Whenever it occurred to a staff member that the process as such, or else media or systems used in the process, could be changed or improved upon – e.g. through product changes, new legal provisions, reorganization of local units or as well as fusion or splitting measures – all it took was a click of the mouse on a particular function within a process or on the process affected by these changes. The recommendations submitted were communicated to the responsible CM manager, who could then in turn co-ordinate further processing of the recommendation.

For the individual staff member, the time required for input and forwarding of the suggested change averaged two to three minutes, comparable with drafting a brief e-mail but actually to much more sweeping effect. In the course of routine cross-checks of the portal against the ARIS database, the recommendations submitted were integrated directly into the process model, where every staff member involved in the change management project then had access to these data.

This also left the CM managers with the option of consulting and evaluating this information whenever they chose, to co-ordinate and prioritize processing of the suggestions collected, and finally to assign to change management subprojects those (groups of) suggested changes meeting the requirements of change management policy.

Essentially, these requirements were oriented towards improving customer satisfaction (particularly e.g. response times, reducing subsequent requests for documentation), standardization (in international comparison, following organizational changes or introduction of new products) and reducing process costs (avoiding duplicated work, eliminating unnecessary process steps, introducing electronic documents, etc.).

Within the ARIS database, the CM manager was now in a position to monitor further processing of the collected suggestions, generate to-do lists for appropriate project staff and thereby co-ordinate the change management subprojects.

These change management subprojects were now responsible for examining the detail processes taken up, against the background of the collected suggestions for improvement and needed changes and, where appropriate, to migrate these to a new process structure. Following this, in a follow-up project, work could begin on implementing the modified process models within the operational system.

5.7 Experience with Day-to-Day Dealings with Change Management

All in all, in light of the evaluation of the change management project, it must be said that such a smooth change management event was only possible with the aid of a communications platform available world-wide and oriented towards the business process. The most important fact for the success of this project was that nearly all data necessary to the country-specific risk management mission on which work was based (country-specific risk policy, databank reports, job-related instructions & forms, etc.) was capable of being integrated in a process model which could then be communicated electronically in the simplest manner to a portal from which feedback from the person concerned could be incorporated, in turn, into the process model.

Here, the entire change management cycle (collecting suggestions for improvement – evaluating, prioritizing, assigning – adapting process models & documentation – implementing modified processes) was integrated within a single tool. This complex set of initial conditions – with a very wide array of persons, systems, legal requirements, bank products and organizational forms distributed throughout the world – presented enormous challenges for the management of this project.

Staff not directly concerned with the CM project must be drawn into the change-management process in great numbers if changes in existing business processes are to be carried out successfully. Experience has shown, however, that staff not directly concerned with the CM project can only be reached if they are presented with simple and familiar means of access to the data they need, and when they can see, on an ongoing basis, that the changes they have suggested are being taken up during project planning and – of course – in subsequent change projects and implementation measures as well.

Particularly in the case of this internationally active bank, it was inevitable that the business field in question, country-specific risk management, be placed on a web-based platform, just as was the actual change process. Realization with ARIS and integration using the processes contained in ARIS were an important component in this respect.

The subproject created to analyze the processes for operational risks is currently still in progress. Still, based on the process analysis carried out, along with system and process changes already enacted, it is already apparent that the quality and security of the business processes involved has increased in large measure.

The integration of change management and risk management has proven inevitable here, as every change can also entail new risks, and every identified risk will be associated with new changes. Together with study of quality management and the process-costs analysis, this gives rise to a target system which defines the requirements for a holistic process-management approach. With ARIS, a link was successfully established among these divergent target dimensions.

6. References

Gartner, Jeff Schulman: "A New View of Architecture Needed for New Business Drivers".

Horvath, Peter, University of Stuttgart, Horvath AG, Reinhold Mayer, Horvath&Partners Management Consulting: "X-Engineering: Neue Potenziale der Prozess-Performance erschließen", in *Information Management & Consulting*, October 2002.

IDS Scheer AG, "Business Process Report 2002".

Kirchmer Mathias, IDS Scheer Inc.; George Brown, Intel, Inc.; and Herbert Heinzel, Siemens AG, SBS: "Using SCOR and Other Reference Models for E-Business Process Networks" in *Business Process Excellence, ARIS in Practice*, Springer Verlag 2002.

Scheer, August-Wilhelm, Institut für Wirtschaftsinformatik of the University of the Saar: "Jazz-Improvisation und Management", in *Information Management & Consulting*, October 2002.

Scheer, August-Wilhelm, "Vom Geschäftsprozess zum Anwendungssystem", Springer Verlag 1998.

Managing Change through Project Management and Process Management

Kelly Talsma, PMP
Project Manager, Quixtar

Trevor Naidoo
Consulting Services Manager, IDS Scheer, Inc.

Summary

While Process Management may not be a project, it can consist of several projects to ensure successful change management within an organization. Inefficient project management can lead to failed Business Process Management Initiatives. This case study illustrates the synergies between these two disciplines.

Key Words

Project Management, Process Management, Project Methodology, Process Selection, Change Management

50

1. Abstract

This chapter will look at how Quixtar Inc. used best practices of project management to manage a business process modeling initiative and management. While processes and projects may seem like very different types of work, in fact, they are very closely related. Projects are comprised of the right combination of processes, and to effectively implement a process initiative, you need to use your best project management skills.

2. Background

2.1 Company Profile

Quixtar Inc. is a Web-based business featuring a blend of consumer shopping, membership benefits and business ownership not found anywhere else on the Internet. Launched Sept. 1, 1999, at www.quixtar.com, Quixtar is based near Grand Rapids, Mich., and currently does business in the U.S., Canada and Puerto Rico.

2.2 Ownership and Management

The families of Rich DeVos and Jay Van Andel, who are among North America's leading entrepreneurs with numerous business ventures in direct selling, sports entertainment, real estate, lodging and hospitality, and other business sectors, founded Quixtar. Quixtar is a member of the Alticor group of companies.

2.3 Products, Services and More

Best known for its Health and Beauty offerings, Quixtar features top brands like ARTISTRY® skin care and cosmetics, NUTRILITE® nutrition and wellness products, SA8® laundry care products, MAGNA BLOC™ Therapeutic Magnets, and more. Quixtar's DITTO DELIVERY^{SM} Service allows customers to create personal profiles of consumable products they use and authorize Quixtar to automatically fill their orders based on schedules they preset.

Quixtar's STORE FOR MORE^{SM} features hundreds of products from leading brand-name companies in many product categories, including apparel, athletic gear, beauty care, photography, electronics, appliances, pet care, furniture, and more.

Quixtar also offers a large variety of Home, Auto, Travel, Financial and Communications Services through affiliated providers including MCI, Visa and other leading providers.

2.4 Business Model

Independent Business Owners register Clients, Members and new IBOs at www.quixtar.com, earning income based on the business volume resulting from their efforts. Unlike many other e-commerce ventures, Quixtar does not advertise, instead rewarding IBOs who provide the "high touch" to Quixtar's "high tech" Web site and infrastructure. Quixtar draws less Web traffic than other top sites, but boasts a much higher sales conversion rate.

3. Goals

As the Quixtar business has grown and matured in the first three years, it became apparent that a better understanding of core processes was needed to facilitate the growth of the information systems. There were two primary goals for the Quixtar Inc. Business Process Modeling Project:

1. To fully develop the infrastructure of the ARIS application, and the infrastructure of modeling practices such as developing a meta-architecture for the models

2. To build models of the core processes for two regions and analyze those models for differences and opportunities for incremental improvements

For the initial project, the focus was never intended to find, recommend or initiate any major re-engineering effort. The team believed that critical infrastructure setup was required. The right tools, methodology, skills and standards are required to ensure a higher probability of success. Building models of our core processes would allow us to test the use and benefit of evaluating our current core processes, and comparing the core processes that exist between two regions.

4. The Roadmap

4.1 The Team

The Business Process Modeling Team consisted of four core members that were dedicated to the project at least 80% of their time. The team was responsible for building the models by coordinating sessions between the representative of the business unit responsible for an area of the process, and the corresponding representative from the IT department responsible for building the functionality to support the process.

The team reported their progress and findings to a management group that consisted of eight functional managers that all reported to the VP of information technology. The goal of the management group was to provide direction for the core team. The first task was to define the core processes and regions to be included into the scope of the project.

4.2 Selection Models - Choosing the Best Processes

As with any project, one of the most important issues to clarify is the priorities of the objectives. Each initiative may consider many objectives, however, in many cases these objectives can and often do compete with each other. Therefore, to narrow in on the target, you need to determine what are the most important priorities to your organization. When a project team does not have a clear understanding of the priorities of the objectives, those priorities can easily change and shift throughout execution of the project. A good selection process will enable the team to gain this clarity of focus and have a better chance at keeping their aim to the goal even in shifting priorities.

Consider if the most important objective to your organization is to reduce cost, then perhaps you need to address the processes that are associated with overhead such as the payroll, accounts payable, procurement or the mailroom. However, if, the most important objective to your organization is to improve service to your customers then you should probably look to those processes that touch your customer, such as the ordering process or shipping processes. Perhaps, the most important objective is to reduce the time to market of your product, and then you should be looking at the product development lifecycle. If the initiative is intended to prepare the organization for an infrastructure move, then looking at those core process that are supported by the systems to be changed might be the best place to start. Without an understanding or agreement of the priorities of the objectives, it can be very easy in a process initiative to shoot at the wrong target.

Quixtar uses a selection process that evaluates two factors; business value and technical difficulty. Alone, these two factors do not make an effective selection model. For example, if a steering committee is reviewing project charters and simply asks the question "What is the business value of this proposed process initiative, those who strongly support the effort might indicate that it is the most important initiative that the company could be involved in with few reasons to support that position. In the same manner the same steering committee to provide me with their judgement of the technical difficulty, those who feel that the proposed initiative is not in the best interest of the company will simply reply that it is the most difficult initiative that could be done, again typically without much support their position. Therefore, the foundation of a selection model is the questions that will best identify what business value and technical difficulty mean to the organization.

4.3 Business Value

Sample Business Value Questions might include:

1. To what degree does this initiative offer us cost savings

2. To what degree will this initiative benefit our customer

3. To what degree will this initiative facilitate the generation of income

4. To what degree does this process strengthen the infrastructure of the organization

4.4 Technical Difficulty

Sample Technical Difficulty Questions might include

1. To what degree would we have to involve legal

2. How many people will have to change the way they work with this process

3. Do we have the necessary skill sets to implement this initiative

4. To what degree would we get upper management support for this initiative

Using this structure you can create a numerical scale, such as 1 – 5, defining characteristics for each number. Next, you would next solicit the judgement of your sponsor or steering committee for the value of the questions with respect to the proposed initiative. The model should be structured in such a manner that you would assign your judgements lowest to highest for the Business Value category and highest to lowest for the Technical Difficulty category. For example if the initiative can potentially save your organization much money, then you would rate that with a high number for business value. If on the other hand, you would need to have heavy legal involvement, you would rate that with a low number for very difficult with respect to technical difficulty. Using this format, when you add up the numbers that have been assigned to each question, the highest totals represent those potential initiatives that offer the highest business value with the lowest technical difficulty.

4.5 Project Methodology

Since the project was intended to only develop AS is models, the project methodology was developed specifically for a lifecycle to develop the AS-IS models and infrastructure. We chose to take a "Horizontal Wave" approach to building models.

The team would complete a full lifecycle for one level before going on to the next level of detail. This approach offered us several benefits. First, it kept the team focused on the level in which we were working. Had we decided to drop vertically into more detail within a given function before finishing a level, the probability of meeting our schedule would be very low. If we spent too much time discussing a given topic, we were able to quickly acknowledge that we were discussing issues that were in a lower level of detail.

As we moved from one level to another, we were able to test the higher level models. Typically, within the first couple of weeks of starting a new level, we would determine minor adjustments to the previous level. I am convinced that going into the depth of a function before finishing a complete level, would not have allowed us the structure to test the validity of each level.

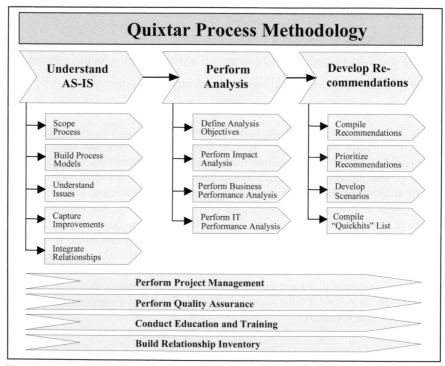

Fig. 1. Project Methodology

The top portion of the methodology represents the lifecycle for each level of the models. First we would scope out the processes to be modeled, clearly defining the inclusions and exclusions for that level. We would then build the models defining only the process.

When the processes were complete, we would spend time reviewing the process with those that worked on the process both from an IT and business unit perspective. We would review any issues with the process and capture recommendations from those who work on the processes.

When the process portion of the model was complete and reviewed, then we would finish this phase by assigning the relationships. When the entire level was complete, the core team would do analysis across the entire level and finally develop and formally submit any recommendations.

If a recommendation successfully made it through the selection process, it would become a full project initiative. The bottom portion of the methodology represents the activities that we needed to do throughout the life of the project, such as project management and quality assurance. The major deliverable represented in the bottom portion of the process methodology is "building the relationship inventory". This represents the work that needed to be done to develop the models for organizational units, systems and data. I refer to these models as inventory because these models are used as a repository for our non tangible assets. Information stored in these models include

- The specific servers located around the world

- The versions of software applications

- Where these versions are located around the world

- Master and Transactional Data

Once the relationships are set up and stored in a central repository, you can go to the "inventory of the relationships" and copy those objects to the functions. We felt that to be fully ready to develop more models, the inventory of the relationships needed to be ready.

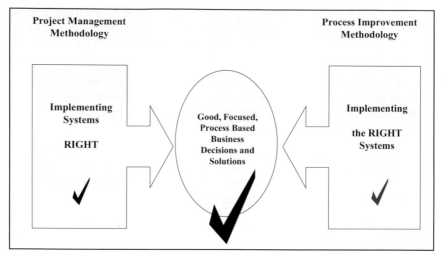

Fig. 2. Processes and Projects

The above figure sums up the need for both a project management methodology and a process improvement methodology to facilitate change management in an organization. Traditionally organizations have focused on creating Project management methodology so that they can implement their systems correctly, manage their projects efficiently and stay within budget and scope. However, if the project does not meet business requirements you would end up with a successful project that does not meet business requirements. The need for a process improvement methodology is vital to ensure that business processes are adequately defined and optimized before being implemented.

The combination of a project management methodology and a process improvement methodology ensures that we understand our business processes before successfully implementing the improved business processes. This combination leads to effective change management in an organization.

4.6 Small Focused Group

Before starting our project, I contacted several other companies that were involved in a business process modeling initiative and asked them what they would do differently if they had the opportunity to do their project all over again. There were many other project teams that struggled with the dynamics of the groups that were formed to build models.

Typically, to build process models, you need people from different perspectives of the company and different perspectives of the processes. This often fosters an environment for conflict. There are two basic challenges when selecting individuals to assist in building models.

First, the number of people who attend the session: More people require more consensus. When initiating the pilot project, we considered building models for one of our largest regions. The rational was that it would be better to build models that offered us a look at our most complex processes. However, the primary goal for the pilot project was to test out the validity of building models, and simply put, we needed models to test the process of modeling. If we had chosen our most complex region to model to meet this goal, the risk was much higher that we would not have been successful in meeting our goals. Why?, because in the most complex region, there were many people that would have to agree on the AS-IS models. In one of the smaller regions there were fewer individuals, in some cases only one, that had to validate a model. The decision paid off, we were able to accomplish the goal and have complete, verified models on time and under budget. By the time we choose to take on a more complex region, we had a better understanding of modeling facilitation techniques.

Another challenge with respect to selecting subject matter experts is to make sure that the individuals are at the level where they perform the work on the process. There was more than one case we encountered this issue. For one reason or another, they began their initiative by having managers come and develop the models. Some choose this strategy because they thought that they would get management support for the initiative. Others chose this strategy because of resource constraints on those that work with the process. In either case, the results were less then beneficial to the project. Managers tend to build AS-IS processes the way they think the process should be and not necessarily the way that it is. In one case, 6 months worth of models needed to be re-done, not to mention the negative support from the management. Subject matter expert selection is critical. From the experiences of others, we decided to keep modeling sessions to small focused groups. We sought to select one to two individuals from both the business unit and the IT department. In both cases they were the individuals who specifically worked on the process. Most modeling sessions were from 3-5 people and that including the facilitator.

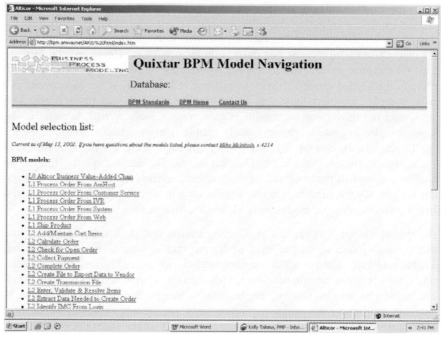

Fig. 3. BPM Web Site

All our projects impact the business in one way or another. It is important for people to know about the change and secondly to know what the future business is going to look like. Our project methodology and process improvement methodology both include a communication plan. Different audiences of the change have been identified with different messages that need to be delivered to them. There are different forms of communication that we will embark on. One of our easiest forms of communication is using our intranet. We used IDS Scheer's ARIS Webpublisher to publish our business process models to our intranet. Once the models were published to the intranet, it made it easier for people to review and provide comments and feedback on their business processes. The webpublisher serves as a training tool for people who are new to a particular process. For those who are familiar with the process it serves as a quick reference. Change is only successful if it is accepted and becomes part of the culture of the organization. Providing the right amount of visibility and communication helps people embrace the processes of the future and webpublisher has helped.

4.7 Inclusions/Exclusions

When defining the scope of any project there are four critical elements to consider; inclusions, exclusions, assumptions and constraints. After reviewing hundreds of scope statements, I can testify that project scope statements missing one of those elements are in danger.

The dynamics of inclusions and exclusions can be used in a variety of ways to help get the project in a box so that it can in fact be temporary. First inclusions/exclusions can help to define the boundaries of the overall project. From an overall project perspective, we defined the boundaries to be the processes that take place from order to shipment.

Another way that you can use the inclusions/exclusions dynamic is to define the boundaries of where one functional group leaves off and another picks up. When managing a very cross-functional project, having each functional group define their inclusions and exclusions can help you quickly find your holes. The IT functional group identified as an inclusion defining the system and data parameters but as an exclusion defining the rules. The business unit had the rules as their inclusion.

Also, you can use inclusions and exclusions is to break up a bigger project into smaller more manageable projects. Our first project was defined as building process models for order to ship, however, after careful scope definition, we defined our first project would be to model an order as if their was nothing unusual about the order; the credit card processed, the inventory was on the shelf, it was picked, packed and shipped. Exclusions to the first project were backorders, item recodes or items that were no longer available.

The next project was defined to build models for the exceptions, but this time the assumption was that the order was only going one way – from company to customer. This excluded the returns process. By narrowing the scope using inclusions and exclusions, the team is able to stay fixed on the defined deliverables without getting off track.

Our organization has had a successful project management methodology but we have now created a process improvement methodology to complement this methodology. We have realized that every project that we embark on impact our business processes in some form or the other so the need to examine our business processes is not optional but an absolute necessity.

5. Challenges

Usually, business process projects are not glamorous compared to other projects that go on in organizations. In many cases these projects appear in the infrastructure category of the companies project portfolio. The most significant challenge is selling the benefits of the initiative as compared to flashy marketing and product development projects.

Even the sales approach to IT is tough, because they are not used to working with process models; therefore, the integration of process models to the development lifecycle is new and must independently be managed as a process revision. Business process models are one of the most beneficial tools in a developer's toolbox, but individuals have to use the tool. Many from the IT department are skeptical because starting models from a higher level, , doesn't give them enough detail to develop code. Using process models is a good tool for the requirements definition phase, but the developer will still need to develop a design document.

An additional challenges is that the expenses of the modeling project might come from IT, but the most significant benefits of business process modeling appear outside of the IT department. There is a cost associated with building model and if they are primarily used for the benefit of other business units, IT will lose interest in funding the initiative, especially when they are facing a full shop of work.

Building models takes time, and will most likely benefit the infrastructure unless you are within an organization that is ready to make a big commitment to major change. Management is usually looking for quick initiatives that will make more money, dramatically reduce cost or mitigate high probability risks.

6. Overcoming the Challenges

The most effective strategy for overcoming the challenges is to actually use the models. Building process models for new development projects demonstrates how they can be used in practical application. For our team it means that we don't go out and sell the need to have a big modeling initiative or create a new functional group. We go out and sell our services to build models for new development projects that are in process or just beginning.

A bottom up approach, one project at a time will facilitate change more effectively than a top down approach where Sr. managers are asked to commit to an initiative that they are not sure of the benefit. If you can push the benefit up, by proving to the IT developers and the business units that models will help make the product faster and with better quality, management will be much more likely to increase their commitments. Ask the project lead on a new development project if you can come in and build models for his or her project, they usually won't say no. Most often, they welcome the help, and if they see the value, they will push it up to their management. Bottom up change, while usually more effective, typically takes longer.

Many people don't know how to facilitate change without a complete top down commitment. It comes down to good old fashion sales and customer service even inside a big company. Whenever possible, get models taped up on walls. Make sure you can print them on large paper, develop models and put them up, get them visible. When you pass models in the hall, stop and start conversations with other people about them. While recently attending a meeting, there were process models taped on the wall for a new development project. During pauses, I would talk about the processes with other participants from the meeting and they were coming from different areas of the company.

7. Successes

An organization can benefit from building process models from several different perspectives. First, by using the models to evaluate core processes for improvements, especially at a higher level of the process. Typically, IT will look for process improvements at lower levels of the processes, sometime evaluating only the functionality, independent of the processes. Process models facilitate the evaluation of the overall processes, which can highlight the most significant, wide sweeping and beneficial improvements.

Building process models should be the key activity to requirements analysis for any new development project. Just the process of building the models ensures that all parties, IT and functional units have had a role in developing the process before the developer ever writes one line of code. Adding this step to the development lifecycle significantly increases the probability for a better quality product. This step added will also, in most cases, reduce the cost to the overall project. Even though it may appear that there is more time spent on the front end of the lifecycle, the actual time for the development phase is usually reduced, and with better quality.

From a communication standpoint, building process models between client groups and IT facilitates strong relationships between the two groups. No longer are they battling over concepts that neither side really understands. If the IT department is constantly being perceived as the bad guy, building process models for new development projects will assist in highlighting the many challenging decisions that IT developers face.

In addition to having a repository of the business processes, organizations benefit from a centralized repository of the business rules. Each process may have dozens of rules associated with that single process. Before process models, the business rules are either stored embedded in the code or typically in someone's head. The models not only represent the overall processes but the business rules, which govern the way the functionality is to be developed. Often, in new development projects, it could take the team weeks or even months to figure out the existing rules, before they can even evaluate for changes. This process adds considerable time to many new development projects. With process models, that time is drastically cut. The entire team can gain access and review the business rules quicker and more effectively, reducing confusion and conflict over the center of the functionality to be built.

Process models have been used as an effective training tool. Specifically within the department that is responsible for testing, quality control and customer service. The process models were initially used to train those that have worked in the department, but as new employees are added, understanding the business processes is one of the key activities for new employee, greatly reducing the 'ramp up' time for productivity.

Another significant application for the models has been using them to troubleshoot functionality. A specific month end process, where affiliates around the world send data to the home office, consistently produced errors. By building models of the processes, we could identify where in the process modifications were needed to reduce the number of transactional errors.

8. Lessons Learned

Building process models and using them to standardize, or optimize, represents major changes to organizations. Organizations and business units within those organizations that are adverse to risk will have a difficult time recognizing the possibilities of a process centered organizations. In such a case, a BPM initiative will represent too much change to some, and too much overhead to others. Implementing such an initiative requires one of two possible conditions.

1. Unified and strong leadership that can keep the vision in view and mentor the change throughout the organization

2. A change agent that is persistent and will push process modeling at the levels where the tools become the most useful for someone to do a good job

A successful BPM project will require extensive project management skills. These types of project will usually be cross-functional, and ambiguous. Successful execution of a BPM project will require, at least, the ability to identify and focus on the goals through an effective selection model, clearly defining the scope using inclusions, exclusions, assumptions, constraints, extensive communication management and change management.

Information & Communication to Prepare for an ERP Implementation

Ed Brady
IT Director, American Meter Company

Marc Scharsig
Director, Consulting Services, IDS Scheer, Inc.

Summary

As both the standard software offerings, and implementation methodologies associated with ERP mature, the remaining area of ERP implementation projects that carries a disproportionate amount of project risk is in change management. As a consequence, this area is beginning to receive more focus, and earlier in project lifecycles.

This case study describes the change management elements of a Business Process Oriented Standard Software Selection of American Meter Company, the first lifecycle stage of an ERP driven improvement initiative. During this stage, the emphasis is more on information and communication. Training will be emphasized during later stages in the ERP project lifecycle.

Key Words

ARIS, ARIS Toolset, BPI, BPR, ERP, Business Process Analysis, Business Process Modeling, Business Process Design, Change Management

1. Project Background

1.1 Introduction

American Meter Company is in the second of a five year plan to overhaul its IT capabilities. The project described in this article involves a preliminary phase of implementing a new ERP system. The project scope was to define a set of "to-be" processes, codify them into a concise set of system requirements, select the optimal standard software to enable these processes, and prepare the organization for the next (implementation) phase.

From a change management perspective, this project intended to address 2 of the 3 areas of change management depicted in Fig. 1 (Information & Communication). The 3rd area (Training) will be addressed during the implementation phase.

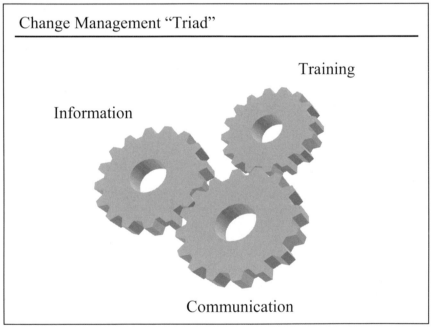

Fig. 1. Change Management "Triad"

1.2 Business Conditions

Market dynamics in the utility industry have driven virtually all major players to refocus on cost efficiency, which represent both a risk and opportunity for American Meter companies to streamline administrative processes, and introduce additional services which provide value and increase satisfaction of our customers. A considerable amount of manufacturing optimization has already been accomplished to satisfy these objectives. The fact that most of the core business information resides in several different ERP databases, which are inherently closed, has rendered their replacement with an integrated ERP system as the next high leverage enabler of continuous improvement.

1.3 Project History

Several projects have been undertaken in the last 12 months to study the strategic IT options, and feasibility of an enterprise-wide deployment of an integrated ERP system to consolidate core business information and leverage common processes. The ERP initiative was selected on the basis of total cost, risk, and flexibility with respect to strategic business plans. The project team recommended, and executive board approved a detailed "to-be" process and system requirements documentation project; to enable tight scope management and clearly articulate benefit targets from the subsequent implementation projects. This phase has been successfully completed and the results were used to finalize ERP software selection and negotiation.

1.4 Company Background

American Meter Company consists of 6 legal entities in 3 countries, primarily servicing the Americas region. There are 13 plant locations, which manufacture a portfolio of products and services serving the gas distribution market. A product model (excerpt) of the company offerings is attached (Fig. 2). The company uses a direct sales model to reinforce its long-standing relationship with the utility industry. The company employs approximately 1400, and anticipates ~350 ERP users.

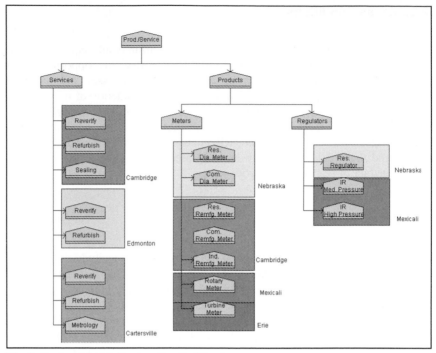

Fig. 2. Product Model (Product Family View)

Organizationally, the company is structured around semi-autonomous divisions, which manufacture exclusive product lines. Business models and manufacturing strategy employed by the plants range from configure-to-order to make-to-stock and repetitive manufacturing in mixed mode, as illustrated as an example in the attached end-to-end process model (Fig. 3).

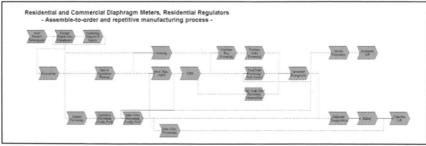

Fig. 3. Level I Enterprise Wide Business Process

2. Project Goals

The objectives of the AMCo ERP project revolve around enabling and realizing the case for change (Fig. 4). The ERP project is providing a forcing function, or catalyst, for making the process and structural improvements across the enterprise, which will position the American Meter companies to effectively compete in the 2000's.

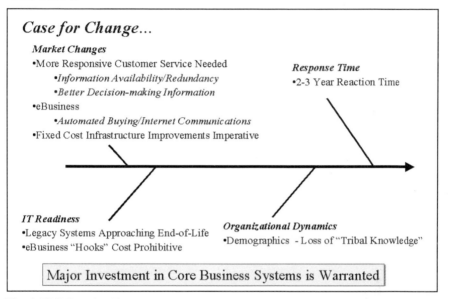

Fig. 4. ERP Case for Change

2.1 Corporate Objectives

- Sustain market leadership in residential gas meters
- Continue producing top of the line quality products
- Enhance profitability
- Improve operational excellence, increasing organizational effectiveness and process efficiency
- Increase business activities in the more profitable/growth market segments
- Reposition AMCo as a prime utility industry supplier, recognized for ease of doing business with and responsive to the changing needs of the industry

2.2 Project Objectives

- Optimize internal processes – Continual improvement in overhead efficiencies
- Harmonize, where possible, business processes across product lines (including best practices)
- Prepare and "set the table" for eBusiness – Anticipate changing buying behaviors
- KISS – Simplify and streamline current business practices
- Capture "tribal knowledge" in a defined, documented, sustainable set of system supported business processes
- Build momentum for future state ERP implementation by securing buy-in from users and local management
- Deliver expected results within given timeline and budget

2.3 Change Management Objectives

- Keep stakeholders fully informed of project developments, dispensing information in manageable "bite size" pieces throughout the project life
- Engage executive management and employees in defining the "future state" vision
- Induce employees to adopt "best practices" to realize sustainable process improvement
- Transform company culture to realize Continuous Process Improvement, adopting prudent risk taking/innovation
- Realize a sense of urgency within the user community for sustainable process improvement

3. Procedure

This chapter describes selected procedures, which were used to achieve the above mentioned change management objectives.

3.1 Information and Communication to Stakeholders

Product models and an enterprise business process model were used in order to communicate the current stage of the development of the future enterprise business processes to executive management and shareholders during this phase of the project. The product models depict all products and services American Meter intends to sell in the foreseeable future. Two product models were developed, one with a product family oriented view and one with a business process oriented view. The product model with the product family orientation (Fig. 2, excerpt) shows also at which physical location products or services will be manufactured or provided, e.g. residential diaphragm meters are manufactured in Nebraska City, NE or automated meter reading devices are manufactured in Scott Depot, WV. The process oriented product model (Fig. 5, excerpt) groups products and services according to business process families, e.g. configurable make to order products or make to stock products. Based on the identified business process families, unique end-to-end processes were developed (Fig. 3, example). In order to be able to present all end-to-end processes in one model it was decided to combine them in one enterprise process model. The selected model types for the product model were "product/service tree" and for the enterprise model "value-added chain diagram". It was an iterative process driven by the input from all divisions until the final versions of these models were developed.

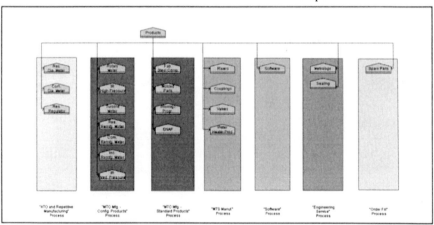

Fig. 5. Product Model (Process Oriented View)

The use of these models facilitated the communication to the executive management, because within a short time all relevant information concerning which products will be manufactured where under the umbrella of what end-to-end process can be provided. It has to be kept in mind that American Meter offers about 30 different lines of products and services, has 13 plants, and has 8 distinct end-to-end business processes. Although considered a mid-size company, the business process complexity and variability cannot be considered less than the ones of large corporations. The saying "a picture is worth a thousand words" truly can be quoted in this case. The forum to communicate with the executive management was primarily the steering committee meetings and the divisional on-site general management briefings and with the shareholders the board meetings of American Meter's parent company.

Additionally, these models will be the roadmap for the upcoming ERP implementation and will be a useful tool to show the scope of the different implementation phases.

In order to inform employees about the designed future business processes, who have not been directly involved in this preparation phase of an ERP implementation, as well as some selected customers and suppliers detailed business process models have been used. These models describe levels 2 (Fig. 6, example) and 3 below the enterprise process model and are linked to the respective objects in the enterprise business model. The selected model type is "extended-event driven process chain". Depending on the point of time these briefings took place either the work in progress of the divisional to-be business processes was used or the enterprise wide harmonized versions of the business processes.

The forum to present these detailed process models were specially arranged communication meetings.

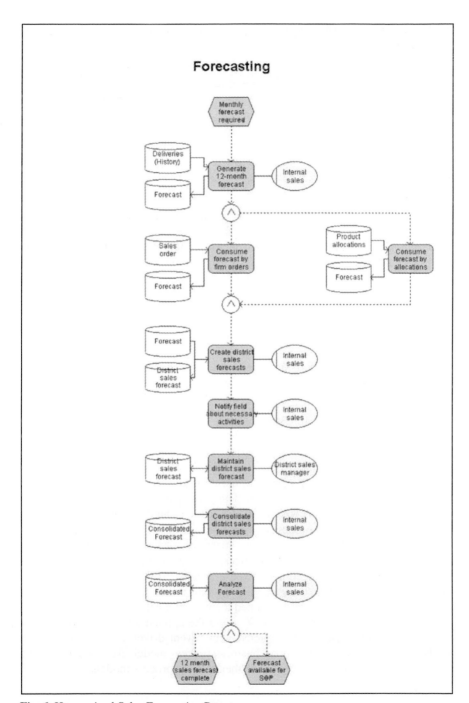

Fig. 6. Harmonized Sales Forecasting Process

3.2 Engaging Executive Management and Employees in Defining the Future State

The product models and enterprise model described in paragraph 3.1 were used to trigger strategic discussions within the executive management about future, mid-term plant locations and the products and services offered at these locations. The objective is to make potential outstanding decisions concerning plant locations and the offered products and services portfolio before the start of the ERP implementation to minimize potential distractions. The executive management team was engaged through the executive project sponsor, with extended discussions in the steering committee meetings.

All 5 business units were involved in the development of the future state processes. To ensure to get the same input from each division the same series of workshops was executed for each division. Depending on the respective products and services adjustments were made, e.g. engineering workshops were not everywhere relevant. To develop the future state processes the following approach was applied:

- Documentation of division and product specific as-is business processes

- Development of division and product specific to-be business processes

- Harmonization of the divisional to-be business processes to enterprise to-be business processes, or in other words products or services driven to-be processes

To benefit most from the future state business process design the objective was to harmonize business processes across the different divisions wherever possible. The taken approach was that the American Meter and IDS Scheer, Inc. project management harmonized the division specific To-Be processes initially. The result served as a strawman for a series of harmonization sessions, which were held in forms of phone or videoconferences. The participants were the respective process owners of the divisions who were also leading the divisional to-be business process design effort. The process owners used the time in between the harmonization sessions to discuss open topics, questions, or concerns with their local teams. Due to this approach best practices, new ideas, and existing experiences were discussed and exchanged across the divisions. At the end of this harmonization process all divisions committed to the future state processes they designed in a joint effort. This approach facilitated the communication across the divisions as well as created transparency. Fig. 7 shows the applied approach. The harmonized business processes were depicted with "event driven process chains" on levels 2 and 3 below the enterprise business process model. At this stage of the project it is not beneficial to develop further detailed process models.

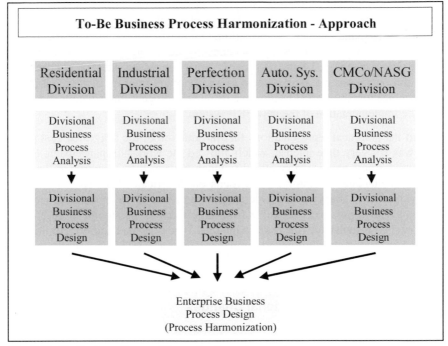

Fig. 7. To-Be Business Process Harmonization - Approach

3.3 Induce Employees to Adopt "Best Practices" to Realize Sustainable Process Improvement

The objective during the To-Be business process design phase was to build on best practices. The approach was to introduce best practices to American Meter in order to allow the divisional project teams to assess and evaluate best practices and thus to create a decision basis whether or not to adopt the suggested best practices. To communicate the features of the suggested best practices business process models were used to in order to explain the logical sequence of the respective process steps, to depict the required input data for and the created output data of each function as well as the executing organizational units. Basically best practice information was provided in the form of reference models. This means for the organizational units that they were kept generic in order to show the participating parties before they were adjusted to American Meter terminology.

As an example can serve the sales and operations planning process, which –properly executed – can help American Meter to maintain the right inventory levels. Although American Meter is applying at some divisions this best practice already, there is still room for improvements, which ranges from having the right audience in the sales and operations planning meetings to using the right data, e.g. product forecast, booked sales orders, product allocations, production orders, planned orders, and inventory information. Obviously the execution of successful sales and operations meetings also depends on the accuracy and the availability of the above-mentioned data. However, American Meter also recognized the sales and operations planning process as an important improvement potential for the organization and started to improve its current process immediately, even before the implementation of the new ERP system.

Due to the graphical representations the introduction of the suggested best practices was not very time intense, which allowed the workshop participants either to dismiss a best practice very quickly, which happened for example to the idea of vendor managed inventory, or to focus on American Meter specific adjustments in order to adapt the best practice into the set of future business processes. It is not always possible or feasible from an efficiency standpoint to describe a best practice completely with process models. Where needed additional information was provided also through additional means, e.g. EXCEL was used to simulate potential sales and operations planning tables.

3.4. Coping with Organizational Changes

Organizational changes can happen on different levels within the organization. In this chapter the focus is on organizational changes American Meter is facing, which have an impact on the divisions as well as on employee level.

As already indicated above in the company background chapter American Meter is organized in semi-autonomous divisions. This means that each of the divisions can make to a large degree their own business decisions and can act independently. But they all maintain also their own supporting functions. Examples for these functions are collections (A/R), payments (A/P), purchasing, human resources, and information technology. This redundancy is of course also forced by the fact that each of the divisions were allowed to make their own business software decisions, which led to a non-integrated system landscape across the divisions, which made it hard or impossible to connect these systems. An improvement potential is to reduce some of these supporting functions. Therefore, in order to reduce the cost of their supporting functions American Meter is seeking to centralize some of them. These functions can be organized under the leadership of a corporate service center. However, this centralization effort does not have to mean that all functions of a certain area can be or have to be centralized. For example the centralization of the information technology function still requires to some degree on-site support for all the sites, e.g. network support or PC support.

Fig. 8 depicts the future American Meter's centralized and decentralized information technology responsibilities.

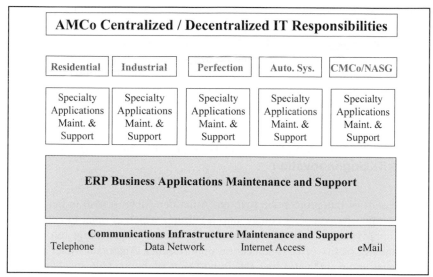

Fig. 8. Centralized/Decentralized Information Technology Responsibilities

The idea of centralizing supporting functions is not new and already implemented by some enterprises, in particular larger ones. Obviously the centralization of business functions means for the divisional general managers that they have to give up some control. This means that the execution of this concept needs to be carried by all impacted general managers. The technical realization with a new ERP system is not the critical issue for American Meter. The more challenging part is to convince management of the business benefits. Therefore, the discussion is still ongoing for some of the support areas. However, the information technology department definitely will go to a more centralized structure.

Obviously with the upcoming implementation of a new ERP system also the working environment of most of the employees will be affected. This does not only mean that the usage of new screens will be trained in the implementation phase. More importantly some positions will experience an enrichment or enlargement of their tasks others will experience a shift of their current focus. American Meter chose to inform strategically important teams and departments, which may face some significant changes in the way doing business in the future, already in this business process design phase. An example is the sales team, which is dealing primarily with residential diaphragm meters, which are configurable products. Today, the members of the sales team who deal directly with customers capture the customer's requirements and let the technical back office make the product configuration. In the future the sales team will be enabled to configure the customer's desired product by themselves with the help of a system supported product configurator. One benefit is that the response time to the customer is shortened.

In order to prepare the sales team early for these rather complex changes information sessions were held with a large portion of the sales team. The objective of these sessions were to educate the sales team about the new processes as well as to get a feeling if the sales team would be willing to buy-in into this new concept and what the upcoming change management effort for the following project phases would be. Also for these communication sessions the main communication tools were the harmonized to-be business processes.

3.5 Transform Company Culture to Realize CPI, Adopting Prudent Risk Taking/Innovation

Since the start of this project one year ago American Meter is also in the process of transforming its company culture into a culture, which is open to continuous process improvement. Due to a tremendous increase in providing information and organizing plenty of communication opportunities American Meter is gaining momentum in understanding the importance of being able to change and adapt in today's business environment. This developing openness to change is also supported by the success of this first project phase, which delivered several dozen quick hits which added immediately value to the enterprise as well as several hundred improvement potentials, which are the foundation of the business case of the upcoming ERP implementation. Due to this project phase the divisions became motivated to think about business process improvement even after the end of the process workshops.

Corporate decided to take this initial business process design phase as the point of departure for a permanent CPI initiative, which led to the decision to acquire all relevant method know-how and ARIS tools in order to support this initiative internally.

3.6 Realize a Sense of Urgency within the User Community for Sustainable Process Improvement

At the beginning of this project, business unit representatives were understandably apprehensive about how an IT project of this nature, led by Corporate, would actually help them locally. As the project evolved, it became clear to these process owners where improvements could be derived. As a consequence, the resistance to change faded, and enthusiasm around the potential accompanying a new ERP system began to supplant it. Several points in the project methodology contributed to making the improvement potential tangible, which in turn raised the level of urgency.

First, the project team was assembled with people experienced in process execution, and exposed to best practices at other similar companies. The team was then dispatched to the site locations to get a real-life sense for the challenges and opportunities. This allowed a quick assimilation of the team and credibility with the process owners to emerge.

Second, a log of improvement recommendations was maintained, which captured the recommendations of users and outcomes of each process workshop. This resulted in documenting an overwhelming composite list of improvement potentials, as well as a feeling among the user community that they were each instrumental in designing the future state. When mapped to existing functionality of current ERP system offerings, the basis for a sound business case developed.

Additionally, 2 areas of the list improvement potentials were isolated for concentration: 1) "critical few" items that contributed most to the business case and were worthy of continued focus from the implementation project, 2) "quick hits" which were not dependant on new software but could be realized right away. This organization served to build momentum and urgency as the project evolved.

To address the perspective of the leaders of the business, we were able to recommend an implementation scope of effort, which addressed the maximum business improvement/ROI with the minimum project and business risk using this detailed improvement potentials as the basis (Fig. 9).

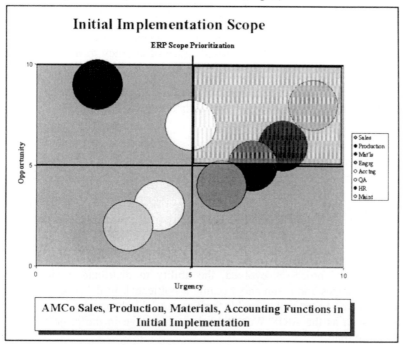

Fig. 9. Urgency/Opportunity Chart

4. Results

The results of this project, and its change management parameters, exceeded our initial expectations. Summarized below, they can be directly related to the stated objectives at the start of the project. In addition, we will incorporate what we learned in this project into future improvement efforts.

- Buy-in from process owners & practitioners into evolving "future state" (communication)

- Enthusiasm of end-users resulting from interactive dialog and diagramming future state processes, documenting of system requirements (information)

- Greater flexibility as project team earned a level of credibility with end-users (communication)

- Increased shareholder satisfaction as they saw the level of fidelity in our analysis (information, & communication)

- Harmonization resulting from interaction of like process owners representing different business units, to arrive at a set of "corporate best practices"

- Common understanding of business unit management regarding where tangible benefits can be derived, and a shared sense of urgency to move forward with ERP implementation.

- Recognition of the value in continuous process improvement, and an endorsement of senior management of this methodology to enable CPI.

5. Lessons Learned

We were pleased with the results of this initiative. As is normally the case, there are several things we would have done differently given the chance to do them over.

ARIS web publisher to enable more widespread review and comment. As our harmonized "to-be" processes evolved, the ability to distribute, review, and communicate changes and comments became a bottleneck in the process. If we had deployed a web-based tool to enable "self service" by the process owners and constituents, such as the ARIS Web Publisher, this stage in the project would have been more fluid.

Tighter communication & interaction with the project sponsor to eliminate or greatly reduce miscommunication. The project team was in the field, and interacted with the senior management largely via steering committee meetings on a monthly frequency. In retrospect, we owed the project sponsor a more frequent, more in depth review of our findings, recommendations & development.

A formal communication plan, to address the needs of each segment of the stakeholder community, which incorporated multiple opportunities to collect feedback. Although the steering committee and shareholders were effectively engaged to solicit feedback, we lacked a consistent strategy for the general employee population.

Using ARIS to Design the Future Logistics Enterprise

Thomas R. Gulledge
George Mason University

Philip Hayes
Teamworks Partners, Inc.

Alexander Lotterer
IDS Scheer, Inc.

Georg Simon
IDS Scheer, Inc.

Summary

The US Department of Defense (DoD) is engaged in a multi-year transformation of logistics planning and execution to support the objectives of Focused Logistics[1], which are integral to achieving the goals of Joint Vision 2020. The Deputy Undersecretary for Defense – Logistics and Material Readiness (DUSD-L&MR) has established a multi-disciplinary, government, industry, and academic team to create an operational architecture to help guide the multi-year transformation from the current DoD logistics environment to the Future Logistics Enterprise (FLE.) This framework, known as the Future Logistics Enterprise Operational Architecture (FLE OA), provides a common language and common structures for articulating requirements, policies, processes, and infrastructure needed to establish the FLE. This chapter describes the use of the ARIS methodology for the development of the FLE OA.

Key Words

Logistics, Business Process Architecture, Supply Chain, SCOR, Standard Software, Public Sector, Department of Defense

---

[1] See Needham (2002) for a discussion of Focused Logistics.

1. Project Background

The US Department of Defense (DoD) has proposed a major transformation of the way that it plans for and executes logistics in support of joint operations. This multi-year effort is called the Future Logistics Enterprise (cf. U.S. DoD, 2002). "The Future Logistics Enterprise (FLE) is an integrated set of six collaborative initiatives to achieve end-to-end customer service within Department of Defense logistics operations. The primary intent of the FLE is to accelerate the DoD's implementation of integrated logistics chains and commercial information systems to meet warfighter sustainment needs and the operational requirements of the National Defense Strategy. The FLE is focused on those mid-term policy, process, and systems changes the DoD must make in order to continue to effectively support our warfighting customers"

The DoD has directed the Future Logistics Enterprise Operational Architecture (FLE OA) project team build a collaborative architectural model that links policy, strategy, metrics, processes and supporting information technologies. The primary intent of the FLE OA is to provide guidance to DoD agencies and military service components responsible for the development of logistics processes and supporting technologies needed to achieve the high degree of interoperability and agility required for modern joint military operations. The DoD established the principle that the FLE OA must provide useful guidance without inhibiting innovation by users of the FLE OA. The FLE OA is designed to evolve as priorities, strategies, and technologies change over time. The collaborative design of the OA anticipates the growing involvement of commercial providers in the full life-cycle support of weapons systems under the concept of full Contractor Logistics Support (CLS.) The FLE OA resides in the ARIS toolset, which facilitates the use, and evolution, of the FLE OA by authorized constituents across the military establishment and from non-DoD communities such as civilian agencies, commercial partners, and military allies.

1.1 The Six FLE Strategies

1.1.1 Depot Maintenance Partnerships

The primary intent of the Depot Maintenance Partnership initiative is to enable DoD-owned maintenance depots to expand partnerships with commercial companies, while fulfilling the national security need for the DoD to retain depot maintenance capabilities.

1.1.2 Condition-Based Maintenance Plus (CBM+)

CBM+ focuses on inserting technology into both existing and new weapon systems to support improved maintenance capabilities and businesses processes. The long-term goal is to integrate condition sensors and self-reporting technology directly into weapon systems so the systems become a direct extension of the logistics chain. The "Logistics Chain" extends the supply chain to include maintenance and transportation functions needed to sustain an operating military force. The advent of this technology requires significant process and policy changes to achieve the dramatic improvements in logistics system responsiveness required to meet DoD strategic goals.

1.1.3 Total Life Cycle Systems Management (TLCSM)

The primary intent of this initiative is to improve weapon system sustainment by establishing clear responsibility and accountability for meeting warfighter performance expectations within the weapon system program management office. The weapon systems program manager will be held responsible for the overall management of the weapon system life cycle to include: timely acquisition of weapon systems, meeting warfighter performance requirements, integration of sustainability and maintainability during the acquisition process, and weapon system sustainment to meet or exceed warfighter performance requirements throughout the life cycle at best corporate value to the Services and the DoD.

1.1.4 End-to-End Distribution (E2E)

The end-to-end distribution initiative is directed toward streamlining warfighter support by providing materiel, including retrograde and associated information, from the source of supply or point of origin to the point of use or disposal, as defined by the Combatant Commanders, Military Services, or characteristics of the commodity, on a worldwide basis. The intent of the initiative is to influence acquisition, sourcing, and positioning to facilitate the flow of materiel to the end user, ensuring that deployment and sustainment are synchronized.

1.1.5 Executive Agents (EA)

The Executive Agents initiative is aimed at improving support to warfighters by ensuring that roles, responsibilities, resources, and capabilities are responsive to the supported Combatant Commanders' deployment and sustainment requirements. The goal is to clarify responsibilities in the complex milieu of crisis/deliberate planning and during deployments of all types.

1.1.6 Enterprise Integration (EI)

To accelerate development of the FLE, this initiative builds upon efforts, underway within the Services and the Defense Logistics Agency, which successfully uses commercial ERP and other commercial solutions to enable the business process requirements across the FLE.

The DoD recognizes that it will take many years to fully implement the FLE, including changes to policy, statute, infrastructure and organization. This transformation requires a mechanism to facilitate on-going planning and analysis while providing a means to communicate changes to successive generations of civilian and military personnel throughout the defense establishment.

1.2 The Scope of DoD Logistics

It is useful to understand how the terms logistics and supply chain are used in the commercial sector and in the military establishments. This is all the more relevant due to the significant, and increasing, role of commercial companies in military logistics and supply chain operations under the concept of full Contractor Logistics Support (CLS) for new weapons systems. Generally, the commercial sector definitions of logistics and supply chain reflect a subset of the broader military use of the terms. The following definitions from the Council on Logistics Management (CLM) and the Institute of Logistics Management (IoLT) reflect prevailing commercial usage.

1.2.1 The CLM Definition of Logistics

"Logistics is that part of the supply chain process that plans, implements, and controls the efficient, effective forward and reverse flow and storage of goods, services, and related information between the point of origin and the point of consumption in order to meet customers' requirements."

1.2.2 The CLM Definition of Supply Chain Management

"Supply Chain Management is the systemic, strategic coordination of the traditional business functions and the tactics across these business functions within a particular company and across businesses within the supply chain for the purposes of improving the long-term performance of the individual companies and the supply chain as a whole."

1.2.3 The IoLT Definitions of Logistics and the Supply-Chain

- "Logistics is the time-related positioning of resources, or the strategic management of the total supply-chain

- The supply-chain is a sequence of events intended to satisfy a customer

- It can include procurement, manufacture, distribution, and waste disposal, together with associated transport, storage and information technology

- The application of logistics is essential to the efficient management of the supply-chain

- Transport is an integral part of the supply-chain, not only between the sequence of events but during the processes

- 'Logistics' is the process of designing, managing and improving such supply-chains, which might include purchasing, manufacturing, storage and, of course, transport."

It is worth noting that prevailing commercial supply chain models and software packages were designed from the point of view of the manufacturer. The result is that business processes as implemented in commercial software solutions focus on a chain of events that begins with a raw material or semi-finished good, adds value to the raw or semi-finished material, and passes (distributes) the value-added item to the next link in the supply chain. The next link could be an end customer or another value-add operation. An idea implicit in commercial supply chain models is that a finished item is eventually handed off to an end user. The latest version of the SCOR model (version 5.0) adds processes for the Return of items from an end user to the final supply chain and for the Return of an item from one supply chain to the source of supply in an upstream supply chain (cf. Supply Chain Council, 2001). In its current form, SCOR does not include a comprehensive model for Maintenance, Repair, and Overhaul.

The DoD logistics definition of a supply chain extends the breadth of the commercial definition to include storage, repair, and movement of items after receipt by the end user. Military logistics processes must address the requirements of military missions such as Mobilization, Movement, Deployment, and In-Theater Distribution. A viable DoD logistics model requires definition of processes such as configuration management, training, and quality assurance. Commercial supply chain models such as SCOR are silent or make only tangential references to many of these areas.

1.3 The Scope of SCOR

A key input to development of the FLE OA is the Supply Chain Operations Reference Model (SCOR) (cf. Supply Chain Council, 2001). "The Reference Model is the product of the Supply-Chain Council (SCC), an independent, not-for-profit, global corporation with membership open to all companies and organizations interested in applying and advancing the state-of-the-art in supply-chain management systems and practices." Initially developed in 1996, the SCOR model has been widely adopted by industry and government as a common basis for expressing the fundamental operational components of a supply chain. At the highest level, SCOR identifies Plan, Source, Make, Deliver, and Return as the macro, Level 1, process types of a supply chain. These five level 1 process types decompose to 30 Level 2 process categories, which decompose into 156 Level 3 processes elements.

SCOR is a framework that provides a common language and common process constructs for communicating supply chain concepts. SCOR provides common ways of expressing ideas within the knowledge domain of supply chains.

The SCOR documentation (cf. Supply Chain Council, 2001) addresses many of the boundaries of the Model:

- "It does not attempt to describe every business process or activity. Specifically, the Model does not address: sales and marketing (demand generation), product development, research and development, and some elements of post-delivery customer support."

- "The Model is silent in the areas of human resources, training, and quality assurance among others."

SCOR was constructed from the point of view of a manufacturer. A quick examination of SCOR level 2 processes confirms this orientation. The first level Source, Make, Deliver, Return processes are in decomposed into second level processes according to the method of manufacture of the product e.g. M1 Make-to-Stock, M2 Make-to-Order, M3 Engineer-to-Order (see Fig. 3 SCOR Version 5 Level 2 Toolkit).

For example, SCOR was not designed to cover the broad spectrum of mission requirements faced by DoD and the military services in moving people, equipment, and material around the world to meet constantly shifting operational needs.

SCOR defines processes at a level above that needed for an executable supply chain design. This overarching framework serves as tool for developing a specific supply chain blueprint. "The [Supply Chain] Council has focused on three process levels and does not attempt to prescribe how a particular organization should conduct its business or tailor its systems / information flow. Every organization that implements supply chain improvements using the SCOR-model will need to extend the Model, at least to Level 4, using organization-specific processes, systems, and practice."

1.4 The C4ISR Framework

The FLE OA conforms to the C4ISR Architectural Framework (cf. U.S. DoD, 1997) standards for expressing operational, systems and technical views of architecture components. Architectures provide a mechanism for understanding and managing complexity. Within the United States Department of Defense exists a standard framework to express Operational Architectures. This framework is called C4ISR (Command, Control, Communications, Computers, Intelligence, Surveillance, and Reconnaissance). The purpose of the C4ISR architecture framework is to express operational architectures that enable the quick synthesis of "go-to-war" requirements with sound investments leading to the rapid employment of improved operational capabilities. The ability to compare, analyze, and integrate architectures developed by the geographical and functional, unified Commands, Military Services, and Defense Agencies (hereinafter also referred to as Commands, Services, and Agencies, or C/S/As) from a cross-organizational perspective is critical to achieving these objectives.

The C4ISR Architecture Framework is intended to ensure that the architecture descriptions developed by the Commands, Services, and Agencies are expressed in a sufficiently common manner to enable communications between and among organizations. This common framework is essential to creating architectural planning tools that may be compared and integrated across Joint and combined organizational boundaries.

The Framework provides the rules, guidance, and product descriptions for developing and presenting architecture descriptions that ensure a common denominator for understanding, comparing, and integrating architectures. The application of the Framework will enable architectures to contribute most effectively to building interoperable and cost-effective military systems.

1.4.1 Definition of the Operational Architecture

The operational architecture is a description of the tasks and activities, operational elements, and information flows required to accomplish or support a military operation. It contains descriptions (often graphical) of the operational elements, assigned tasks and activities, and information flows required to support the warfighter. It defines the types of information exchanged, the frequency of exchange, which tasks and activities are supported by the information exchanges, and the nature of information exchanges in detail sufficient to ascertain specific interoperability requirements.

88

Table 1. C4ISR Operational Views

Operational	OV-1	High-level Operational Concept Graphic	Essential	High-level graphical description of operational concept (high-level organizations, missions, geographic configurations, connectivity, etc.)
Operational	OV-2	Operational Node Connectivity Description	Essential	Operational nodes, activities performed at each node, connectivities & information flow between nodes
Operational	OV-3	Operational Information Exchange Matrix	Essential	Information exchanged between nodes and the relevant attributes of that exchange such as media, quality, quantity,, and the level of interoperability required
Operational	OV-4	Command Relationships Chart	Supporting	Command, control, coordination relationships among organizations
Operational	OV-5	Activity Model	Supporting	Activities, relationships among activities, I/Os, constraints (e.g. policy, guidance), and mechanisms that perform those activities. In addition to showing mechanisms, overlays can show other pertinent information
Operational	OV-6a	Operational Rules Model	Supporting	One of the three products used to describe operational activity sequence and timing that identifies the business rules that constrain the operation
Operational	OV-6b	Operational State Transition Description	Supporting	One of the three products used to describe operational activity sequence and timing that identifies responses of a business process to events
Operational	OV-6c	Operational Event/Trace Description	Supporting	One of the three products used to describe operational activity sequence and timing that traces the actions in a scenario or critical sequence of events
Operational	OV-7	Logical Data Model	Supporting	Documentation of the data requirements and structural business process rules of the Operational View

1.4.2 Definition of the Systems Architecture

The systems architecture is a description, including graphics, of systems and interconnections providing for, or supporting, warfighting functions. For a domain, the systems architecture shows how systems link and interoperate, and may describe the internal construction and operations of particular systems within the architecture. For individual systems, the systems architecture includes the physical connection, location, and identification of key nodes (including materiel item nodes), circuits, networks, warfighting platforms, etc., and specifies system and component performance parameters (e.g., mean time between failure, maintainability, availability). The systems architecture aligns physical resources and their performance attributes to the operational architecture and its requirements per standards defined in the technical architecture.

Table 2. C4ISR System Views

Systems	SV-1	Systems Interface Description	Essential	Identification of systems and system components and their interfaces, within and between nodes
Systems	SV-2	Systems Communications Description	Supporting	Physical nodes and their related communications laydowns
Systems	SV-3	Systems² Matrix	Supporting	Relationships among systems in a given architecture; can be designed to show relationships of interest, e.g., system-type interfaces, planned vs. existing interfaces, etc.
Systems	SV-4	Systems Functionality Description	Supporting	Functions performed by systems and the information flow among system functions

Table 2. (continued)

Systems	SV-5	System Information Exchange Description	Supporting	Mapping of system functions back to operational activities
Systems	SV-6	System Information Exchange Matrix	Supporting	Detailing of information exchanges among system elements, applications an H/W allocated to systems elements
Systems	SV-7	Systems Performance Parameters Matrix	Supporting	Performance characteristics of each system(s) hardware and software elements, for the appropriate time frame(s)
Systems	SV-8	System Evolution Description	Supporting	Planned incremental steps toward migrating a suite of systems to a more efficient suite, or toward evolving a current system to a future implementation
Systems	SV-9	System Technology Forecast	Supporting	Emerging technologies and software/hardware products that are expected to be available in a given set of time-frames, and that will affect future developments of the architecture
Systems	SV-10a	Systems Rules Models	Supporting	One of three products used to describe systems activity sequence and timing – Constraints that are imposed on systems functionality due to some aspect of systems design or implementation
Systems	SV-10b	Systems State Transitions Description	Supporting	One of three products used to describe systems activity sequence and timing – Responses of a system to events
Systems	SV-10c	Systems Event/Trace Description	Supporting	One of three products used to describe systems activity sequence an timing -- System-specific refinements of critical sequences of events described in the operational view
Systems	SV-11	Physical Data Model	Supporting	Physical implementation of the information of the Logical Data Model, e.g., message formats, file structures, physical schema

1.4.3 Definition of the Technical Architecture

The technical architecture is the minimal set of rules governing the arrangement, interaction, and interdependence of system parts or elements, whose purpose is to ensure that a system satisfies a specified set of requirements. The technical architecture provides the technical systems-implementation guidelines upon which engineering specifications are based, common building blocks are established, and product lines are developed. The technical architecture includes a collection of the technical standards, conventions, rules and criteria organized into profile(s) that govern system services, interfaces, and relationships for particular systems architecture views and that relate to particular operational views.

Table 3. C4ISR Technical Views

Technical	TV-1	Technical Architecture Profile	Essential	Extraction of standards that apply to the given architecture
Technical	TV-2	Standards Technology Forecast	Supporting	Description of emerging standards that are expected to apply to the given architecture, within an appropriate set o time-frames

1.4.4 C4ISR Compliancy and the ARIS Toolset

The C4ISR Architecture Framework does not define the supporting tools to be used to build an architecture. As it should be with a flexible architectural framework, multiple tools could be used to express the required C4ISR views.

The advantage of the ARIS methodology and associated toolset is that it is fully compliant with the C4ISR framework. ARIS supports all essential and supporting views and combines them in one object-linked repository. The following table shows a mapping among the C4ISR views and related ARIS methods:

Table 4. ARIS and C4ISR Compliancy

C4ISR	ARIS Method
OV-1	Value Added Chain Diagram (VACD): The value added chain diagram allows you to describe the high level functions that support the mission or the vision of the organization. Organizational responsibilities, information objects, location etc. can be associated with this model.
OV-2	ARIS UML Activity Diagram: The ARIS UML activity diagram describes a process as a sequence of activities. The information flow & connectivity's is represented by the decision conditions & connection role type available in this model type. Also activities performed at each node can be assigned organizational responsibilities using "swim lanes"
OV-3	EPC (Event Process Chain): The even process chain is used to describe the process in either a detailed or an overview format. A combination of events & functions (along with the data in the form of inputs, outputs, systems, organizational units) are used to describe the information exchanged between the various nodes. Relevant attributes that are used to describe who, what, where, whom & how can be captured with each event or function to derive the required level of information exchange & interoperability.
OV-4	Organization Chart: The organizational chart is a form of representing organizational structures. A chart of this kind reflects the organizational units (as task performers) and their interrelationships, depending on the selected structuring criteria such as command, control, and co-ordination.
OV-5	EPC (Event Process Chain): The even process chain is used to describe the process in either a detailed or an overview format. A combination of events & functions (along with the data in the form of inputs, outputs, systems, organizational units) are used to describe the information exchanged between the various nodes. Relevant attributes that are used to describe who, what, where, whom & how can be captured with each event or function to derive the required level of information exchange & interoperability
OV-6a	EPC (Event Process Chain): The event process chain is used to describe the process in either a detailed or an overview format. A combination of events & functions (along with the data in the form of inputs, outputs, systems, organizational units) are used to describe sequence and timing of operational activities. Logical business operators are provided in this model type to help identify & represent the business rules that constraint the operation.
OV-6b	UML State Chart Diagram: The UML State Chart diagram focuses on the object states. It describes the sequence of states that an object can assume in the course of its existence. Furthermore, it can contain actions related to the state.
OV-6c	EPC (Event Process Chain): The event process chain is used to describe the process in either a detailed or an overview format. A combination of events & functions (along with the data in the form of inputs, outputs, systems, organizational units) are used to describe sequence and timing of operational activities. Logical business operators are provided in this model type to help identify & represent the business rules that constraint the operation.
OV-7	Entity Relationship Model (ERM): The ERM is used to document the data requirements & structural business process rules through the use of entities, relationships and attributes.
SV-1	Application System Type Diagram: The application system type diagram can be used to identify the different systems, components, interfaces, and modules. It can also be used to capture the functions that are supported by the application systems along with the supported objectives. This model type captures different levels of information for the design and implementation specifications.

Table 4. (continued)

SV-2	Network Diagram: The network diagram is used to represent the exact location of every network, network node, and network connection within the company. The inter-relation between the different elements can be captured using the different connection types.
SV-3	Application System Type Diagram: The application system type diagram can be used to identify the different systems, components, interfaces, and modules. It can also be used to capture the functions that are supported by the application systems along with the supported objectives. This model type captures different levels of information for the design and implementation specifications.
SV-4	Application System Type Diagram: The application system type diagram can be used to identify the different systems, components, interfaces, and modules. It can also be used to capture the functions that are supported by the application systems along with the supported objectives. This model type captures different levels of information for the design and implementation specifications.
SV-5	EPC (Event Process Chain): The event process chain is used to describe the process in either a detailed or an overview format. A combination of events & functions (along with the data in the form of inputs, outputs, systems, organizational units) are used to describe sequence and timing of operational activities. Logical business operators are provided in this model type to help identify & represent the business rules that constraint the operation.
SV-6	Application System Type Diagram: The application system type diagram can be used to identify the different systems, components, interfaces, and modules. It can also be used to capture the functions that are supported by the application systems along with the supported objectives. This model type captures different levels of information for the design and implementation specifications.
SV-7	Application System Type Diagram: The application system type diagram can be used to identify the different systems, components, interfaces, and modules. It can also be used to capture the functions that are supported by the application systems along with the supported objectives. This model type captures different levels of information for the design and implementation specifications.
SV-8	Use Variants from the ARIS repository to model the incremental steps in migrating from a current state of systems to future state of systems.
SV-9	C3 method: The C3 method is used to define the emerging systems, products, organizations, processes and applications that are affected during the development of the architecture.
SV-10a	OMT (Object Modeling Technique): Functional and Dynamic Modeling of the OMT methodology can be used to describe the constraints that are imposed on system functionality due to systems design or implementation.
SV-10b	State Chart Diagram: The UML State chart diagrams depict automatic status focuses on object states. It describes the sequence of states that an object can assume in the course of its existence. Furthermore, it can contain actions related to the state. These actions are either prerequisites for the entry of a state (*entry*), are executed during the state (*do*), or are executed upon leaving the state (*exit*).
SV-10c	State Chart Diagram: The UML State chart diagrams depict automatic status focuses on object states. It describes the sequence of states that an object can assume in the course of its existence. Furthermore, it can contain actions related to the state. These actions are either prerequisites for the entry of a state (*entry*), are executed during the state (*do*), or are executed upon leaving the state (*exit*).
SV-11	Table Model: The physical implementation of the information into data model can be represented using the table model. A database system's tables and fields can be described in the table diagram.
TV-1	Structuring Model + Reports: The structuring model can be used to document the standards of the technical architecture and reports can be run on the same to extract the standards
TV-2	Structuring Model + Reports: The structuring model can be used to document the standards of the technical architecture and reports can be run on the same to extract the standards

The C4ISR framework only defines "what" should be described, not "how" it should be described. Table 4 shows examples of methods in ARIS that could be used to address the requirements of individual views. Each C4ISR view could in fact be constructed from one or more of the hundreds of methods supported by the ARIS Toolset.

2.   Approach

The Future Logistics Enterprise Operational Architecture provides a common language and common structures for articulating the requirements, policies, processes, and infrastructure needed to build the Future Logistics Enterprise. The FLE OA identifies processes required to meet the broad DoD logistics requirements and the service components. The FLE OA addresses two important requirements of the FLE. First, it provides specific guidance to support logistics decision making during the term of the Five Year Defense Plan. Second, it is an adaptable and extensible framework to support longer-term evolutions of logistics strategy and infrastructure. A key intent of the FLE OA is to provide a tool that is useful for planning and decision making, without hindering the design and implementation of logistics chains.

The FLE OA documents and connects policy, doctrine and metrics in the highest layer to business processes at the middle layer to information systems and other enabling infrastructure in the lowest layer. This concept is presented in Fig. 1.

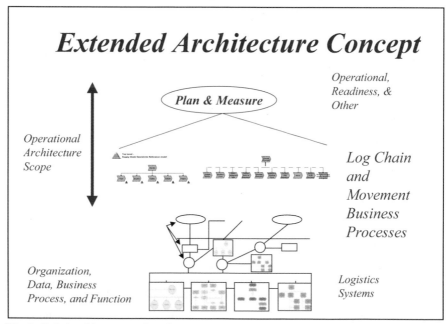

Fig. 1. Relationships among Levels

The architecture encompasses DoD logistics as a component of the larger defense enterprise. Logistics is cross-functionally aligned with readiness business processes as well as those processes that enable joint operations planning and execution. Hence, the OA must respond to all the performance requirements that are imposed by this larger environment. The top layer of the architecture links external performance measures that align organizational performance with the DoD logistics processes.

The business process layer of the architecture is built around the framework of the Supply Chain Council's Supply Chain Operational Reference (SCOR) model. Some adjustments have been made to the level-three SCOR business processes to ensure that the framework adequately speaks to FLE requirements. For example, for specialized movement, the to-be OA from the U.S. Transportation Command was used.

The systems and infrastructure layer of the architecture link logistics processes to the diverse systems that enable the FLE. Since full implementation of the FLE will occur over many years, this mapping of automated information systems (AIS) is time dimensioned to define a transition path for retiring old AIS environments and creating new environments. Support for this transitional mapping of application systems within an evolving technical architecture satisfies an essential requirement of the implementation plan for the FLE. The mapping from the OA processes to information technology infrastructure is less specific than what will be needed for implementation of production supply chain systems. Like SCOR, the OA provides a framework as opposed to a design. Users of the three layer OA process models will need to design specific processes and specific enabling systems at least one level more detailed than the lowest OA process level. This limitation of the depth of the OA is driven by the evolution of operational requirements and technologies over the long life of the architecture and the logistics enterprise.

2.1 The Functional Scope of the FLE OA

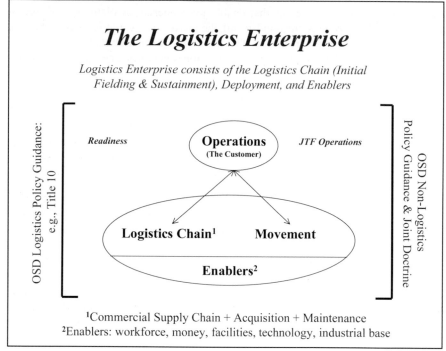

Fig. 2. Architecture Scope[2]

The scope of the architecture encompasses the overall DoD logistics domain in-cluding forces and materiel. This is indicated in Fig. 2.

The customer[3] for "Logistics" is "Operations," which calls for the performance measure linkages that are derived from the policy requirements on the vertical bounding brackets on Fig. 2:

- Office of the Secretary of Defense (OSD) guidance for logistics, which defines the requirements for peacetime readiness

- Joint Doctrine for Joint Task Force operations, and

- OSD policy guidance for non-logistics, which bounds the enablers

---

[2] In DoD C4ISR Architectural Framework terminology, this figure is equivalent to the highest level Operational View; i.e., an OV 1.

[3] Strictly speaking, Operations is a consumer, since they don't pay for the assets and com-modities that they receive. However, for the purposes of this chapter, we adopt the com-mercial terminology.

The scope of the architecture is defined this way to capture the broad requirements of the military establishment. These requirements include the commercial definition of a supply chain as well as the requirements to rapidly reconfigure and move forces, consisting of people, equipment, and material, to meet operational needs. This architectural construct captures an "end to end" view of business processes from the battlespace all the way to weapon system acquisition and sustainment functions.

2.2 The Operational Architecture in ARIS

This chapter describes how the OA was built in ARIS following the requirements of the C4ISR framework. Our tasking required that we develop the Operational Views that comprise the OA, so other views are not discussed. The OA (i.e., the Business Process Architecture) is bound by strategies, which in this case are the six FLE strategies. The Architecture is defined in the following sections.

2.2.1 Initiatives, Objectives, and Measures

The primary intent of this section is to define the FLE requirements that lead to the underlying operational architectures. The six initiatives are defined as strategies in a Balanced Scorecard for the Future Logistics Enterprise[4]. There are three types of strategies:

- Readiness and Sustainment

- Cost

- Customer Satisfaction

Each FLE initiative has specific implementation objectives, critical success factors, and related measures. These measures enable the DoD to quantify the implementation success of the architecture, as well as providing architectural implementation requirements. Fig. 3 shows the linkages across the concepts.

---

[4] For our implementation of the Balanced Scorecard, we adopt the study by the Logistics Management Insitute (Klapper, 1999), and supplement is as needed.

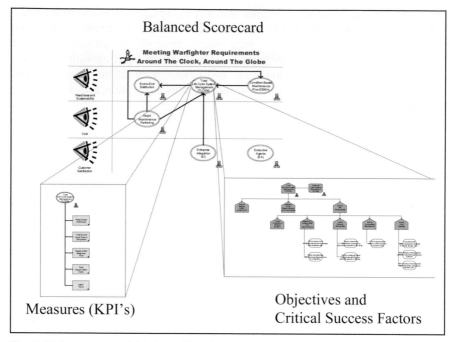

Fig. 3. Linkages among Initiatives, Objectives, and Measures

2.2.2 Operational Views

The Operational Views support all FLE requirements from the management level to the implementation level.

The OA consists of the following views:

- The OV-1 "Project and Sustain the Force" identifies the scope of the FLE OA

- The OV-2s define the scenarios; i.e., the involved roles/nodes and their interoperability within the scope of the FLE OA

- The OV-5s represent the the required functional components/activities to enable the FLE OA

- The sequential detail for each OV-2 is presented in the OV-6s. There are multiple levels of detail expressed by the OV-6 standard

Examples for each view are presented in Fig. 4.

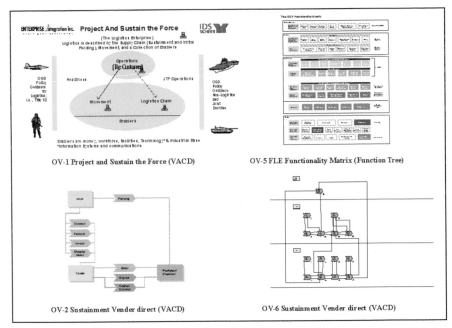

OV-1 Project and Sustain the Force (VACD)

OV-5 FLE Functionality Matrix (Function Tree)

OV-2 Sustainment Vender direct (VACD)

OV-6 Sustainment Vender direct (VACD)

Fig. 4. Operational Views in ARIS

2.3 The Information Technology Alignment Approach

The FLE OA links and validates, logistics policy, logistics processes, and logistics enabling technology, including automated information systems. This comprehensive linkage in a single repository facilitates analysis of the disparate elements required to define and manage the logistics enterprise. Such analysis is currently impractical because the necessary information is dispersed in policy documents, a variety of disparate and incomplete process models, vendor sales and technical documentation, and, in some cases, computer code in existing systems.

The FLE OA enables planning and management of the DoD logistics application portfolio, which comprises a large and capital-intensive component of the logistics enterprise. Mapping existing and proposed software applications to the OA identifies gaps, conflicts, and duplication in automated information systems. These mappings proceed at a variety of levels. Higher-level mappings provide resource sponsors and senior managers with a tool to understand the relative distribution of investment for existing systems and new development efforts in the context of the overall logistics environment. The higher-level mappings use business process maps that provide an aggregated view of logistics business processes. The lower level business process models are used for more detailed analyses of logistics business process requirements. These lower level models help program managers and business unit leaders set and control the scope of software implementation projects. They also provide an estimating tool to determine the cost impact of business process reengineering.

2.3.1 The Business Process Map

The business process map simplifies the task of relating OA business process requirements to the functional capabilities of enabling information systems. Over time, the OA business process map is expected to evolve into a comprehensive tool that captures the broad spectrum of DoD logistics business process requirements and maps those processes to the underlying DoD application portfolio. As a requirements repository, the business process map supports the evaluation of existing software systems as well as the implementation of new solutions.

The objectives for the analyses supported by the business process map are:

- To discover requirement gaps and conflicts in the current application portfolio that must be filled in order to achieve FLE business process requirements. Knowledge of these gaps and conflicts will enable logistics decision makers to effectively guide application implementation efforts and to influence the development efforts of commercial solution providers

- To discover business rule gaps or conflicts among DoD logistics business process requirements and current DoD policy, statute, and regulation. The intent is to convey these gaps for appropriate action by the DoD and by software solution provider

- To facilitate more effective communication between the logistics communities and solution providers and sustainers in the public and private sectors by providing a common frame of reference, which is, in turn, directly linked to the process architecture employed by the logistics operators

2.3.2 The High-Level Comparisons

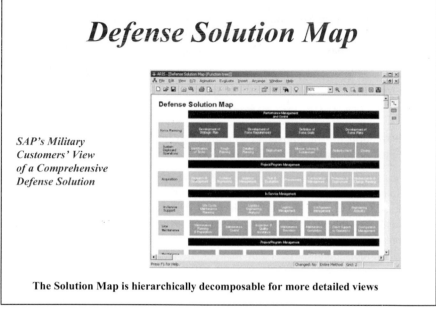

Fig. 5. The Top Level of a Business Process Map

A business process map is a simple matrix that portrays the business processes required to meet enterprise requirements. The "cells" in the top level matrix allow users to "dill down" to successively more detailed process views depending on the granularity required for a particular analysis. Lower level process views show linkages to corresponding capabilities within automated information systems including an indication of the status of the capability such as:

- Component available
- Capability planned for future release(s)
- Capability not planned
- Capability available from alternate source
- Capability planned for future release from alternate source

Business process maps provide one methodology for aligning the software applications with the DoD enterprise. The OA is being used to compare leading ERP solutions to the OA across two broad business areas:

- The DoD Enterprise – A DoD specific business process map has been developed and aligned with business process maps developed by commercial solution providers as an overall baseline for the defense enterprise. This methodology will be applicable to subsequent analysis of existing DoD owned information systems and additional commercial packages.

- Logistics Chain & Movement – A Logistics Chain and Movement specific business process map has been developed and aligned with commercial solution maps as a baseline for the logistics enterprise

These comparable business process maps allow us to complete a high-level gap-fit analysis of

- Each solution relative to the DoD enterprise

- Each solution for the logistics chain and movement relative to the FLE business process models

These mappings are discussed in more detail below. Business process maps are similar to commercial presentation tools used with senior executives. Therefore, it seems reasonable that the format is valuable for providing management overviews of different logistics solutions with the capability to expose more detail process definitions as needed. The direct connection of the matrix format to more detailed analytical models enables decision makers, functional managers, and technical analysts to operate within the same information base. This reasoning led to the selection of business process maps as an effective tool for process analysis and portrayal of FLE alignment with the broader defense enterprise.

2.3.3 Alignment with the Logistics Enterprise

At the highest level, we construct a customer specific business process map for the US DoD as a baseline for comparison to the commercial baseline process maps. These models provide a complete overview of the US DoD (from an OSD perspective.) They form the base customer-specific process map for comparison with commercial business process maps. Therefore, the highest-level analysis compares the commercial business process maps with a customer-specific business process map. The analysis identifies gaps in those functional capabilities that are clearly associated with logistics.

2.3.4 Alignment with the Logistics Chain

This level is specifically focused on the detailed logistics business processes that underlie the FLE. The logistics chain process models were adapted from SCOR 5.0 and are consistent with SCOR level 3 processes. Expanded distribution process models are adapted from the operational architecture developed by he US Transportation Command (TRANCOM) using the C4ISR Architecture Framework. The models were implemented in ARIS and then used to build a customer-specific business process map. Once again, we compare the functionality in the customer-specific map with the comparable level of commercial business process maps.

3. Conclusions

The objective of the FLE OA is to provide an architectural framework that will serve as a tool to help guide the multi-year transformation from the current logistics environment to the Future Logistics Enterprise. This framework provides a common language for articulating requirements, policies, processes and infrastructure needed to build the FLE. One function of the FLE OA is to understand the degree to which the FLE can be enabled by commercial standard software solutions. This chapter documents the methodology used for comparison of FLE processes to commercial capabilities using two primary tools:

- High-level business process maps, and

- Detailed business process models

FLE business process representations are compared to similar process representations of leading commercial application packages.

The business process maps provide a basis to document functionality gaps in current and planned releases of application software, relative to the requirements of the FLE. Using business processes, we compare the commercial business processes with the business processes in the OA repository. The resulting analysis identifies functional gaps and overlaps, which enables management to take appropriate actions such as recommendation to software vendors or the initiation of a request to alter DoD policy.

4. References

Kirchmer, Mathias, Business Process Oriented Implementation of Standard Software. New York: Springer-Verlag, 1999.

Klapper, Larry S., Neil Hamblin, Linda Hutchison, Linda Novak, and Jonathan Vivar, Supply Chain Management: A Recommended Performance Measurement Scorecard, LG803R1. McLean, Virginia: Logistics Management Institute, 1999.

Needham, Paul, Getting There: Focused Logistics, In H. Binneddijk (ed.), Transforming America's Military. Washington, DC: National Defense University Press, 2002.

Scheer, A.-W., Architecture of Integrated Information Systems: Business Process Modeling. Berlin: Springer-Verlag, 1999a.

Scheer, A.-W., Architecture of Integrated Information Systems: Business Process Frameworks. Berlin: Springer-Verlag, 1999b.

Supply Chain Council, Supply-Chain Operations Reference-Model, SCOR, Version 5.0. Pittsburgh, PA: Supply chain Council, 2001.

U.S. Department of Defense, C4ISR Architecture Framework, Version 2.0. Washington, DC, 1997.

U.S. Department of Defense, Future Logistics Enterprise: A Way Ahead, Internal Document of the Joint Logistics Board, March 27, 2002.

U.S. Department of Defense, Quadrennial Defense Review Report, Washington, DC, 2001.

Process-Centric Approach for ERP Evaluation Using ARIS Methodology in a Midsize Group of Companies

Low Siow Hoon
Senior Manager, MMI Holdings Ltd., Singapore

Christian Rieger
Vice President, IDS-Gintic Pte Ltd., Singapore

Summary

ERP feasibility studies are often seen as an activity that is lowest in priority in companies planning to embark on ERP projects. Often it is thought that the additional time and resources spent at the beginning constitutes a luxury that can be avoided. The authors show in the following article that a well-planned, business process-oriented approach in a feasibility study provides substantial benefits which by far outweigh the additional time and costs incurred in a feasibility study. The structured approach allows a review of existing business processes and matches them to "best practice" of business processes that will underpin the training of users in new functionalities when selecting the appropriate package. It also provides a systematic way to implement company-wide processes that are seamless and synchronized through the use of enabling templates.

Key Words

ARIS, ARIS Toolset, BPR, Change Management, Standard Software Selection, ERP

1. Project Background

An electro-mechanical systems integrator and contract manufacturer in the hi-tech industry, MMI's business includes contract manufacturing, data storage as well as factory automation equipment. It has about 4000 staff across Asia and achieved a turnover of 346 million SGD or about 200 million USD in the last business year ending July 2002. One of its subsidiaries is IMT (Integrated Magnesium Technologies Pte Ltd.), the business activities of which involves magnesium and aluminum die-casting, fuller manufacturing of both components, high-level mechanical assemblies as well as engineering design services for new product development. Typical products are base parts used in mobile phones and mechanical components supplied to sister companies within MMI Holdings. It has operations in Singapore as well as Malaysia, the latter for capacity expansion and value adding assembly work. Business is expected to increase due to work from new customers.

IMT used BPCS financial software to support its financial business processes as well as to consolidate its accounts to that of MMI Holdings. The sales, manufacturing and logistics operations were mainly supported by Microsoft Office applications. Information flow in the company was not integrated and transparent with increasing dependence on human effort to facilitate the capturing, flow and sharing of information across departments/functions as projects are being executed and managed. Being a relatively new company, IMT was also gearing up to improve its present ISO-9002 quality procedures from the computerization of its enterprise resource planning activities. In the process of computerization, it was hoped that good industry practices can be introduced to improve the present business pro-cesses and to implement new ones, wherever necessary.

MMI Holdings as a group was also planning to revamp its information infrastructure and used IMT as the pilot company to carry out its plan. IMT was chosen for the study since its business is representative of the more complex business pro-cesses of the group.

2. Project Objectives

The primary project goal was to support the MMI vision in terms of IT infrastructure regarding information as one critical enabler for best business practices. MMI's vision is to define a distinctive market position as a mechanical systems contract manufacturer serving growth industries in global markets such as data storage, telecommunications, semiconductors and computer peripherals. This vision will be achieved through leveraging the group's core competencies and building new capabilities to capitalize on the new industry trends of global outsourcing by OEMs and consolidation and integration of the manufacturing supply chain.

Derived from this goal a special emphasis was put on enabling the organization to adapt world-class processes supported by an enhanced ERP package achieving a quantum leap in a short time rather than stretching improvements over a long period of time. As the funds were limited, the solution had to be cost-effective too.

From a task perspective this meant that the main purpose of this project was to assist MMI and to work closely with its project team to carry out a company-wide feasibility study to computerize the enterprise resource-planning activities in a goal-oriented fashion in the two plants in Singapore and Malaysia. The outcome of this project had to result in business process improvement as well as the specification, evaluation and selection of the most suitable ERP solution which in turn would lead to a timely, reduced risk and cost-effective implementation of the selected ERP system in the two factories.

This project therefore aimed to achieve a significant improvement in the overall effectiveness and efficiency of the mechanical contract manufacturing business of the company. This computerization was expected to enable IMT to realize the following goals when the new ERP system was implemented in 2001:

- Reduced operating costs

- Better utilization of manpower – from reduced manual and laborious work and improved business processes through an integrated ERP system ensuring data entered only once

- Shortened cycle times

- Streamlined business processes – this will result from simplification and/or improvement of existing business processes, as well as from new ones made possible by information and Internet technologies

- Faster query and reporting capabilities as well as higher visibility of process results for decision-making

- Improved integration among IMT's factories and with its parent company and the supply chains of its key suppliers and customers

- Readiness to embrace e-business strategy with ERP system as the backbone of the company's e-business application architecture – other applications for supply chain management, business-to-business transactions, business-to-customer transactions, customer relationship management, and e-learning can then be implemented systematically when the need arises

- Long-term quality improvement – employees with reduced manual and laborious work will focus more time on adding value and improving the quality of their work

- More effective ISO-900x quality procedures – derived from the business process improvement and the implementation of the ERP system

- Employees educated and trained in advanced IT knowledge and skills/change management – this will have a positive impact on staff motivation and will lead to increased productivity. It will also prepare them for future projects of a similar nature.

3. Scope of Work

Fig. 1 shows the two phases of an ERP project, i.e. selection phase and implementation. The roles and contents can be divided into the following 3 stages:

- Stage 1:
  Feasibility study – business process improvement, specification, evaluation and recommendation of an ERP system

- Stage 2:
  Project and program planning and technical consultation for ERP implementation

- Stage 3:
  Project management and technical consultation for ERP implementation

The implementation phase was planned to be staggered implementing the whole MMI Holdings Group within less than 2 years.

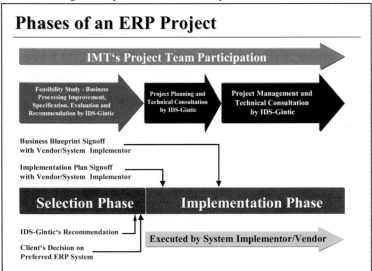

Fig. 1. Project Phases

The scope of work for this project covered the following departments/functions:

- Finance
- Logistics
- Quality Assurance
- Engineering and Production
- Human Resources (with Payroll) – only their interfacing requirements with other departments/functions were considered in the study. Existing software supporting these two functions were retained

The main business processes studied in this project comprised of:

- Sales order processing
- Master scheduling
- Production planning
- Material requirement planning
- Capacity planning (rough cut)
- Purchasing
- Inventory management
- Shop floor tracking (limited to features available in ERP systems)
- Shipping
- Billing
- Incoming QA
- Quality management
- Costing
- Accounts receivable processes
- Accounts payable processes
- General ledger processes
- Financial consolidation processes

These are shown in Fig. 2 in an overall framework consisting of an ERP system and other enterprise solutions such as MES ("manufacturing execution system"), SFC ("shop floor control systems"), and APS ("advanced planning and scheduling system"). This framework was important as the MMI group was committed to "thinking big, but starting small", meaning additions to the base ERP such as

APS (advanced planning and scheduling) or connectivity to suppliers and customers were to be considered in the selection of the system.

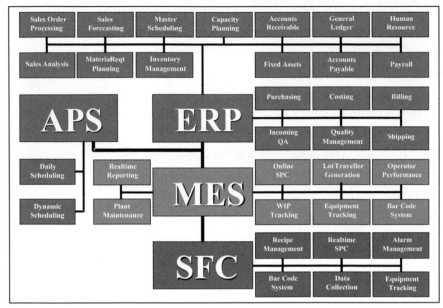

Fig. 2. A Typical Functional Framework of an Enterprise Information System

4. Project Approach

Our project approach for the study (as stage 1 of the overall ERP project) consisted of two major elements – a proven 5-step procedure in which business process modeling and reengineering is integrated, and the selection of the system.

The activities to be carried out included the following:

(a) To carry out a situational review (as-is analysis) at the two factories of IMT to:

- Establish a working understanding of the company's organization, business and goals

- Review the current business operations in terms of the workflow, information flow, interdependencies to related operations, work policies, management reporting and control systems

- Obtain an overview of the computer architecture, hardware and software applications portfolio presently in use in the company

- Design the high-level as-is models of the major business processes in the company, which is also the starting point from which the to-be models will be designed

- Gather the problems and concerns faced by the end users in their work, as well as their suggestions for improvement

(b) To develop the high-level and system-independent to-be models of the major business processes in the company and, related to this, to specify the functional and technical requirements of the ERP system and the computer hardware required. These to-be processes will consist of existing business processes, those that are improved, and new ones.

(c) To source, evaluate and determine the feasibility of a new ERP system, and recommend the most suitable ERP system and the appropriate computer hardware for the company.

(d) To recommend the most suitable ERP solution and its system implementer.

Special consideration was given to the process and interaction aspect comprising 2/3 of the project time (see Fig. 3).

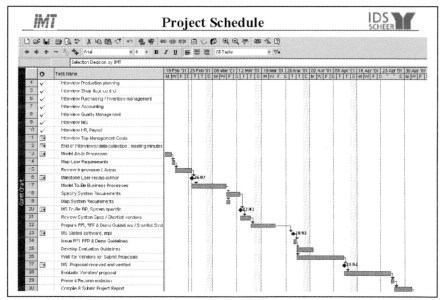

Fig. 3. Project Plan (Extract)

The ARIS methodology was used extensively to model as-is as well as to-be processes and to facilitate change management. The ARIS eBusiness Suite of products provided the method and tools for developing innovative business models via newly designed value added chains and processes that go beyond company

110

boundaries using global information and communication technologies. In the following it is assumed that the reader is familiar with the basic ARIS principles.

For IMT's case three model types have been chosen. For the first level of the process hierarchy, a value added chain diagram depicting the application areas provides an overview of the business processes (see Fig. 4 below). Application areas are detailed by function tree diagrams on the next level (e.g. production planning, see Fig. 6). These provide an overview of the referring processes which are detailed on level 3 by EPCs (event-driven process chains). EPCs are explained in the next paragraph as they are the main object of the process modeling.

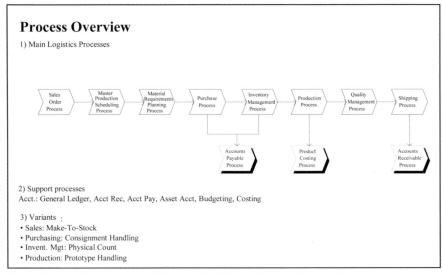

Fig. 4. Process Overview with Value Added Chain Diagram (Level 1)

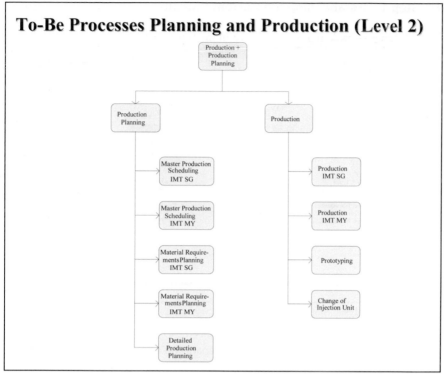

Fig. 5. Process Example with Function Tree Model (Level 2)

4.1 Step 1 – Establishing the Current Situation

The 1st step was broken down as shown in the figure below:

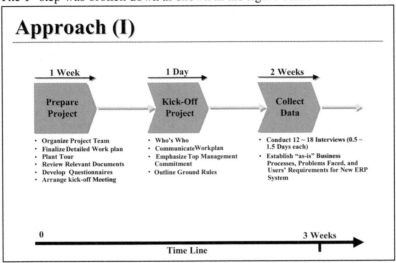

Fig. 6. As-Is Analysis, Step 1

The start of the project involved project preparation activities such as plant walk-about, analyzing work-related activities, interviews and discussions with key executives of the manufacturing operation and its main interfacing functions. It also included browsing through relevant documents such as operation procedures (e.g. ISO-900x manual), product literature, management reports, hardware and software manuals. Reports and/or information on similar work already done or in progress were gathered and used to help reduce the efforts and shorten the time required to deliver this project.

The kick-off meeting dealt with the detailed procedure ahead, organizational assignments of key users as well as involvement of end users and emphasized the importance of user involvement. Data collection was then facilitated using interviews with the process owners in charge and questionnaires were used to record and confirm processes as well as requirements concerning those processes.

With the information gathered on the knowledge of technology and experience from projects of a similar nature, the team proceeded to draft out the major high-level as-is models of the business processes. IDS Scheer's ARIS eBusiness Suite and methodology was used to carry out the process modeling and analysis. Review sessions with IMT's project team were done to validate the business processes for completeness, errors and consistency. Also, the user requirements were gathered and structured using Word templates.

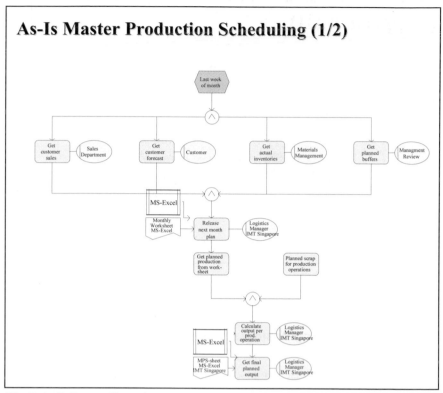

Fig. 7. As-Is Process Example

Based on this, the improvement areas from a consultancy point of view as well as problems, concerns and suggestions raised by the end users were compiled for review with IMT's project team in the next step and used as consideration for business process improvement potential and development of new processes. A document on the as-is business process models for IMT was prepared and submitted at the end of this step.

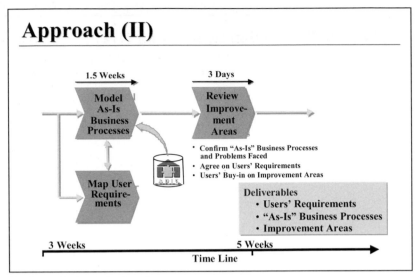

Fig. 8. As–Is Analysis, Step 2

4.2 Step 2 – Improving Business Processes

In this step, a series of discussion sessions with IMT's project team were organized to review and confirm the findings from the earlier stage. These findings included weaknesses of the present business processes in the manufacturing operation and their interfacing processes, as well as the limitations of the present information assets to support these as-is business processes. They also revealed weaknesses in internal control systems and human-related issues.

These discussion sessions aimed to identify the main improvement areas, in particular those which can exploit new technologies to further improve the efficiency and productivity of the company. The relevant problems, issues and suggestions, upon confirmation, were considered when developing the high-level to-be business processes.

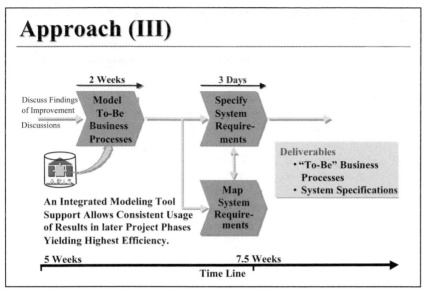

Fig. 9. To-Be Business Process Steps

The next step then was to improve the core as-is business processes and, where necessary, to generate new to-be business processes for the company (examples of possible improvement alternatives are shown in Fig. 10). Best practices from the consultants technological knowledge, experience and ARIS reference models were applied to generate the to-be business processes.

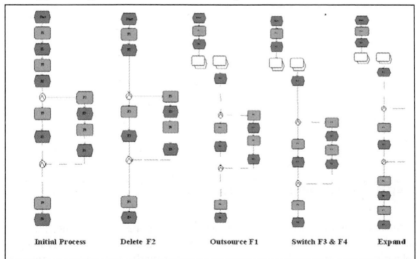

Fig. 10. Example of Using ARIS eBusiness Suite and Methodology to Carry Out Business Process Analysis and Improvement

116

Special emphasis was given to the reduction of activities (delete) and automation of activities to increase efficiency as well as new functions (expand) to improve decision-making and the quality of processes. The ARIS Toolset database and reporting tool, which allowed powerful comparisons concerning objects used, was very helpful in this regard.

A document on the to-be business process models for IMT was prepared and submitted at the end of this step. The findings from the brainstorming sessions were also reported in this document. As shown in the example below, improvements often took place when combining changes, i.e. applying new technologies (the ERP system symbol below) and modifying functions or their sequence. To illustrate this point: the to-be process shown previously in Fig. 8 has more parallel functions compared to the as-is process in Fig. 7, thus shortening the cycle time.

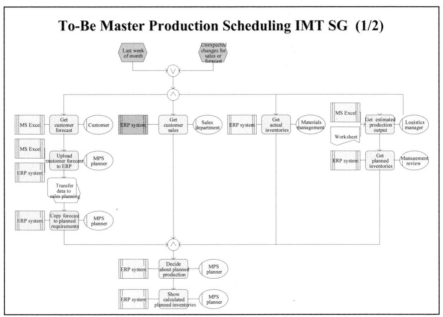

Fig. 11. To-Be Process Level 3 (Example)

4.3 Step 3 – Developing System Specifications

The information gathered from the first two steps was used to generate the functional and technical requirements. These requirements were grouped as mandatory, desirable and optional based on user input. Finally, the user requirements were transformed into system specifications in IT-compatible language which were reviewed and agreed upon mutually. Especially the process-related information entered in the ARIS database was helpful for focusing the team on system-related specifications rather than describing everything possible and ensured completeness of important process or output-related specifications.

4.4 Step 4 – Sourcing

In this step, RFI (request for information), RFP (request for proposal) and DG (demo guideline) documents were prepared. These documents include the specifications established in step 3, vendor's submission requirements, and terms and conditions for proposal submissions from vendors; as well as the scenarios for the conference room demonstration to show the main capabilities of the proposed solutions by the vendors. Especially the last document is an important step in securing user commitment for the implementation and to reduce implementation-related risks.

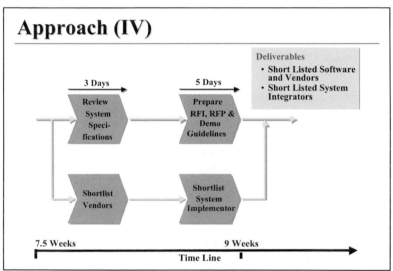

Fig. 12. Approach for Preparation of Sourcing

Prior to the release of these documents to the vendors, the team recommended two vendors (SAP and JD Edwards) whose software packages for enterprise resource planning were considered as suitable for evaluation. Later a third product (Oracle) was included based on MMI's request. As for SAP, the team decided to select two system implementers – the main reason being to generate price competition, as SAP is relatively more available and also often regarded as a rather expensive solution. These selected vendors, together with their respective chosen system implementers, were asked to submit their replies to the RFI and RFP documents. At the same time, the DG document was issued to get them to prepare for their conference room demonstrations.

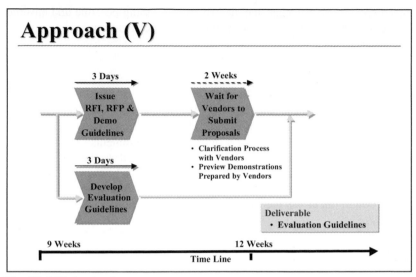

Fig. 13. RFP Approach

A period of approximately 2 weeks each was provided for the vendors/system implementers to hand back their proposals and to prepare for their demonstrations.

In this step, we also developed the process and defined the criteria for evaluating the responses from the proposals submitted by the vendors/system implementers. Each demonstration by a vendor/system implementer to IMT's project team and including key end users took about 2 days.

4.5 Step 5 – Evaluation and Selection

Each proposal received was screened against the evaluation criteria. These criteria included technical compliance, capabilities of vendor/system implementer and their project team as well as financial costs over a 5-year period. To test the confidence of the implementers, customer reference sites were also validated.

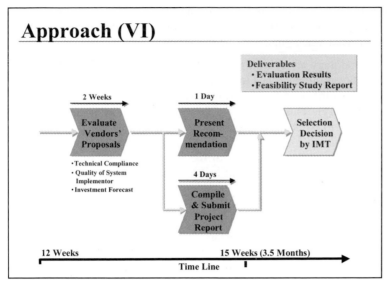

Fig. 14. Evaluation Approach

From the evaluation results, the team was able to determine whether a new ERP system could be implemented in IMT to help achieve the objectives of this project as well as which is the most suitable one. The team confirmed the rule of thumb that it is unlikely that any ERP system could achieve a 100% fit to the system specifications required by IMT. The selected packages offered fit levels between 80-90% overall, which is well within the range of the typical and acceptable fit level of about 80% without major customization of the ERP system.

Assessing the implementation of the projected goals as feasible, the team then recommended the most suitable ERP solution to IMT as SAP, which was confirmed by the senior management of MMI and IMT. Rather than price, the overall fit of the software and the team quality were decisive factors. The decision concluded the first phase of the project with IDS actively involved as consultant in the subsequent phases of group-wide implementation.

5. Benefits of the ARIS-Enabled Feasibility Study Approach

The approach proved to be efficient in terms of information and communication between consultants and users. IMT and MMI Holdings acquired an in-depth understanding of an appropriate ERP system before implementing it. Due to the structured approach, only 3.5 months plus another 6 weeks for one more vendor to be evaluated were needed to give a comprehensive picture of the requirements and processes to be matched in the ERP system of their choice. Combined with a grant from the Singapore government, it was a worthwhile investment in terms of avoiding pitfalls later when implementing the system.

The ARIS methodology along with the ARIS Toolset enabled the users to gain insights of the current situation and to visualize desired processes from an overall perspective, without the need for major training (merely an overview of the procedure was necessary). This allowed the consultants and the users to talk the same language and to point out improvement potentials together. As the discussions were in "simulation" mode, changes were allowed and made in the interest of the overall picture. Often, awareness of the process predecessors and successors was only obtained after mapping the end-to-end process.

The ARIS methodology with the agreed conventions also enforced the consistency of data collection, reducing errors through subjective description of facts.

From a business process engineering perspective, it enabled the project team to focus on streamlining related processes, i.e. no duplication and to identify potential ways to shorten cycle times and stabilize processes. Due to the assignment of organizational units in the models, roles were assigned which help the users to understand the degree of change to be expected.

From a human resource perspective, employees were educated and trained on advanced IT knowledge and skills, i.e. ready to handle future projects of a similar nature. This also had a positive effect on employee motivation and productivity.

The processes and requirements have been reused as a template to examine the implementation phases after project completion as well as to derive the scope of other group companies and therefore helped to avoid functionality mismatches.

6.   Lessons Learned

Selecting and implementing the most brilliant state-of-the-art ERP system is a waste of time and effort unless people accept and use it effectively. As such, good change management is important and is part of overall risk management when running a business. In some cases, the computer system never operates correctly on the computer, in other cases the system works properly, but does not work successfully in the organization as people are not using it in order to improve their processes. In the project described, change management was an integral part of the study. Based on the theory of change (Lewin/Schein), change management involves three major steps: unfreezing, moving and refreezing.

Unfreezing involves creating an awareness of the need for change and a climate of receptivity to change. In the feasibility study, this effect was accomplished by the benefits of the study. As a result of the potential benefits outlined earlier, the group management of MMI, especially the Executive Director, supported the decision to go ahead with an ERP implementation in spite of the difficult economic situation the company was facing. It is the most critical step, as people who are not convinced attempt to block the success of the implementation in subsequent phases. From the experiences of our study it also became clear that these efforts to show benefits to the staff need to be periodically repeated in order to change mindsets.

Moving means changing the forces and behavior that define the old situation and comprise new methods, learning new attitudes and processes to get things done. The integrated planning process was such an example faced in the study. The new process comprised more steps but helped to cut down many manual steps and checks done before. However, as the study was on a high level, this step is prepared in the evaluation project and has to be reinforced in the blueprint and testing steps of the subsequent implementation project. It is paramount that enough time be given to this aspect which requires high social skills and not to leave this topic out due to the technical focus of the project.

Refreezing means reinforcing the changes that have occurred, thereby institution-alizing new processes and work practices. This step is directly linked to the effectiveness of the implementation and the amount of training carried out and should therefore be undertaken during the implementation. However, refreezing activities should be part of the planning during the feasibility study. IMT and MMI are giving importance to this point by assigning senior staff as team leaders to oversee the transition to the new system. Due to the nature of their involvement, their incentives are tied to the project success, although more in a loosely coupled fashion. Still, it requires more than a one-time effort to communicate the desired outcome of the processes and their importance to all team members and users and to convince people to change and to assimilate and then internalize this new mindset. If not enough emphasis is given to this point, this leads to rejection later.

In our project, it was most important to have the project manager from MMI, with a solid company background and experience in critical logistics, to convince users of practices which had to be changed. It is interesting to note that it required relatively more effort to train the accounting functionality compared to logistics as the users need the system more frequently for a bigger part of their work and also have to manage a bigger change in an integrated system by controlling the quality of processes in front of them (e.g. incorrect sales order entries might result in incorrect account postings).

7. Next Steps

After the decision was taken to implement SAP, the chosen ERP system, for the whole group, the top management also decided on an approach with several steps which should be accomplished in as short a timeframe as possible. The whole group included 11 business entities (the Holding alone with 5 subentities) to be

122

implemented in 18 months. Companies were grouped in three phases at 6 months each and contract manufacturing entities commenced in Singapore including the Holding and Malaysia. As of the time of writing this article, MMI is halfway through the group-wide implementation, having implemented two companies, with four more commencing operations in the next two months. The well-designed approach allowed the team to increase the number of companies to be implemented from two to four and to add more complicated business scenarios such as engineer-to-order into the last phase starting next January and above all, it allows the group to enjoy "time-to-benefit" from their ERP system investment.

8. References

Kurt Lewin, "Frontiers in Group Dynamics", Human Relations Journal, Vol. 1

Change Management –
Health Care Reform in Bulgaria

Boyan Doganov
Director, World Bank "Reform in Health Sector"

Gencho Nachev
Director, National Health Insurance Fund of Bulgaria

Ralf Martin Ester
Managing Director, IDS Scheer Schweiz AG

Summary

*To ensure high-quality medical and dental care for the population, the health in-
surance system in Bulgaria and all relevant social relations, the Bulgarian Parliament adopted the Health Insurance Act, which aims to change the whole health
system from a socialist system to a modern Western European-style health care
system. The reform is partly financed by the World Bank, Washington D.C. One
important component during this huge change is the definition of new health care
processes and the conception and implementation of a new information system
and infrastructure.*

Key Words

*Change Management, Health Care Reform, Health Insurance, Information Sys-
tem, IT Infrastructure, Ministry of Health, National Health Insurance Fund, Process Change, Software Requirements, VPN, World Bank*

1. Project Background

1.1 Health Care in Bulgaria

During the socialist era, health care in Bulgaria was free of charge for every citizen, according to constitution. Everybody had free access to polyclinics, medical diagnostic laboratories and hospitals all over the country. The only aspect which patients had to pay for were drugs in outpatient care (drugs in hospitals were free of charge). All medical and paramedical staff were paid on a fixed salary scheme fully financed by the state budget. Therefore the system had at least two major disadvantages: first of all there was a motivation problem for people working in medical care and secondly the state budget was at risk every year. Both effects were caused by a rather unsatisfying system of incentives.

To avoid these disadvantages, the main goal of the health care reform in Bulgaria is to ensure high-quality medical and dental care to the population. One of the ways to achieve this goal is to rebuild the doctor-patient relationship, to restore their mutual trust and to reestablish the "family doctor" institution. The health insurance system in Bulgaria and all relevant social relations was introduced in 1998, as the Bulgarian Parliament adopted the Health Insurance Act. It is the legal basis for changing the Bulgarian health care system and for the introduction of both compulsory and voluntary health insurance in the country.

1.2 The Health Care Reform Project

The Health Sector Reform Project supports the government of Bulgaria in implementing a fundamental reform of its health sector that is designed to improve access, especially for the disadvantaged and people in remote areas, to quality health services, and to ensure financial and operational sustainability. Most of the project's components are financed by the World Bank.

- The first component facilitates the reform and sustainability of the primary and ambulatory care sector. It provides practical equipment for primary health care, funds physician office information systems, provides training in general practitioner (GP) practice management, funds an information campaign, finances a health reform investment program to provide low-interest loans to physicians, and funds a labor adjustment strategy

- The second component helps implement a reform of the hospital system, including funding hospital information systems, financing a health reform investment program, and funding a labor adjustment strategy to shift surplus hospital staff

- The third component helps the National Health Insurance Fund (NHIF) to establish the technological infrastructure for operating the insurance system, including the hardware and software systems needed as well as the training and technical assistance required

- The fourth component strengthens the management and institutional capacity of the health ministry, the NHIF, and the health system in general[1]

1.3 The World Bank

Founded in 1944, the World Bank Group is one of the world's largest sources of development assistance. The Bank, which provided 19.5 billion USD in loans to its client countries in fiscal year 2002, is now working in more than 100 developing economies, bringing a mix of finance and ideas to improve living standards and eliminate the worst forms of poverty. For each of its clients, the Bank works with government agencies, non-governmental organizations, and the private sector to formulate assistance strategies. Its country offices worldwide deliver the Bank's program in countries, liaise with government and civil society, and work to increase the understanding of development issues. The World Bank is owned by more than 184 member countries whose views and interests are represented by a Board of Governors and a Washington-based Board of Directors. Member countries are shareholders who carry ultimate decision-making power in the World Bank. The Bank uses its financial resources, its highly trained staff, and its extensive knowledge base to help each developing country onto a path of stable, sustainable, and equitable growth. The main focus is on helping the poorest people and the poorest countries, but for all its clients the Bank emphasizes the need for:

- Investing in people, particularly through basic health and education

- Focusing on social development, inclusion, governance, and institution building as key elements of poverty reduction

- Strengthening the ability of the governments to deliver quality services, efficiently and transparently

- Protecting the environment

- Supporting and encouraging private business development

- Promoting reforms to create a stable macroeconomic environment, conducive to investment and long-term planning[2]

---

[1] World Bank, Project Appraisal Document Date: 2000/05/30.
[2] see www.worldbank.com.

1.4 National Health Insurance Fund (NHIF)

The Health Insurance Act established the NHIF as a public organization and set forth principles defining the relationship between the NHIF and the health care providers. The NHIF is responsible for the development, operation and management of the compulsory health insurance scheme in Bulgaria. The compulsory health insurance scheme is a system for social health protection of the population, which guarantees a package of health-related services and is administered by the National Health Insurance Fund and carried out by its territorial divisions – the 28 Regional Health Insurance Funds. The voluntary health insurance is optional and is carried out by shareholder companies, registered according to commercial law.

2. The General Approach

New technology plays an important role in achieving the described goals. Emerging technology changes the game (cf. Adomeit et al 2001). The whole reform project is divided into several sections:

- Training

- Financial Management

- Contracting and Payment Methods, Medical Audit

- Media Campaign

- Labor Adjustment Strategy

- Hospital Management

- Process and Information Management

Consultant agencies from Australia, Bulgaria, Germany, Greece, the United Kingdom, the United States of America, Slovenia, Spain and Switzerland have been chosen to support the various activities.

As part of the described third part of the Health Care Reform Project IDS Scheer Schweiz AG started in September 2001 to help NHIF to establish a new technological infrastructure, which is derived from the business requirements of the business processes which are analyzed and defined according to the ARIS methodology.

2.1 Change Management

A precondition for effectiveness and productivity is the availability of relevant information at the place where the information is needed. The direct way for this is along the process chain. The design of the process chain becomes the design of change (cf Doppler & Lauterburg 2002).

The main central elements of integrated change management are:

- Development of strategy
- Organizational analysis
- Leading through target definition
- Bosses as moderators
- Personal feedback
- Process-oriented project management
- Building up communication
- Management of conflicts
- Team-building
- Change of the culture
- Improvement through business process optimization
- Coaching (cf Doppler & Lauterburg 2002)

2.2 Process Change

Radical process-based change means that organizational elements, namely strategy, structure, people's responsibilities and appraisal criteria, collaborative behaviors and information systems will change.

Table 1: Content of Changes (cf. Braganza 2001)

Strategy	• Companies / Institutions change • Notion of customer (patient) service • Stakeholder satisfaction
Roles and Responsibilities	• Spreading of responsibility downwards and outwards • Greater empowerment, where people in the process decide how and when work is done • Decision-making authority is increased for the person responsible for the process • Defined along the horizontal or process dimension rather than on a vertical or functional basis

Table 1. (continued)

Appraisals	<ul><li>Performance reviews</li><li>Improvement measures</li><li>Introduction of performance related pay</li><li>Team-based compensation</li><li>Compensation linked to profitability of the process</li><li>Linked to broader process goals</li><li>Linked to the individual's and group's contribution to improving the process</li><li>Rewards should be in the form of bonuses linked to value created the process</li></ul>
The Reward Structures	<ul><li>Support of the new roles and responsibilities</li><li>Flattened hierarchy in terms of the number of levels</li><li>Decrease in the number of vertical functions</li><li>Size and power of the functions decrease</li><li>Organize by process rather than function</li></ul>
Behaviors	<ul><li>Implementation of a new culture</li><li>Notion of teamwork</li><li>Employees believe they work and take ownership of customers</li><li>Enhancing trust, communication, information sharing and willingness to change in the organization</li><li>Demolishing old assumptions</li><li>Change business practices</li></ul>
IT-Systems	<ul><li>IT as enabler for change</li><li>Development of new systems that support the process</li><li>A mix of old an new systems</li><li>Tailored IT solutions</li><li>Shared databases</li></ul>

2.3 Process Change with ARIS – Process and Information Management

The purpose of any health care provision system is to prevent or cure disease. This system must function in an environment of cost control, quality assurance, open access and equity of delivery. To do this it must have information. The entire health care system is built on the appropriate people having the appropriate information at the right time in order to provide the patient with the best possible care. This information is critical. Information systems have a key role in the provision of health care (cf. Pierskall & Woods 1988). Information systems assess the level of risk, clinicians, nurses and other providers can call on protocols, algorithms and other models to aid in prognoses, diagnoses and treatment (cf. Glaser et al 1986).

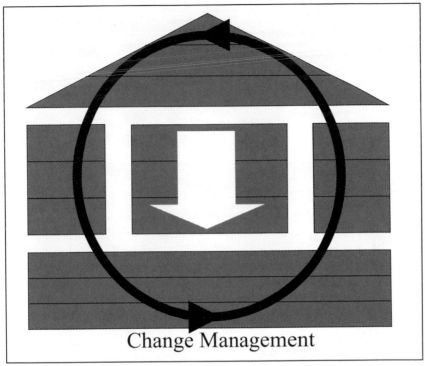

Fig. 1. Main Tasks – IT Infrastructure According to Business Processes

The integration of the different views – people and organizations, health care processes, technology and the way all of these parts will transfer from a socialist to a Western European system through a methodological approach which enables the change management process.

130

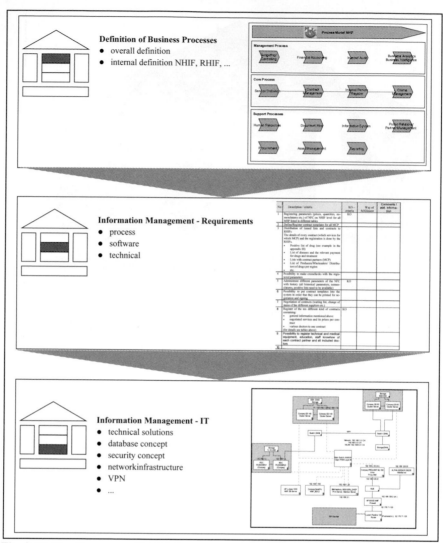

Fig. 2. Linking Processes with IT Infrastructure

3. The Project Approach

The activities are carried out in several phases as shown in Fig. 3.

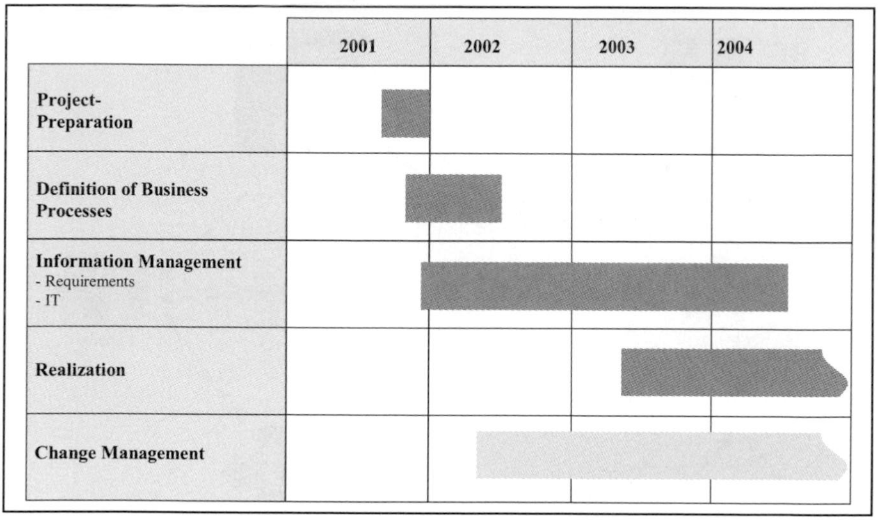

	2001	2002	2003	2004
Project-Preparation				
Definition of Business Processes				
Information Management - Requirements - IT				
Realization				
Change Management				

Fig. 3. Project Plan Process/Information Management

3.1 Project Preparation

In the first phase the organizational activities are completed. The scope of the further phases are exactly defined, the team out of the central IT staff of NHIF, local Bulgarian consultants and fellow consultants from IDS Scheer must be defined. Out of the large number of participating consultant agencies there must be intensive coordination between the different companies, the different project scopes and results.

3.2 Definition of Business Processes

One of the most important activities for the success of the overlapping processing between the different players (NHIF, RHIF, GP, ...) is the integrated view of the business processes and the definition of the IT concept.

132

3.2.1 The Bulgarian Health Care Value Chain

The following shows the results of the analysis the fundamental value chain of the Bulgarian health care system.

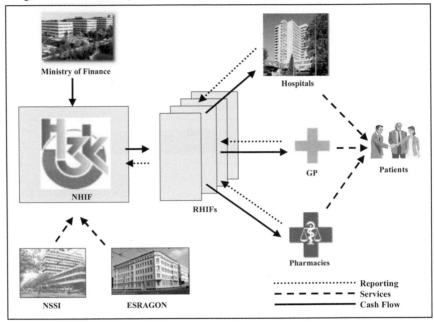

Fig. 4. The Value Chain of the Bulgarian Health Care System (Extract)

The key players are described below.

National Health Insurance Fund (NHIF)
According to the recently established Health Insurance Act, compulsory health insurance in Bulgaria is managed by the National Health Insurance Fund (NHIF), a corporate body with its headquarters in Sofia. By law NHIF is not allowed to possess or maintain any medical or dental infrastructure – i.e. ambulatories, surgeries, laboratories, hospitals or pharmacies. The budget of the NHIF is kept separate from the general state budget. Nevertheless about half of the NHIF budget is derived from the "normal" state budget. These special contributions are destined for state administration, pensioners, children up to 18 years of age, unemployed persons and the disadvantaged. In the case of a short-term shortage, an interest-free loan from the state budget or loans from other institutions can be used. The budget consists of a basic financial plan for revenue and expenditure with respect to the whole compulsory health insurance. The budget of the NHIF shall be worked out and realized in such a way that the expenses shall not exceed the revenues within one budget year.

According to the regulations for the organization and activities of the NHIF, the following functions can be stated:

- Determination and control of the NHIF budget

- Registration of contracts with drugs wholesalers

- Analysis and control of all drug claims data for the purpose of payment confirmation

- Registration, control, analysis and summary of all drug claims data with payments directly to the wholesalers of drugs

- Development of methodologies for the RHIF regarding how to deal with the contents of NFC as part of daily business

- Development of a technology designed for a complete information exchange (in Excel format) from the municipal offices and the RHIFs to the NHIF

- Development, management and control of a national health insurance information system

Regional Health Insurance Fund (RHIF)
As mentioned, NHIF is a corporate body with its central management and headquarters in the national capital Sofia. In the Bulgarian health care structure a certain aspect is given to a decentralized system of health care management and health care provision. According to the 28 regions in Bulgaria, 28 Regional Health Insurance Funds (RHIF) were also established.

The main functions of an RHIF can be described as follows and must be covered by a future information system:

- Registration of contracts with medical care suppliers and pharmacies

- Registration of those with compulsory health insurance in the general practitioner's patient list

- Registration of receipt booklets and protocols of chronically ill patients

- Registration of dispensary for ill patients

- Registration and summary of patients participating in Health Priority Programs

- Registration, control, analysis and summary of all medical care provider claim data

- Registration, control, analysis and summary of all drug claims paid to pharmacists and paid directly to wholesalers

National Social Security Institute (NSSI)
The National Social Security Institute is a public organization which, on the basis of the Code for Obligatory Public Insurance, guarantees the citizens' right to pen-

sions and benefits. The Institute provides for quality service and manages the funds of the state social security in an effective and transparent way. The Supervisory Board is the highest management body of National Social Security Institute comprised by representatives of the state and the national representative organizations of workers and employers. The National Social Security Institute administers the mandatory insurance programs for disability, old age and widows' benefits, sickness and maternity, work injuries and occupational diseases as well as collection, control and information services for all obligatory contributions.

General Practitioners (GP)
In his/her core processes of providing primary outpatient health care – among other things – the general practitioner (GP) prescribes drugs in accordance with the "positive list". When it is necessary to prescribe drugs not listed in this, the GP must inform the RHIF about his/her intention and has to explain the reasons for every single prescription. The RHIF has to decide whether or not it wishes to pay.

The GP can dispose of a number of referral cards for consultation with a specialist and/or for joint treatment. The number of referral cards is set monthly for every GP by the RHIF according to his/her patient list and his/her reports from the previous months. The GP is obliged to write down his/her requests in the referral card addressed to the specialist. In the referral card for joint treatment, the GP has to specify his/her motivation for it and also the types and the numbers of scheduled services destined to be performed by the different health care providers.

The GP takes action to hospitalize the patient if the healing processes cannot be achieved by measures and conditions of outpatient care.

3.2.2 Core Processes

The business process model below shows how the processes can be structured into management, core and support processes within NHIF.

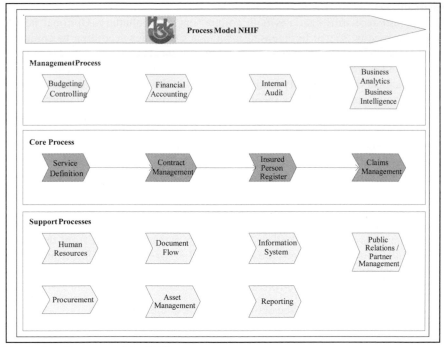

Fig. 5. Core Processes of the NHIF

The main core processes are:

Service Definition
The core process of the service definition contains the definition of all health services by nomenclature, range, volume, quality and prices paid by the NHIF for each medical care provider (MCP). That means that the NHIF states which drug they pay for (partially or fully), which services of specialists and laboratories, which medical attendance. According to the Bulgarian law laid down in the Health Insurance Act the above-mentioned details must be defined in the National Framework Contract (NFC):

Contract Management
The core process of contract management contains all activities in the context of individual contracts with all MCPs. The NFC is the basis for all further activities and it consequently has to be signed before performing any contract negotiations with MCPs. The terms and conditions underlying these contracts are defined in the Health Insurance Act and in the NFC. In a first step the NFC, and as an integrated part of that the positive list, has to be negotiated and signed. Afterwards in a second step the contract management starts.

136

Insured Persons Register
Health insurance in Bulgaria is both compulsory and voluntary. Optional health care insurance is offered by licensed insurance companies according to commercial law. Voluntary health insurance is not part of this tender scope. Everybody in Bulgaria is obliged to be insured and has to pay a monthly health care contribution to the National Social Security Institute (NSSI). At the moment the contribution is fixed up to 6% of the monthly income for employed persons. The amount is paid partly by the employer and partly by the employee. According to the Health Insurance Act, the aim is to establish a 50-50 spread between both parties as of 2007. The state budget pays 1 lev per month for each child up to 18 years of age. Self-employed persons are insured on the basis of their monthly income according to the salary declaration but not below 6% of the double amount of the minimum salary for the country.

Claims Management
The claiming process should allow the NHIF to manage invoices from the MSP, check if the contract conditions are fulfilled and to give the certified claims the final payment confirmation to the RHIF, unless they were not returned to the provider because of completion errors.

As an example Fig. 6 shows the claiming process to the pharmacies.

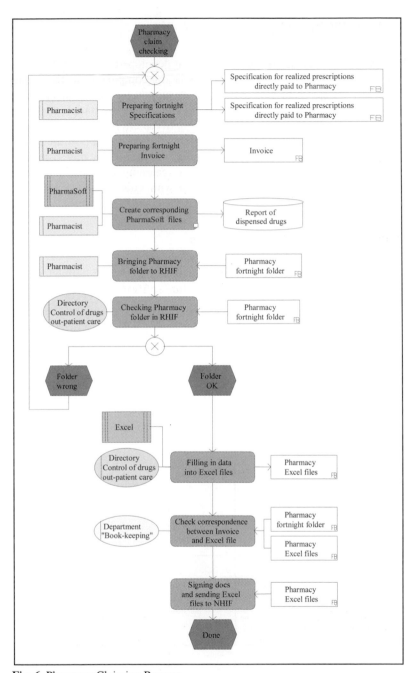

Fig. 6. Pharmacy Claiming Process

3.3 Information Management – IT Requirements

Historically, the technology infrastructure has been developed in a reactive manner, driven by IT professionals, extending and replacing components as they were needed. If the IT strategy is to play a full role in supporting and enhancing the business strategy, it must endeavor to link the planning and exploitation of the IT infrastructure directly with business drivers and improvement initiatives (cf. Ward & Griffith 2000). The need to extend the IT systems in order to support the newly identified processes was recognized in the change program. Changing computer systems is not something which is perceived to be threatening to people's immediate livelihoods and as a result will generally meet with little resistance (cf. Braganza 2001).

3.3.1 Definition of Software Requirements

Out of the needs represented by the business processes IDS Scheer defined an extensive list of the required functionalities of the future software solutions.

Table 2. Business Process-Defined Software Requirements (Extract – Example)

No	Description/Criteria	Elimination Criterion	Means of Fulfillment	Comments/ add. Information
1	Registering parameters (prices, quantities, nomenclatures etc.) of NFC on NHIF level for all MSP listed in different tables	KO		
2	Define/Register contract templates for all MCPS			
3	Distribution of issued lists and contracts to RHIFs The details of every contract (which services for which MCP) and the registration is done by the RHIFs. • Positive list of drugs (see example in appendix III) • List of diseases and the relevant payment for drugs and treatment • Lists with contract partners (MCP) • List of producers/wholesalers/distributors of drugs per region • etc.			
4	Possibility of making cross-checks with the registered parameters			
5	Administrate different parameters of the NFC with history (all historical parameters, nomenclatures, positive lists need to be available)	KO		
6	Possibility of putting contract templates into the system in order that they can be printed for negotiation and signing			
7	Negotiation of contracts (waiting list, change of status of the different suppliers, etc.)			

Table 2. (continued)

8	Register of the ten different kinds of contracts containing: • General information mentioned above • Negotiated services and prices per contract • Various doctors to one contract (for details see tables above)	KO		
9	Possibility of registering technical and medical equipment, education, staff, know-how of each contract partner and all doctors involved			
...				

3.3.2 Information Systems Infrastructure

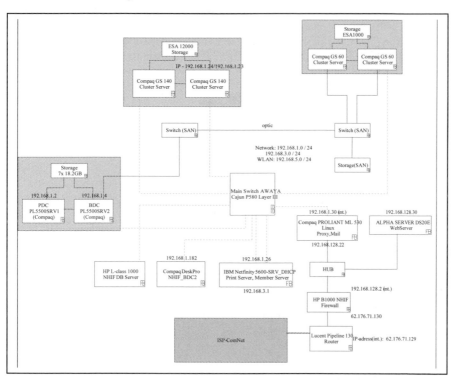

Fig. 7. Existing IT Infrastructure (Extract)

According to the needs of the business processes IDS Scheer has to design a concept of a new IT infrastructure which will fulfil the special requirements of the whole health care system:

• Country-wide, decentralized solution

• High diversity of functional requirements (funds, doctors, hospitals, pharmacies, ...)

- High diversity of IT training levels

- Underdeveloped IT infrastructure especially on a regional scale

- High security requirements out of the personnel illness data

- Need for a disaster center

As an example of a concept according to the business and software requirements the following figure shows the analysis of the current firewall concept, the weak point analysis and the future concept.

Firewall Concept – Description of Current Architecture
The NHIF currently uses a Checkpoint Firewall-1 25 User installed on an HP-UX machine. This setup is meant to be a test installation but will not satisfy the needs of the NHIF. The firewall must handle the complete network traffic for all internet services like HTTP and mail. In addition, the firewall must control all VPN connections to the central database.

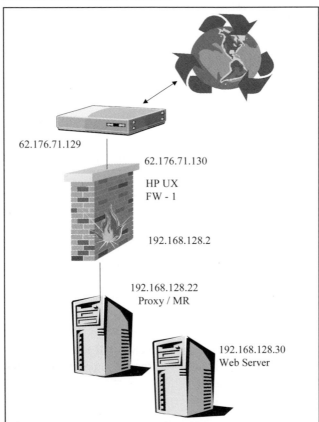

Fig. 8. Current Firewall Architecture

As shown in the overview, there is no physical interface within the firewall to provide a separate DMZ. The NAT (network address translation) is done by the proxy running Linux. This machine is responsible for the complete internal routing too. In addition to these facts, the 25 user licenses for the firewall will not cover the planned implementation of a centralized firewall.

Table 3. Weak Point Analysis & Measures

No	Weak Point	Evaluation/ Consequences	Measures	Pre-Conditions
1	Current firewall license is limited to 25 users	Legal operation is not possible	Upgrade of firewall license as described in firewall proposal	Approval on overall communication concept; approval on firewall concept
2	No physically separated DMZ	Security issue: secure operation is not possible with a DMZ machine inside the LAN	Installation of dedicated proxy in DMZ	Upgrade of firewall as described in firewall proposal
3	The firewall is installed on only one machine	Single point of failure because all traffic (internal/external) is controlled by firewall	Implementation of high availability solution as described in firewall proposal	Approval on overall communication concept; approval on firewall concept
4	The hardware is not capable of handling estimated traffic	Performance bottleneck: database synchronization might not be possible	Upgrade of firewall hardware as described in firewall proposal	Approval on overall communication concept; approval on firewall concept
5	No intrusion detection system in place	Security breaches behind the firewall cannot be detected	Development and implementation of concept for intrusion detection	Upgrade of firewall; approval on requirement of intrusion detection system
...				

Future/Long-Term Firewall Concept

The graphical overview shown in Fig. 9 describes the basic configuration of a firewall cluster based on Sun Microsystems. Additionally, there will be DMZs for proxy/mail and VPN terminators. This solution is redundant and highly expandable.

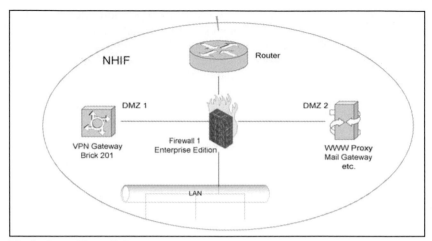

Fig. 9. Future Firewall Concept

The proposed future concept will provide a stable and bulletproof firewall that will protect the NHIF/RHIF systems against potential attackers. For all VPN connections the Lucent Brick 201 VPN terminator will be installed within one DMZ, allowing the NHIF full control over all VPN connections through the firewall. A second DMZ is used for the installation of the proxy and mail gateway. If additional secure connections (for MSPs/hospitals) are needed, the CheckPoint VPN client can be used to connect remote clients over a VPN to the NHIF network.

3.3.3 Ongoing Support

To be successful with the new processes and the new IT environment, the knowledge of all participants must grow step by step. Furthermore as the whole project runs until 2004 it is essential to have a robust workaround of the as-is business processes in the meantime, so another side focus of the project is to support the NHIF through ongoing support and enhancement of the running solutions through activities in Microsoft, Hewlett Packard/Compaq, Oracle, Network LAN and VPN via close cooperation with local Bulgarian experts in these areas.

3.4 Realization

As shown in the project plan (Fig. 3) the realization phase is to be finished in 2004.

4. Conclusion

With this ambitious project, Bulgaria will reach the international standards in health care, an important precondition for joining the European Union in 2007 (planned). The use of modern information technology helps to reach the targets. In defining the new processes and IT systems a huge project was set up in 2001. The initial phase was very successful.

But the new processes and the new IT systems alone can not fulfil the expectations – only an integrated change management approach will be successful.

5. References

Adomeit A., Baur, A., Salfeld, R.: A New Model for Disease Management, The McKinsey Quarterly, 2001, Number 4.

Braganza, A.: Radical Process Change, John Wiley & Sons Ltd., 2001.

Doppler, K., Lauterburg, C.: Change Management, Campus Publishing Company Frankfurt/New York, 2002.

Ester, R. M.: Performance Measurement Onto the Operation of Standard Business Software, IM & Consulting, 2000.

Glaser, J. P., Drazen, E. L. et al: Maximizing the Benefits of Health Care Information Systems. Journal of Medical Systems, Vol. 10, No. 1, 1986.

Pierskall, W. P., Woods, D.: Computers in Hospital Management and Improvements in Patient Care – New Trends in the United States, Journal of Medical Systems, Vol. 12, No. 6, 1988.

Scheer, A.-W., Jost, W.: ARIS in Practice, 2002.

Scheer, A.-W.: Architecture of Integrated Information Systems: Business Process Modeling. Berlin: Springer-Publishing Company 1999.

Ward, J., Griffith, P.: Strategic Planning for Information Systems, John Wiley & Sons Ltd., 2nd Edition, 2000.

6 Conclusion/...

With this ambitious project Bulgaria will reach the international standards in ... by joining the European Union in 2007 ...

Slovenian Railways Process Reengineering Project

Peter Lovšin
Work Process Development Department, Slovenian Railways

Josip Orbanić
Manager of Quality and Environment System, Slovenian Railways

Miro Sobocan
IDS Scheer Slovenia d.o.o.

Summary

This report discusses the efforts on the work process reengineering project of Slovenian Railways. The reengineering project was developed with the wish to obtain a transparent inventory of company processes and the tool ARIS proved a suitable solution. The project was started in 1999. We had to assure not only the basic equipment but also the appropriate human resources to cover individual work areas by specific knowledge. Having formed the group, we started to train the people and model the function trees. The next step was to set up the organizational structure and create the first eEPC diagrams. Due to company reorganization, the organization structure chart changed as well. This caused a short delay in process analysis because we had to adjust the changed company organization to the status of ARIS data base. The processes were analyzed by means of a questionnaire / identifier from which we derived the required data. The data collected in this manner will serve as a good foundation to confront the anticipated changes in the company; these changes concern cost-efficient business operations, adjustment to the market and adaptation to EU directives. Our further work will be based on the products / services that we provide to the market. We will accordingly adapt our optimal work processes and, on this basis, implement the quality system, in harmony with the new ISO 9001:2000 standard which involves process approach and continuous improvements.

Key Words

ARIS, Process, Process Architecture, Reengineering Project, Railways

1. Background of the Company and its Subsidiaries

1.1 Slovenian Railways

Railways came first to our country in 1846 (Celje) and in 1849 to our capital Ljubljana. In the past, the railways on the territory of present Slovenia were part of Austrian, Italian and Yugoslav railways systems. Since 1991, they have been operating as independent railways. Today, Slovenian Railways have about 9000 employees and their main activity is providing transport services – transport of people and goods, and management, maintenance and modernization of railways infrastructure.

At the moment, Slovenian railways are organized as a public company, in the form of a 100 % state-owned joint-stock company. In addition to the parent company there are six subsidiaries which provide complete railways activities in Slovenia. Some general data about Slovenian railways (cf. Annual Report 2002):

- Transported loads: 14.9m tons, 2837m ntkm, 90 % in international traffic

- Transported passengers: 14.5m passengers, 715m pkm, 16 % international traffic

- Average daily traffic: 736 trains, 509 passenger and 227 freight

- Railway lines length 1226 km, 41 % electrified, 26 % double-track, 129 stations

- Employees: about 9000 in parent company and 2200 in six subsidiaries

- Locomotives: 87 electric, 92 diesel, 5 steam (museum)

- Motor trains and passenger wagons: 42 electric, 78 diesel, 186 wagons

- Freight wagon: 5569 wagons, average capacity 48.5 tons

- Annual turnover: SIT58 billion (EUR260m)

Market share of railways in passengers traffic is about 18 %, and in freight traffic 45 %. The above data refer to statistically tracked carriers. Actually, this share is significantly lower if we take into account private transports, as is evident from the diagrams in Fig. 1 and 2 (cf. White Paper 2001, cf. Statisticni letopis 2001). The market share has a long-term falling trend, as a consequence of increased road traffic and because the railways lag behind with regard to speed, quality and logistics. A great success was achieved in combined traffic which, in the period from 1996-2000, increased by nearly 50 % and participates in total traffic with 11 %.

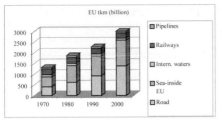
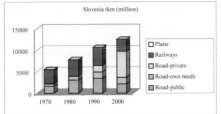

Fig. 1. Modal Split of Freight Traffic in EU and Slovenia

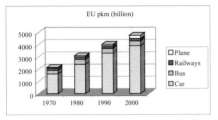
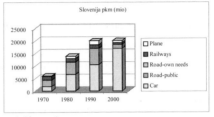

Fig. 2. Modal Split of Passenger Traffic in EU and Slovenia

1.2 Railways Management

Railways management is very complex. Railways are a large system which encompasses numerous activities such as infrastructure and fleet management, maintenance of resources and equipment, training of personnel, organization, leading, etc.; in addition to this, railways are extended over a wide area of countries and continents. At the beginning, railways were private systems which gradually became very extensive and strategically so important that the State started to interfere with their structure and ownership. Most railways were State-owned and they mostly remain so.

The concept of general railways management model is based on hierarchy (see Fig. 3).

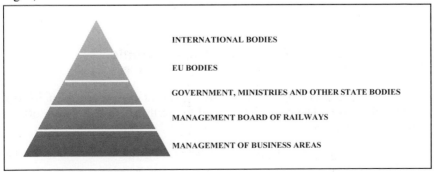

Fig. 3. Railways Management Hierarchy in EU

Railways management is based on EU directives, international, State, and internal regulations, and individual railways programs. EU Council has issued eight important directives which establish the legal framework of EU railways operation. These directives are (cf. Official Journal of the European Communities 2001):

1. Council directive of 29 July 1991 on the development of the Community railways (91/440/EEC)

2. Council directive 95/18/EC of 19 June 1995 on the licensing of railway undertakings

3. Council directive 95/19/EC of 19 June 1995 on the allocation of railway infrastructure capacity and the charging of infrastructure fees

4. Directive 2001/12/EC of the European Parliament and of the council of 26 February 2001 amending Council directive 91/440/EEC on the development of the Community's railways

5. Directive 2001/13/EC of the European Parliament and of the council of 26 February 2001 amending Council directive 95/18/EC on the licensing of railway undertakings

6. Directive 2001/14/EC of the European Parliament and of the council of 26 February 2001 on the allocation of railway infrastructure capacity and the levying of charges for the use of railway infrastructure and safety certification

7. Council directive 96/48/EC of 23 July 1996 on the interoperability of the trans-European high-speed rail system

8. Directive 2001/16/EC of the European Parliament and of the council of 19 March 2001 on the interoperability of the trans-European conventional rail system

Slovenia has passed three laws and more than 30 by-laws which regulate railways operations. They all, with internal regulations, business plan, and management strategy, form the basis for defining and executing the railways work processes. Slovenia is a candidate for EU membership and is obliged to adjust all work processes and operations to EU requirements.

2. Process Approach - What are our Goals

In 1999, there was a demand for a clearer survey of the processes of SŽ d.d. (Slovenian Railways). The company decided to use the tool ARIS which offered suitable solutions.

The starting points of the work process reengineering project (cf. Projektna naloga... 2000):

- Present work processes are based on past practices which, in the contemporary conditions of market-oriented business management, informatization and globalization, do not allow sufficient transparency, efficiency and market-orientation

- Work process documentation is based mainly on manual recording and work execution that does not assure adequate efficiency in this information age

- Some discrepancies have been stated in the process of establishment and implementation of the quality system according to the ISO 9001 standard, that cannot be eliminated without a modern approach to work process description and process management

Concrete goals related to general project objectives were:

- Determine clear and user-friendly processes (visualization)

- Optimize the processes by discarding the activities that do not contribute to new added value (optimization)

- Document the processes on uniform foundations and assure consideration of up-to-date technological developments (updating)

- Prepare the foundations for information support of work processes (informatization)

- Introduce a continuous improvement system in order to keep pace with the demands and needs for development (continuous improvement)

The project is closely connected with other strategic social projects: information system restructuring, new organization, new regulations, quality and environment projects, etc. By means of reengineering we wish to achieve the set goals and to efficiently record and execute work processes.

From the very beginning, the work on the project had a long-term character. The first stage of status reconnaissance was followed by analysis and changes of the processes. This stage will be followed by continuous process improvement as the prerequisite for further development and fine-tuning of the results, achieved by means of the reengineering.

In addition to the hardware that we started to purchase this year, we had to assure also a corresponding human resources structure which would be able to implement such a complex project. The company management decided that the project would be covered by one representative from each business unit.

3. Reengineering Project

The project is organized on the principle of project management. Strategic level of decision-making consists of the Slovenian Railways Quality Team, led by the President of the Management Board. The creative level is represented by the project team, led by the manager of the section for Quality Development and Environment Protection, and is coordinated by the Head Engineer. The project group comprises members from the areas and headquarters services. The execution level consists of members of the group, each for his own work area, who include all the interested sides. These teams realize individual tasks that have been set on the strategic and tactic levels.

Fig. 4 (cf. Projektna naloga... 2000) shows the structure at the beginning of the project in 1999:

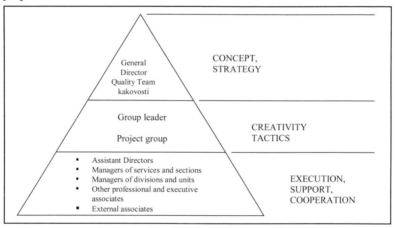

Fig. 4. Structure at the Beginning of the Project

From the start, the work process reengineering project comprised the activities in Fig. 5 (cf. Projektna naloga... 2000):

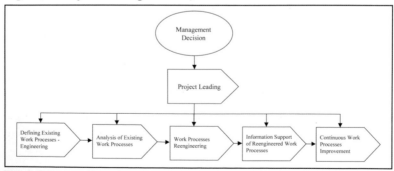

Fig. 5. Processes Reengineering Project

4. Using ARIS Methodology

4.1 First Steps

At the beginning, we gathered basic knowledge about process management and ARIS (cf. Orbanic 1998, cf. Schher 1999).

Before we began working with the tool ARIS we also had to:

- Train the ARIS team for tool operation

- Obtain appropriate equipment and install the tool on user's PC

- Prepare users conventions

- Define the structure of data base, basic modules and accesses

- Determine the timetable for using the licenses

Training was carried out in two groups of 6 participants and was completed in July 1999. At the same time, we prepared the regulations for work convention. They comprised the data about the method of working with the tool ARIS. A glossary of functions formed a constituent part of the regulations. Its purpose was to prevent uncontrolled use of terms for function names – the goal was to achieve a uniform nomenclature.

The work with ARIS intensified in September 1999. Each member of the group was made responsible for a particular group of processes in organizational units.

The data base structure derived from a uniform organization model and function tree (Fig. 6). The work was organized in such a manner that each member of the group worked at his own working place and was connected to the server via LAN. The assignment for working with the tool ARIS was full-time, with some exceptions; e.g. Purchase and Material operations were covered by two members who carried out everyday work tasks within their organization unit.

The models we used for working with ARIS were Functional trees (level 1 to 6); on the second level we made also a Value-added chain diagram for illustration of time dependency of the functions. We put a special stress on eEPC diagrams (event-driven process chain diagram) which were made for level 6, and partly also for level 5, in case the functional trees were not branched in level 6.

In the starting stage, we decided that there would be 6 written levels of the function trees, but in practice, this proved to be a very broad approach, and it would perhaps be better if there were less levels – especially for the purpose of clarity.

The work progress was reported at regular meetings, first each week and then every fortnight, where we discussed the actual issues. In practice, most problems occurred in obtaining concrete information about individual processes, which was a bit surprising, considering that the project was supported by the top management. By April 2000, most processes of the company were registered, the organization scheme was arranged and data carriers in the so called eERM diagrams were structured. At the proposal of the consultant - who was at that time still from the company Enel d.o.o., but is today part of the company IDS Scheer Slovenia - we started to contemplate a two-days' workshop at which we would present to the management of the company the work that had been done on the project and the opportunities for further work. At ARIS ProcessWorld 2000 in Düsseldorf, we agreed about the last details about the meeting which took place from 18 to 19 May 2000.

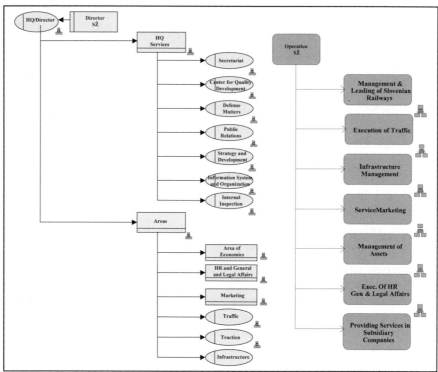

Fig. 6. Organization scheme of SŽ Company at the Beginning of the Project, with Basic Function Tree

4.2 Workshop SŽ – IDS - Enel

The work completed until then was presented in the introductory session of the workshop:

Until the workshop, we had completed 391 models of eEPC, entered 3620 functions and 3874 data carriers. The most important conclusions of the workshop were related to the next steps that we can sum up in the following subparagraphs:

Results:

• detailed

This should be followed by:

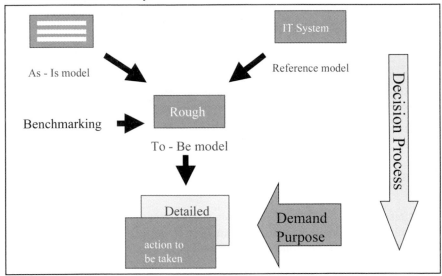

Fig. 7. Further Decisions, on the Basis of the Workshop

During the workshop, the consultants from IDS Scheer AG and the management of SŽ came to a general agreement concerning a longer workshop that would take place in July at Slovenian Railways and that we named the IDS Workshop, with the purpose of setting up the starting-point architecture and proposing further measures for company management.

We decided for a workshop because we wanted to obtain the guidelines for a successful integration of ARIS into company operation. The workshop took place from 4 to 17 July 2000.

We presented the situation as is to the team from IDS-Scheer (Fig. 8) – with indicated changes of organizational structure which actually happened in September 2000, after the workshop.

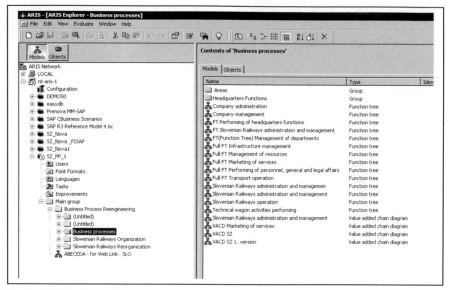

Fig. 8. IDS Workshop Base

Main stress of the workshop was on the executive company level – traffic and infrastructure, and a smaller stress on the support processes. The workshop had the following contents (cf. Protfolio of Measures 2000):

1. As-is situation and project contents

2. Process architecture of Slovenian Railways d.d.

3. Portfolio of measures

4. What next

The project contents referred to:

1. Planning of Slovenian Railways process architecture

   • Defining the organizational units and the information systems

   • Forming the basis for the to-be plan

2. Development of the 'measures portfolio'

   • Defining the existing project activities

   • Description of measures for business process optimization

3. Creation of the basis for process management

   • Base of processes of Slovenian Railways

   • Introduction of process management as a continuous activity

The core of the workshop consisted of conversations with Slovenian Railways management, moderated by the representatives of IDS Scheer AG. The structure of the questions referred to the organization, method of working, connection with other organization units, etc.

An architectural concept was developed, based on the conversations, experience and consulting, which is partly represented in Fig. 9.

The following measures for business operations improvement were proposed:

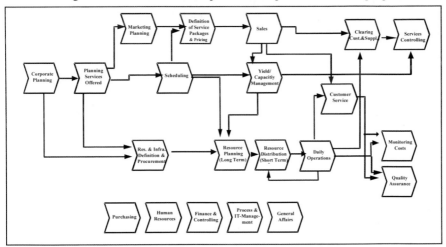

Fig. 9. Process Architecture of SŽ d.d.

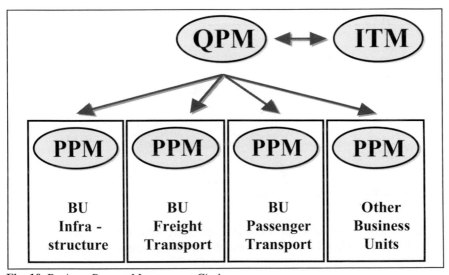

Fig. 10. Business Process Management Circle

4.3 New Organization

The processes had to be modified based on the law on railways traffic that determined adjustment of Slovenian Railways to EU directives. After the IDS Workshop, Slovenian Railways were reorganized in accordance with the European legislation. The reorganization process caused delay in the work with ARIS because the organization structure had to be adjusted to the new situation. Working place systemization was changed, too. This meant changes of working place nomenclature in the data base and changes of all eEPC models.

Fig. 11 shows the new organization structure:

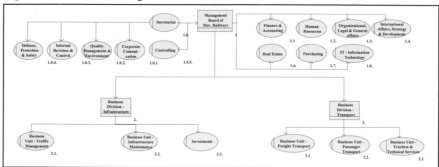

Fig. 11. Organization Structure after Reorganization

We based the changes of processes on the architecture, the creation of which began by a draft, shown in Fig. 12:

Fig. 12. Draft Work Processes Architecture

The model was subjected to many changes and quite some time passed until its final form was achieved. Fig. 13 shows the default architecture (cf Orbanic & Lovsin 2002):

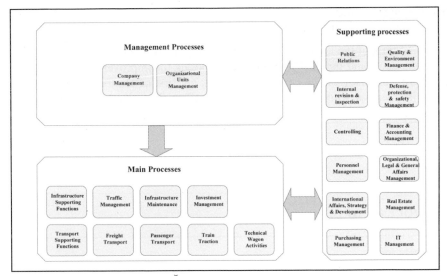

Fig. 13. Process Architecture of SŽ

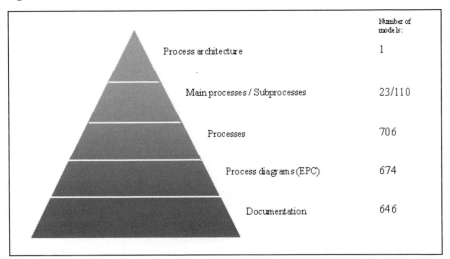

Fig. 14. Process Hierachy

The adjustment to new organization was a good opportunity to improve our work processes. In the next stage, we passed to process analysis by means of identifiers. We formed the process identifiers with the aim to obtain the most useful data for changing the business operations methods and, consequently, for reducing the costs.

Initially, the analysis was planned in the form of questionnaires. However, it seemed that the selection of 2 x 14 questions was to wide and that, during the performance of the analysis, we would probably be met by reluctant employees, so that the effect would be contrary to the desired one– interest of the employees in the processes and proposals for improvement.

The final form of the identifier is presented in Fig. 15 (cf. Scheer 1999). The stress is on the goals and indicators and on the proposals for improvements. In the next stage we will tackle the process improvement, but first of all, the change of processes into such a form that they would not reflect the organization structure to such extent as until now.

Slovenske železnice d.d.

PROCESS CARD:

Superior process:

Process scope	
Indicators for process quality/ efficiency	
Process costs	
Number of employees	
Performing frequency	
Process weak points	
Proposals for process improvements	
- **increasing efficiency / quality** (what, how, how much, who, wen?)	
- **cost cutting** (what, how, how much, who, wen?)	
- **IT support - proposals**	

Inferior processes: -

Date: . .	**Responsible person:**

Fig. 15. Process Card

The data gathered in the identifiers provide the most complete survey of the processes and their evaluation, with goals, indices, number of employees, description of weaknesses, with proposals for increased efficiency, cost reduction and information support. Next steps will lead to process improvement.

5. Future Goals

It is obvious from the above presented materials that a lot of things have been done but that much more could be done about the matters related to company restructuring and intensity of work in specific periods.

The goal for the future is to upgrade the present work with opportunities offered by the PPM and Scout packets. The first would serve for a comprehensive survey of work process implementation and, above all, for supporting the management in leading the company.

We decided to continue the project by defining the product range offered to the market by our company. The products/services diagram will serve as the starting point. We must define the main product support processes and related sub-processes whose business effect is a partial product. The starting diagram will be the Product allocation diagram (Fig. 16) and, like when we analyzed the processes with identifiers, we will create also the product identifiers (Fig.16).

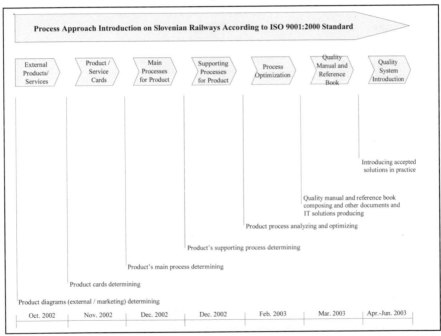

Fig. 16. Introduction of Process Approach

This stage will be done within the organization restructuring and adjustment to the requirements of the ISO 9001:2000 quality standard.

160

Slovenske železnice d.d.	

PRODUCT CARD:

Superior product:

Scope, purpose and description of the product	
Indicators for measuring efficiency / quality of the product	
Sources for product (short description): - Material sources (quantity, description) - Human sources (number, description) - Financial sources (000 SIT, description) - Other sources (quantity, description)	
Product revenue by market (000 SIT)	
Processes needed for product execution: - main - supportive	
Connections with other products (which, how, weak points?)	
Product weak points from - market point of view - internal point of view	
Proposals for product improvements - **increasing efficiency / quality** (what, how, how much, who, wen?)	
- **cost cutting** (what, how, how much, who, wen?)	
- **increasing sales volume and revenues** (what, how, how much, who, wen?)	

Subordinate product:

Date: . .	Responsible person:

Fig. 17. Product Card

In further project implementation we plan to use the ARIS Web Publisher, ARIS for mySAP.com, ARIS Process Performance Manager, ARIA Activity Based Costing, ARIS Quality Management Scout etc.

6. References

Annual report 2001, Slovenian Railways, 2002

Official Journal of the European Communities, L 237/25-28/,24.8.1991; L 143/70-73/, 27.6.1995; L 143/75-78/, 27.6.1995; L 75/1-75/25, 15.03.2001; L 75/26-75/28, 15.03.2001; L 75/29-75/46, 15.03.2001; L 235/6-235/24, 17.09.1996; L 110/1-110/27, 20.04.2001

Orbanic, J.: Sistem kakovosti v logisticni gospodarski druzbi, s posebnim ozirom na zelezniski promet, doktorska disertacija, EPF Maribor, 1988 (Quality System in a Commercial Logistics Company with Special regard to Rail Transport, Doctoral Thesis EPF Maribor, 1998)

Orbanic J. & Lovsin P.: Program nadaljnjega dela in dopolnjeno porocilo o prenovi peocesov dela (A Program of Further Activities and a Supplementary Report on Pocess Reengineering), Slovenske zeleznice, Ljubljana, 2

Portfoli of Measures "Design of Process and IT-Systems", Slovenian Railways and IDS Scheer AG, 2000

Projektna naloga za prenovo procesov dela (Process Reengineering Project task), Slovenske zeleznice, Ljubljana, 2000

Scheer, A., W.: ARIS – Business Process Modeling, Springer, Berlin, 1999

Statisticni letopis (Statistical annual report/yearbook), Statisticni urad Republike Slovenije (Statistical Bureau of Republic of Slovenia), 1971, 1981, 1991, 2001

White paper (European transport policy for 2010: time to decide), Commission of the European Communities, COM(2001)370, Brussels, 12/09/2001

5. References

Evaluation of Business Processes – Basis for Successfully Changing the Organization of ERA© Ltd., a Slovenian Retail Company

Iztok Pustatičnik
Project Manager, ERA, d.d.

Summary

The paper presents the methodology of evaluating business processes used in the Slovenian retail company ERA Ltd. Since evaluation plays an important role in the comprehensive approach to business process reengineering within the company, the presentation starts with the introduction of the project Business Process Reengineering at ERA and the ARIS methodology as a tool for process modeling reengineering. This is followed by a short presentation of business process modeling in relation to purchasing in retail outlets. The established existing situation represents the starting point for the evaluation and analysis of the purchasing process. The paper then outlines some applications of the methodology of business process evaluation along with their practical application value and advantages of the evaluation methodology to the company. The evaluation process enables the identification of more time-consuming functions (activities) that represent significant cost centers, comparisons of work processes between different organizational units – internal benchmarking (in this case between retail outlets), evaluation of proposals for changing the processes of the organization and so on. Such insights and conclusions facilitate the decision-making in relation to the introduction of more radical changes into the organization (change management) aimed at improving the overall company performance.

Key Words

ARIS Methodology, Business Processes Reengineering (BPR), Change Management, Changing the Organization, Changing Process, Communication, Continuous Process Improvement (CPI), Function (Activity), Methodology of Evaluating Business Processes, Purchasing Processes in Retail Outlets

1. Introduction

Issues like improving company business processes by reducing costs and time involved while increasing quality and speeding up the business communication process, are just some of the challenges that today's managers are facing on a daily basis. In order to be able to improve a business process within a company, we first have to have a thorough understanding of what it does and how it works. Since business processes typically include a number of sequential or concurrent activities, it makes sense to use process modeling to show the flow of these processes and their integral parts. There are various tools available for the design of process models. The design of process models represents the starting point for conducting the necessary assessment of the existing business processes. The main objective of the evaluation process is to identify the weaknesses in the business operation along with the rectification options aimed at eliminating the established shortcomings. This way it becomes easier to identify specific changes that need to be introduced into the business processes to bring about a significant improvement in business performance, while also keeping in mind the interests of customers, employees and company shareholders.

Thus, evaluation of business processes is an integral part of business process reengineering. It is often a demanding task in terms of expertise, time and costs involved; therefore it is essential to apply a well-defined, uniform methodology.

The objective of this paper is to present a case study involving the methodology for the evaluation of business processes used at the ERA retail company. The practical application value of the methodology has been assessed in relation to the purchasing process in ERA's retail outlets.

The starting point for the evaluation of business processes at ERA is the project Business Process Reengineering. The main phases of this project are presented in Item 2. This Item also includes a brief introduction to the concept and practical application value of the ARIS methodology (as a tool for the modeling and reengineering of business processes). The outline of the purchasing process in retail outlets is presented in Item 3 along with the modeling of the purchasing process using the ARIS Toolset. On the basis of the results of the modeling of the existing purchasing process, the methodology and practical application value of the evaluation of the selected business process are presented in Item 4.

2. Background

2.1 Reengineering of Business Processes at ERA

Having an understanding of the company's own business processes is the key to implementing them in an effective and efficient manner. To this end, in the year 2000 ERA[1] launched the project Business Process Reengineering. In the initial phase of the project, ERA's vital and support business processes had to be identified and placed in the context of the value added chain as shown in Fig. 1.

Next we had to select the methodology and define the context of modeling of the existing business processes identified and presented in Fig. 1. As already mentioned, ERA is using the ARIS (Architecture of Integrated Information System) methodology for the modeling of business processes. This methodology serves to determine the flow of the existing processes and their integral parts by building process models. The process models themselves are defined by interviewing the 'owners' of the business processes and their associates at a lower level.

The next phase required us to define the methodology for the evaluation of the business models designed. The evaluation should expose the activities that represent the weaknesses in the business operation as well as enabling us to determine the degree to which the existing information subsystems of individual business functions have been integrated into a comprehensive information system at the corporate level. This would give us an idea as to the level of information support of the individual business operations, any task duplications and possible ways of reducing or eliminating them should a more appropriate information support system be introduced.

---

[1] ERA is a business system with 50 years of tradition. We are primarily a retail business operating within our own network of retail stores and the retail network of our joint venture partners and associated members of the ERA Group. We are also wholesalers of beverages and alimentary as well as non-alimentary products throughout Slovenia. In addition ERA acts as a nationwide distributor and supplier to petrol stations. The last few years can best be characterized as a period of dynamic company growth.
Other important information about Era:
Address: Prešernova 10, 3504 Velenje, Slovenia
Phone No: +386 3 8960 100
Fax No: +386 3 8960 146
E-mail: era@era.si; http://www.era.si
Organization: Ltd. with daughter companies in Slovenia, Croatia, Montenegro, Serbia, Bosnia and Herzegovina, Macedonia and Italy and joint ventures in Austria and the Czech Republic
Number of Retail Stores: 137
Annual Sales Volume: 221.1 million €
Number of Employees: 2,256

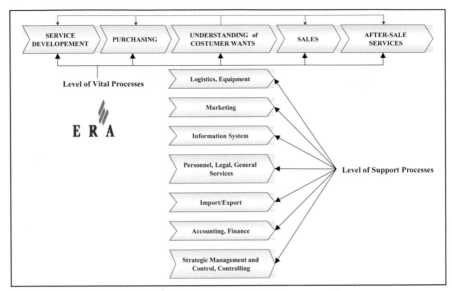

Fig. 1. ERA's Key and Support Business Processes in the Context of the Value Added Chain

As shown in Fig. 1, there are a number of key and support processes present at ERA. Therefore we decided to take a gradual approach to the modeling and reengineering of the business processes. Initially we focused on the key processes in Purchasing and Sales in retail outlets, and relevant support processes in two general function areas: Accounting and Finance. This was to be followed by the modeling of the key processes in Purchasing and Sales in ERA's wholesale stores along with the relevant support processes in the general function areas. This approach allowed us to split the project Business Process Reengineering into separate subprojects along the lines of functional subsystems. This way we reduced the risk of project failure since individual process units require significantly fewer process models as opposed to the modeling of all processes simultaneously. The latter often produces misleading results since the usefulness of process models is a function of their reliability, which decreases in reverse proportion to their number.

2.2 ARIS Methodology

The ARIS methodology is characterized by the reduction in the extent of comprehensive descriptions of business processes and a 'level' approach to business process reengineering. Due to the complexity of business processes the advantage that ARIS offers is in allowing us to view them from different perspectives (cf. Scheer 1998):

- **Functional view** describes the functions (activities) in the company, their interrelatedness and hierarchical structure

- **Data view** defines the objective situations arising in the company

- **Organizational view** describes the organizational units and human resources involved in the processes, and their mutual relationships

- **Control view** integrates the three overviews above into a comprehensive whole

When using ARIS to describe processes, the business system is perceived as a whole that is gradually broken down into increasingly smaller but interconnected subsystems until the desired level is reached ('top down' approach). Business processes are described in terms of 'objects': functions (activities), events, situations, users, organizational units and means of information technology.

The ARIS methodology supports the systematic collection and analysis of various data in relation to business processes. The data are available to all users simultaneously. The methodology enables the merger between the modeling concepts and methods for monitoring performance and company efficiency (Balanced Scorecards – BSC), and cost control (Activity-Based Costing). The method also allows for the data to be presented as information that the users can define in accordance with their thought model.

3. Purchasing Process in ERA's Retail Outlets

The main functions (activities) within the existing purchasing process in ERA's retail outlets are sequential, as follows:

- Purchasing planning (i.e. planning within the framework of the company Annual Plan and planning at the operational level by stores' managers)

- Selecting the source of supply (there are several different sources of supply available, some of which are more cost-effective for the company than others)

- Placing of orders for merchandise (peculiarities in relation to the way orders are placed and manner of delivery)

- Receiving the delivery of merchandise (quantity/volume control; entry of the delivery docket into the records and pricing; making an inventory record; and completion of the purchase order at the store)

- Receiving and processing the account (verification of the account form and content)

- Entering the account into the accounts payable ledger and general ledger

- Payment of the account

All of the above activities were first consolidated into three key links in the value added chain diagram (see Fig. 2).

- **Order creation** (includes planning, selection of supply sources, manner of placing orders and delivery of merchandise)

- **Receiving delivery of merchandise** (quantity/volume control with a complaint option; entry of the delivery docket into the records, and pricing; making an inventory record; and finalization of the purchase order at the store)

- **Completion of purchase** (receiving the account, verification of the account form and content, entering the account into the accounts payable ledger and general ledger, payment of the account)

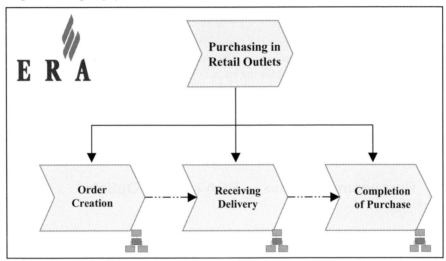

Fig. 2. Value Chain of the Purchasing Process in ERA's Retail Outlets

For every key element in the established value chain we next had to define its key functions (activities). Since "Order Creation" and "Receiving Delivery" differs when it comes to alimentary and non-alimentary retail outlets, we used the Process Selection Matrix in order to determine the key functions (activities). Likewise we used the Process Selection Matrix for "Completion of Purchase" since the manner of completion is subject to the type of the account payable. An example of a process selection matrix is presented in Fig. 3. Fig. 3 also illustrates the differences between functions (activities) in relation to "Receiving Delivery" in alimentary and non-alimentary retail outlets.

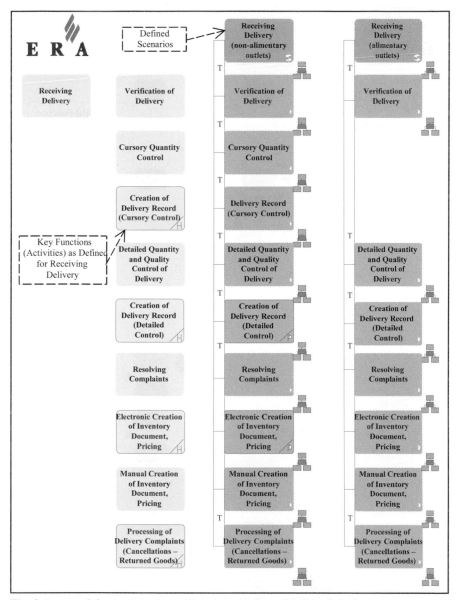

Fig. 3. Process Selection Matrix for "Receiving Delivery" in Retail Outlets

For all the scenarios identified we next defined process models (eEPC diagrams), where the flow of the business process was determined in detail using functions (activities), events and situations. An example of a process model for the scenario "Receiving Delivery" in alimentary retail outlets is presented in Fig. 4.

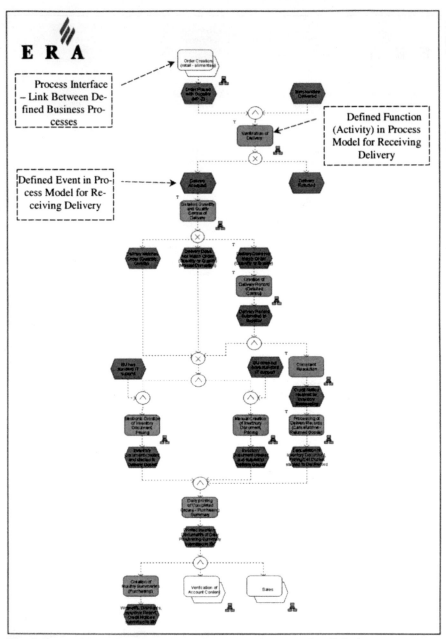

Fig. 4. Process Model for "Receiving Delivery" in Alimentary Retail Outlets

It was also necessary to determine whose role (persons responsible, organizational units) it was to ensure that the identified functions (activities) were being carried out, along with the information technology requirements and other tools necessary for the execution of the individual functions (activities). The latter was defined using a function allocation diagram. An example of a function allocation diagram is presented in Fig. 5.

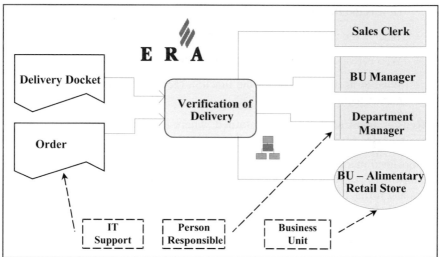

Fig. 5. Function Allocation Diagram For "Verification of Delivery" in Alimentary and Non-Alimentary Retail Outlets

Using the diagrams shown, the entire purchasing process at ERA's retail outlets was defined in detail. To summarize, the main steps involved in the modeling of the existing situation in the purchasing process (retail) are as follows:

- **Scope of the project**, including:

    - Project implementation study

    - Breaking down the key processes into relevant support processes and activities (value added chain)

    - Determining the depth of the modeling of the business processes (the type of models used)

    - Defining the uniform terminology for the objects involved in the function execution (documents, computer applications, databases, organizational units, job/position titles)

    - Creating a timetable for conducting the interviews

- **Interviewing and modeling**, including a chart illustration of the flow of the process defined with the help of the person being interviewed. At the interviews the following questions are asked:

  - What criteria need to be met to trigger the execution of a certain function (activity)?

  - How is the function (activity) performed?

  - What is the result/outcome of the function (activity)?

  - Who is responsible for the execution of the function (activity)?

  - What tools are required for the function (activity) to be carried out (information technology)?

- **Reassessment of the models obtained**, where any amendments are made and the model is finalized and accepted

The obtained models provide insight into the purchasing process in retail business and how it works, which is crucial for the introduction of new retail outlets, associates and forms of business. The models also enable existing work procedures to be amended and redefined, which is the basis of business standardization in the company. At the same time they represent the starting point for the evaluation of the existing purchasing process in ERA's retail outlets, as will be shown later on.

4. Evaluating Purchasing Processes in Retail Outlets

4.1 Purpose and Objectives of the Evaluation

The main *purpose of the evaluation* was the analysis of the process models (eEPC diagrams – see Fig. 4) obtained by modeling the existing purchasing processes in ERA's retail outlets. The chief objective of the evaluation was to identify the functions (activities) in the purchasing process that represent weaknesses in the business operation. The key criteria for the evaluation of the functions (activities) were as follows:

- Total time and cost involved in the execution of individual functions (activities)

- Time spent by the person responsible for the execution of each function (activity)

- Identification of the level of information support of individual functions (activities)

The evaluation of functions (activities) is a demanding job. It therefore made sense to use a predefined, uniform methodology. The aim was to arrive at the accurate definition of the method for the evaluation of functions (activities) in the process models. Thus the necessary degree of uniformity was achieved between the individuals involved in the analysis of the process models obtained. The uniformity was required in order to acquire more useful and comparable data needed for further analysis of the functions (activities).

4.2 Evaluation Methodology

The methodology of business process evaluation used at ERA comprises six working packages as shown in Fig. 6.

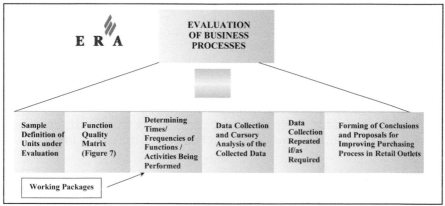

Fig. 6. Working Packages in the Phase of Business Process Evaluation

For the first working package we had to define the sample of the units under evaluation, i.e. where we monitored the flow of the purchasing process in retail outlets. To this end we selected[2] two representative alimentary and four representative non-alimentary retail outlets (the type of stores with development potential were chosen). We also closely monitored the flow of the purchasing process through the three sections of the general function of Finance (Completion, Payments, Accounts Payable) and two sections of the general function of Accounting (Inventory Bookkeeping, Financial Bookkeeping).

The second working package required us to produce a rough estimate of the desirability of the identified functions (activities) within the defined process models of the existing purchasing process. Our focus here was on determining the level of efficiency of the value-adding functions (activities) from a customer perspective. Apart from the functions (activities) already mentioned we also considered those

---

[2] In the case of the retail outlets we selected the stores whose managers we had already interviewed in the phase of purchase process modeling.

174

support functions (activities) necessary for the smooth and successful running of ERA's business (e.g. order preparation, transmission of order to supplier, etc.). For this purpose the Function Quality Matrix approach was used, as shown in Fig. 7.

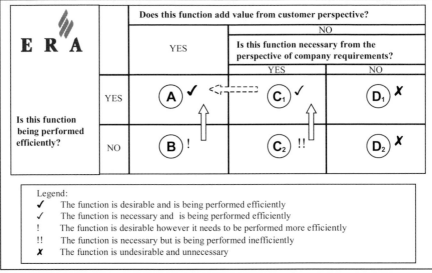

Fig. 7. Function Quality Matrix from a Company Perspective[3] (cf. Tekavčič 1997)

The third working package was used to measure the times and frequency of individual functions (activities) being performed as identified in the models of the purchasing process. This was conducted in the timeframe of one month within the defined sample of the units under evaluation. To this end the persons appointed for the individual units of the defined sample (retail outlets and identified departments within the general functions of Accounting and Finance) filled our tabular forms specifically designed for this purpose. The objective of each table was identified in the table heading. For example, the form "Functions/Activities" in the "Receiving Delivery" model was designed for the purpose of evaluating the

---

[3] Without a doubt, the most desirable functions (activities) in the company are Type A functions (activities). These functions (activities) add value from a customer perspective and are performed efficiently by the company. Type B functions (activities) in the company are also desirable, however we have to find a way for them to be performed in a more efficient manner. Type C functions (activities) are less desirable since they do not add value from a customer perspective but cannot be entirely eliminated since they are required by the company. However we need to be careful to reduce the number of such functions (activities) to a minimum while ensuring they are being performed as efficiently as possible, preferably in a manner that corresponds to customer needs and wants. Type D functions (activities) are not desirable under any circumstances whatsoever since they do not add value from a customer perspective nor are they needed by the company, therefore it makes no difference whether they are performed efficiently or inefficiently. We need to aim to eliminate Type D functions (activities) altogether.

set of functions (activities) related to the receipt of merchandise delivered to the retail stores. The table included all the functions (activities) recorded in the "Receiving Delivery" model (eEPC diagram – see Fig. 4). Functions (activities) in the table were sequentially listed in the same order as they were recorded in the model (i.e. from top down and from left to right). An example is shown in Table 1.

Table 1. Functions (Activities) in the Model Receiving Delivery in Alimentary Retail Outlets

Table: Functions (activities) in the model Receiving Delivery

FUNCTION (ACTIVITY)	Department	Person responsible for the execution of the function (activity)						Average time of the execution of function (activity)	Average costs of function	
		Department manager		Sales clerk		Store manager			type	estimated amount
		avg. time	frequency	avg. time	frequency	avg. time	frequency			
Verification of Delivery										
Detailed Quantity and Quality Control of Delivery										
Creation of Delivery Record (Detailed Control)										
Complaint Resolution										
Electronic Creation of Inventory Document, Pricing										
Manual Creation of Inventory Document, Pricing										
Processing of Delivery Records (Cancellations – Returned Goods)										
Daily printing of Completed Orders – Purchasing Summary										
Creation of Monthly Summaries (Purchasing)										

When filling out the forms the desired data had to be entered into the columns as follows:

- **Column Department;** in order to facilitate identification and monitoring of the functions (activities), this column had to contain the information about the relevant department for which an individual function (activity) was performed (e.g. the function Order Creation as performed for the Meat Department; when an order was being created for the outlet as a whole, "BU" (Business Unit) was to be entered into the column). Identifying the department was significant in relation to the next column: Person responsible for the execution of the function (activity)

- **Column Person responsible for the execution of the function (activity);** the column identified a selection of relevant persons responsible for the execution of the function (activity). For each identified person responsible it had to be determined how many times he/she carried out or was involved in the execution of an individual function (activity) as well as the average time needed for the execution of that function (activity). In order to make things simpler we monitored the execution of the functions (activities) by department (e.g. for the Meat Department: the department manager prepares orders by himself 25 times per month; on average, an individual order creation takes about 30 minutes. The sales clerk is involved in the order preparation on average 13 times, each time for 10 minutes. The store manager checks such orders on average 3 times a month, which takes 5 minutes each time)

- *Column Average time of the execution of function (activity);* on the basis of the average time taken by the individual person responsible that was entered in the column, the person appointed for the unit under evaluation (BU manager, department manager) calculated the average estimate of the time required to carry out an individual function (activity). The time was to be expressed in minutes

- *Column Average costs of function (activity);* for each function (activity) the person appointed for the unit under evaluation (BU manager, department manager) also estimated (using own judgment) the significant costs involved in the execution of the function (activity). All costs were identified in terms of type and estimated amount (e.g. significant types of costs could be phone costs, shelf labels, transport costs (car use), cost of manual terminals …)

In the working packages #4 and #5 there followed the data collection and verification of the collected data. Within this package a cursory verification of the gathered data was required. On the basis of such audits we decided to repeat the data collection in some units.

In the working package #6 we analyzed the collected data. We also formed conclusions and proposals for improving and changing the purchasing process in retail outlets. The data were analyzed for each sample unit under evaluation. The results and practical application value of the evaluation are presented next.

4.3 Results and Practical Application Value of the Evaluation

The results of the evaluation of the purchasing process in retail stores can be divided into two groups, i.e. the group of alimentary and non-alimentary retail units and the group of departments within the general business functions of Accounting and Finance.

In the case of *alimentary and non-alimentary retail outlets* the evaluation allowed us to identify:

- The most time-consuming functions (activities) within the purchasing process in alimentary and non-alimentary retail outlets

- The available work time that the store managers, department managers and sales clerks in such retail outlets spend on individual functions (activities) of the purchasing process

- The departments that are the most time-consuming in relation to the purchasing process in retail stores

Table 2 presents some of the functions (activities) identified in relation to "Receiving Delivery" in non-alimentary retail outlets, from which the following can be established:

- The functions (activities) that are the most time-consuming (detailed quantity and quality control of delivery, manual creation of inventory document and pricing)

- The average time spent and frequency of involvement with the functions (activities) on the part of store managers, department managers and sales clerks, and

- The departments that are the most time-consuming from the perspective of purchasing (glass, china, cosmetics)

Table 2. Times of Functions (Activities) for "Receiving Delivery" in a Non-Alimentary Retail Store

FUNCTION -ACTIVITY	Department	Person responsible for the execution of the function (activity)						Average time of the execution of activity/function	Monthly Frequency
		Department manager		Sales clerk		Store manager			
		avg. time	frequency	avg. time	frequency	avg. time	frequency		
Coursory Quantity Control	technical goods			10	53			10	53
	glass, china, cosmetics			9	44			9	44
	textile	2	14	2	8			2	20
Detailed Quantity and Quality Control of Delivery	technical goods			37	53			37	53
	glass, china, cosmetics			86	65			86	65
	textile	88	14	116	14			114	25
Creation of Delivery Record (Detailed Control)	technical goods	7	9					7	9
	glass, china, cosmetics	7	5					7	5
	textile	7	5					7	5
Creation of Delivery Record (Detailed Control)	technical goods	3	7	3	2			3	9
	glass, china, cosmetics	8	5					8	5
	textile	3	5					3	5
Manual Creation of Invetnory Document, Pricing	technical goods	16	38	9	15			14	53
	glass, china, cosmetics	38	48	19	17			33	65
	textile	22	25					22	25
Processing of Delivery Records (Cancellations - Returned Goods)	technical goods	6	9					6	9
	glass, china, cosmetics	7	5					7	5
	textile	6	5					6	5

Practical application value of the evaluation in alimentary and non-alimentary retail outlets can be found in that:

- It enables comparisons of the purchasing process between similar retail business units – internal benchmarking (see Table 3 that allows a simple compari-

178

son to be made between different retail stores; the table shows the comparison between two alimentary retail outlets)

- It enables the comparison between the purchasing process in alimentary and non-alimentary retail outlets[4]
- It enables the assessment of the proposed changes aimed at improving the purchasing process in retail stores[5]
- It promotes mutual exchange of ideas between individual retail outlets (improved communication)
- It encourages employees in retail stores to strive towards continuous process improvement (CPI)
- The results of the evaluation can serve as a platform for the setting of time (performance) standards in retail stores
- The obtained results of the evaluation become the foundation for further changing and rationalization of business operations – focusing on the processes and functions (activities) that are more time-consuming and costly

Table 3. Comparison (Internal Benchmarking) between Two Alimentary Retail Outlets

	BU 1	BU 2
Number of employees involved in the purchasing process at the store	22	**28**
Total time spent on the purchasing process at the store [monthly]	336 hrs	**408 hrs**
Total time spent on the entire process of Order Creation at the store [monthly]	164 hrs	**202 hrs**
Total time spent on the entire process of Receiving Delivery at the store [monthly]	173 hrs	**205 hrs**
Percentage of work time spent on the entire purchasing process at the store	**8.8%**	8.4%
Percentage of work time spent on the entire process of Order Creation at the store	**4.3%**	4.1%

---

[4] In alimentary retail outlets the percentage of available work time spent on purchasing is around 8% while it is significantly higher in non-alimentary retail stores – between 12 and 15%.

[5] The evaluation allowed us to propose specific changes aimed at improving the purchasing process in retail stores. The information obtained in the process enabled us to assess the effects of the proposed changes. For instance, for the function (activity) Order Preparation within the process of Order Creation we proposed that manual terminals be introduced into retail stores (as a tool for Order Creation and Receiving Deliveries from suppliers where there is no electronic delivery docket). This measure reduces the time required for Order Creation by more than 20%. Other proposed changes could be assessed in a similar manner.

Table 3. (continued)

Percentage of work time spent on the entire process of Receiving Delivery at the store	**4.5%**	4.2%
Minutes spent daily by the BU manager on the purchasing process at the store	144 min	**162 min**
Minutes spent daily by every department manager on the purchasing process at the store	**21 min**	20 min
Minutes spent daily by every sales clerk on the purchasing process at the store	25 min	**27 min**
Percentage of work time spent by the BU manager on the purchasing process at the store	34.4%	**38.7%**
Percentage of work time spent by every department manager on the purchasing process at the store	**4.9%**	4.8%
Percentage of work time spent by every sales clerk on the purchasing process at the store	5.9%	**6.5%**

In the case of departments within the general business functions of Accounting and Finance, **the evaluation allowed us to identify:**

• The functions (activities) within individual departments that are the most time-consuming (e.g. account/price matching, entering the account into the common accounts payable database ...) and

• The level of information support of the individual functions (activities)

In addition we could also establish the time required for the processing of individual accounts payable. The time required to process an account payable depends on the type of account (retail, wholesale, internal account, transferable delivery docket ...).

Practical application value of the evaluation within the departments of general business functions can be found in that:

• It enables the assessment of the proposed changes aimed at improving individual functions (activities) within these departments[6]

---

[6] For the function Analytical Account Bookkeeping that represents one of the more time-consuming activities in the department Inventory Bookkeeping, a proposal for gradual introduction of electronic transfer of receipts from the retail outlets to the process of Completion 2 has been accepted. With the implementation of this proposed change, the average time of processing each account payable will be reduced by more than five minutes, which at the current number of accounts payable received translates into a monthly saving of more than 400 available work hours. The effects of other proposals for a more efficient execution of individual functions (activities) could be assessed in a similar manner.

- It enables the calculation of costs in relation to the processing of accounts of individual suppliers[7]

- The obtained data become the basis for establishing the cost of individual functions (activities) – Activity-Based Costing – as the foundation for allocation of general costs (overheads)

- The evaluation of functions (activities) generates documentation and accumulation of knowledge, which is the basis for efficient business operation

- The understanding of activities encourages the managers of individual departments to continually reconsider how the set level of quality can be achieved using the minimum of time and resources required for the functions (activities) to be carried out

- The obtained results of the evaluation become the foundation for further rationalization of business operations – focusing on the processes and functions (activities) that are more time-consuming and costly

An important advantage of the evaluation of process models – that however is difficult to quantify – is that it gets the employees to think about their job and the way they go about it as an integral part of all business processes in the company. This increases their awareness of the impact their work has, directly or indirectly, on the way the other processes and activities, which are not their direct responsibility, are carried out.

5. Conclusion

Initially, company initiatives for change management and improvements of business processes were a response to the need to reduce costs and shorten the time involved in the execution of business operations, and to improve the quality of the output at the same time. Today change management and improvements of business processes also go hand in hand with the development of new technologies that enable the introduction of electronic business operations between geographically separate company organizational units, between the company and its suppliers, between the company and consumers, etc. It is important to realize that numerous processes neither begin nor end at the door of an individual company. Often they reach along the value added chain all the way – either back to the suppliers of spare parts and raw materials, or forward to the customers and their desires.

In order to undertake the improvements of company business processes we first have to have a thorough understanding of these processes. In addition to the processes that add value from a customer perspective and those that are required from

---

[7] Significant as an integral part of costing when establishing the supplier impact on profitability, based on the established net difference in price.

a company perspective, we frequently also find processes that neither add value from a customer perspective nor are necessary for company purposes. Such processes can only be discovered by systematic modeling and evaluation of business processes. How to approach the modeling and evaluation of business processes is the main purpose of this paper. The approach described can also be applied in other companies provided their specific characteristics are taken into account.

6. References

Hammer M. in Stanton S.A. *The Reengineering Revolution.* 1st ed. New York: Harper Business, 1994, p. 336.

Scheer A.W. *ARIS – Business Process Frameworks.* 2nd ed. Berlin: Springer, 1998, p. 186.

Scheer A.W. *ARIS – Business Process Modeling.* 2nd ed. Berlin: Springer, 1999, p. 218.

Tekavčič M. Obvladovanje stroškov. Ljubljana: Gospodarski vestnik, 1997, p.193.

URL: http://www.ids-scheer.com

It Pays to be Prepared

Andrej Devečka
CEO, ZSE Bratislava

Václav Kalenda
Senior Consultant, IDS Scheer CZ

Ján Sirota
Product Director, IDS Scheer SK

Summary

Západoslovenská energetika (West Slovakia Energy Utility) is the largest Slovak electric energy distribution company. In 2001 it started to implement comprehensive restructuring of the company with the aim to prepare for liberalization of electric the energy market. IDS Scheer Slovakia offered its experience from the Czech energy sector, and joint solution teams then developed a comprehensive project of process-oriented company restructuring. After the entrance of the strategic partner E.ON Energie, this project became the basis for the project of implementing of changes throughout the company.

Key Words

Design of Process-oriented Comprehensive Restructuring of the Company, Business Process Optimization

1. Project Starting Points

ZSE Bratislava is a regional distribution company operating in four regions of Western Slovakia and the capital city, Bratislava. It focuses on the purchase, distribution and sale of electric energy. In a territory covering 16 thousand km^2, the company serves more than 0.5 million customers. In November 2001, it was transformed from a state enterprise into a joint-stock company, and in the privatization tender in May 2002 the company E.ON acquired a 49% stake. Before its transformation, the company had 3,500 employees.

At the beginning of 2001, the top management of the company was confronted with the task of preparing for imminent liberalization of the market in relation to EU Directive No. 92/96 and for expected privatization, one, however, lacking a define time frame. It was clear to the company´s top management that the competition for lucrative customers in industry and trade areas would start long before the Directive on Liberalization came into force since on the European market competition for customers – households had started before and with greater ferocity than expected. The top management realized that the struggle for customers on the electric energy market within the EU would take place under difficult conditions and would involve eliminating competition, and also expected that after the transformation of the state enterprise into a joint-stock company there would be "absorption" of ZSE within the privatization by strategic partners from the "Big Three".

Yes, it was possible to wait several (?) years until this situation took shape. Which scenario would follow? If ZSE did not make use of opportunities in the transition period, it would lose its best customers. And after the arrival of the new owner, dramatic ridding of the company of all activities which do not bring immediate direct profit would follow. This worst-case scenario has already played out in several distribution companies in Europe and has always entailed mass lay-offs and deprived such distributors of the possibility to co-decide about their own development.

There was also another possibility, which had been applied by many Czech utilities too. To start preparing for liberalization immediately. To demonstrate to their possible owners their viability and to create the best possible conditions for future survival.

What were these steps? When it came to distribution, it mainly involved dramatic streamlining of system management, maintenance and development. In the area of trade, it was the achievement of maximum efficiency of sales to mass customers and the creation of good relations with large and important customers. It also concerned the use of all such originated redundant capacities in developing further directions in business of doing business beyond the electricity distribution area.

It was clear that this course is connected with sweeping changes in work practice. However, it provided higher certainty that in the future the company would not only survive, but also be among the major players.

Therefore, ZSE announces the project Restructuring and sought in the tender a reliable partner for this painful course of action. The international consulting company IDS Scheer won the tender since in this stage of development it had helped several Czech distributors to survive and had sufficient experience from the already liberalized European market.

2. Project Goals

Why was the Restructuring Project commenced:

1. Within several years the energy market will be opened and only those firms who have prepared will have a chance to survive

2. In the distribution area it means dramatic streamlining of work

3. In the trade area it involves keeping key customers and making services for households effective

The project brief was defined as follows: "Drawing up an analysis of the current status in ZSE and proposing a comprehensive solution to change the existing status with respect to current functioning in relation to EU Directive No. 92/96 with emphasis on the optimal structure of arrangement, stating the optimal number of employees and recommending a suitable Time Schedule for implementation of the target solution".

The objective of the project was not a one-off reduction of employee numbers or substantial cost reduction, but, given the current degree of room for maneuver (state, trade union organizations, social situation, etc.), **to create a process-oriented organization structure and management system** which makes it possible to carry out the following activities according to the defined development scenarios:

- Rapid and effective merge with the new owner

- Radical reduction of costs

- Considerable increase in trade performance

- Development of vertical and horizontal integration, and creation of alliances

3. Project Procedure

3.1 The Course Selected

Using to the model of the most successful energy-market players in Europe and worldwide, we decided to abandon our hitherto semi-military way of management and to become a process-oriented company. What did it mean?

The key term of the change was the word "**process**", i.e. a sequence of activities forming added value paid by the customer at the end of the chain. A series of processes of various types was analyzed in the enterprise. If the result of a process served directly for the outside customer, we spoke about a key process. Processes which serve to support a key process were termed supporting processes. Processes with strategic importance aimed at ensuring the company's long-term prosperity and cohesion were called control processes.

A process-oriented company is able to concentrate on its key processes and supporting processes, which it can either carry out so efficiently that it is worthwhile for the company to do so itself, or the company simply purchases services or products of these processes. Let's give an example. A motorcrane for assembly work could be ensured by ZSE´s internal transport or could be ordered from outside. For the company's own professional transport, to make economic sense, the motorcrane´s maximum price must be identical with the price for its leasing on a free market with identical speed of delivery parameters.

It was clear that it would be difficult to achieve the same efficiency in supporting internal processes that was achieved by firms beyond ZSE which were not burdened by the enterprise's overhead expenses and could offer their services on a considerably wider market. Therefore, for all these processes it was also necessary for the company to try to provide services on the market outside ZSE so as to be able to optimally set the size of capacities for their suitable capacity utilization (economies of scale). It was always necessary to balance quality and price. In our example – ZSE can have 20 motorcranes and then they will be immediately available, but their capacity utilization will be only 50%, or the company can have 10 motorcranes with favorable costs, however, their availability will be much lower. Or there will be 20 motorcranes which will also be used for work for other companies.

Therefore, it was necessary to ensure for each such process whether it would be possible to succeed on the market with one product or service also outside ZSE. If not, unfortunately it was the only way – the process had top be canceled and the services purchased. If so, it was possible to start this type of business. Provided, of course, that there were in this area capable persons possessing an entrepreneurial spirit and who, after starting such secondary enterprise, would be able to lead this area to full separation (from a contextually directed company up to clear financial investment).

The second basic feature of the process-managed firm was absolute preference for processes as against organizational structures. In ZSE processes ran across organizational structures. This was historically caused by the division of labor when, due to the non-qualified labor force, it was possible to assign to an employee only a piece of a wide-range of activity to manage at the required quality level. Such groups of employees had to be supervised by the manager, who was able to manage and advise any of his subordinates. These managers were in turn supervised by the most intelligent (or, unfortunately, also the most pushy) managers, etc. The initial structure of ZSE was an example of a company managed in such a manner. In the case of a process somewhere between employees from different management branches, this problem passed to higher and higher management structures and it was not surprising that the top management of the company mainly resolved such operative problems. In most cases, completely different problems than those in practice because by passing through series of management levels these problems become blurred.

Of course, there was a solution. The first point was to do away with the absurd division of labor. It was derived from the well-established precondition that most employees of the company are too intelligent and capable to carry out merely a piece of work. The most appreciated person was not the expert, but the person who managed a wider spectrum of activities. In many cases it was supported by modern information technologies. The condition for this was well-documented and standardized processes up to the level of working procedures. Possible experts were called in only to resolve of extraordinary situations.

The second point was work in teams instead of detailed specification of the working duties of each individual employee. People in teams assume common responsibility for the final result of their work, they have the same motivation and they share their knowledge. This required an entirely different corporate culture than was common in the hierarchically structured company.

The third element was, functionally the in-house market. Individual processes mutually "sell" their products to each other and individual teams are motivated both by their "market" performances and by satisfying internal clients.

The Restructuring Project sought to bring about the following changes:

1. To straighten out and defragment key processes, and to remove from them activities which do not bring any value

2. To do business from supporting processes which is also capable of competing beyond ZSE and to prepare it for outsourcing, or to define SLA for purchased products and services

3. To support an organizational structure based on teams and appropriate information technology

188

4. To implement an in-house market

5. To initiate the building-up of a new company culture

3.2 Project Staging

The project was officially started in April 2001. It had 2 introductory stages, followed by individual implementation projects.

3.2.1 Stage 1: Analysis (as-is)

The declared objective of this very quick introductory stage was to formulate as completely as possible ideas about project implementation goals, restrictions, expectations and conditioning factors.

This stage lasted 7 weeks and included a series of activities, the most important being rapid mapping of the existing status of processes on the basis of comparison with reference-model utilities and analysis of critical points with the support of benchmarking.

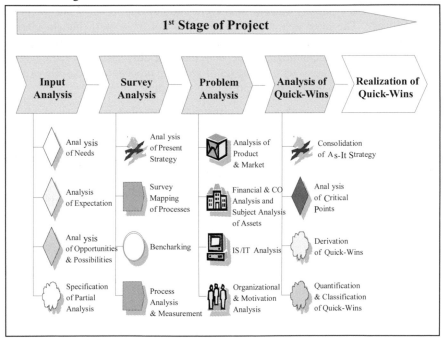

Fig. 1. Contextual Contents of Stage 1

Five consultants of IDS Scheer participated in this stage animating the work of 42 appointed employees of ZSE in 6 analytical teams focused on individual groups of processes. The linkage of analyses was ensured by the main team, consisting of heads of analytical teams and selected members of the top management. The Steering Committee played a key role in the dynamism of the project. It was headed by the sponsor of the project, the CEO, who was informed on a weekly basis about the course of analyses and actively worked on the consolidation of company strategy.

The results of the analyses defined the scope of problems the target status had to eliminate and made it possible to compare the initial status of the company before transformation with a similar situation in selected distribution firms in the Czech Republic.

Table 1. Results of Process Analysis (Example from Assessment of Critical Points)

Group of Processes	Critical	Problematic	Acceptable	Score	Overall Assessment	Standard
Controlling	100%	0%	0%	1,00	critical	critical
Planning	100%	0%	0%	1,00	critical	critical
Legal Matters	100%	0%	0%	1,00	critical	suitable

3.2.1 Stage 2: Analysis (to-be)

The objective of the 2nd stage was to create a prospective target solution and to define acceptable ways of implementing this solution. This stage lasted 11 weeks and finished in the middle of August 2001. Between the stages there was a 2-week break to regenerate the labor forces of the working teams.

190

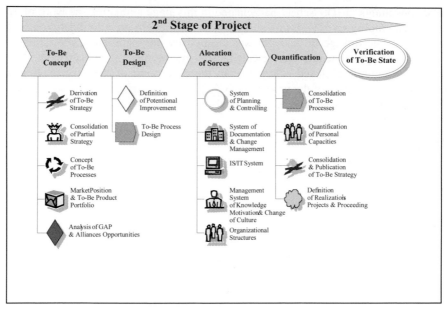

Fig. 2. Contextual Contents of Stage 2

The target status of the company is defined with the corresponding volume of changes and in sufficient detail to be implemented while keeping risks within manageable limits. Outputs included definition of implementation risks and suitable measures for their elimination. The most serious risks were considered to be the following:

- Postponement of implementation of management and organizational changes due to transformation into a joint-stock company – loss of project dynamism, consequently, half-implemented solutions, risk of the most capable employees leaving due to uncertainty.

- Implementation of changes without sufficient support from the consulting company – half-implemented solutions, unintegrated management of the change project, risk of discontinuities in jurisdiction

- Unmanaged resistance to change, in particular, among existing middle-management in regions – refusal to implement the project, non-passing of jurisdiction or jurisdiction disputes, local problems

- Insufficient communication of changes up to the level of executive managers – only formal changes without changes in thinking

- Unmanaged outsourcing – unverified financial relations, unsettled management, difficulties of subsidiaries on the external market

- Postponement or unnecessary prolongation of factual process changes – loss of dynamism, risk of differing development of individual areas of the enterprise

- Late decision about innovation of the ERP system – additional costs related to the modification of existing controlling

- Organizational changes carried out without change in management and support of controlling – uncontrollable company performance

- Occupation of management positions according to the key of existing positions – conservation of existing approaches and relations, not finding the real value of individual employees and their potential

- Non/specification of target surplus employees – conservation of working performance, not carrying out re-qualification, not searching for new business opportunities

For the 2nd stage the teams were reconstructed and adapted in terms of employee numbers and personnel to the expected target solution. The statute of the main team was kept – the task of the team was considerably strengthened due to the necessary process integration and standardization. Sixty-four ZSE employees were actively involved in this stage, headed by 5 ISD Scheer consultants. A 9-member opponent team was appointed for effective quality control of the project. They did not directly participate in the design of the target status, but regularly verified project outputs. At the same time, they acted as an interface to the existing enterprise structures. Project participants underwent a considerable change of attitude in the direction of process understanding of the company. Therefore, it was recommended that these participants have the opportunity to bring into being the entire proposed target status of the company, and hence they were appointed to the relevant management positions (with a few exceptions).

In both stages the results of the project were regularly communicated inside the company through cascade meetings and the enterprise magazine "Prúd".

4. Project Results

Within the proposed target status of the company, the following areas are defined:

- Management of the company on the basis of the in-house market

- Target adjustment of processes

- Selection of processes suitable for outsourcing

- Organizational assurance of processes

- Procedure for implementing target status

It is necessary to point out that the target status was defined as the status of a fully liberalized electricity market.

4.1 Management System

The system of strategic management was proposed, integrating the system of planning and passing of strategic tasks on to operative management. The executive management of the company was created and the internal market for internal business units was defined, both oriented to increasing the profitability of assets. The system of controlling was defined making possible real management of this system.

4.2 Outsourcing

The basic outsourcing strategy was defined - ZSE will concentrate on key business in the area of electricity distribution and sale. Business opportunities beyond the area of primary business, if they are complementary to client needs and seem promising, will be transferred to subsidiaries.

None of the groups of processes analyzed made it possible to separate them immediately. Despite this fact, processes were divided into 2 categories:

- Parts which can be separated within several months, for which arrangement of independent divisions was carried out in such a manner that this outsourcing is possible after the development of economic parameters has been assessed and the risks resulting from separation have been eliminated

- Parts separated later, after one year or longer, for which within the implementation benchmarking will be defined, making it possible to monitor permanently both internal performance of processes as well as the situation on the market so that in the case of revision of the strategic plan possible outsourcing could be considered again. For these processes, the setting up of independent departments was defined (BU)

4.3 Target Processes

Target processes were proposed for all areas of the company with definition of their products, process flow and interface, input and output documents, data files and application support. Types of places (roles) (cooperating, deciding) were defined for all activities.

Staff was proposed as being very slim and centralized. Some entirely new processes were defined in the areas of strategic management, process change management and controlling. Self-contained economic management was prepared for the potential of the new information system. The mail branch and archive were centralized.

Consistent process management was applied in **distribution,** with the key role of DS management and management on the basis of performance. Target-oriented centralized DS management was defined. Management of DS development was integrated. It was decided that the implementation of client service would from the viewpoint of DS be through Electricity Trading. Failure services were streamlined and centralized. Measurement and readings were assigned to DS, linkage to OTC was proposed through self-service. Diagnostics was defined as an independent BU (on the basis of measured performances), as were Repairs and Maintenance (low-voltage/high-voltage) and Engineering and Projects – with the aim of gradual preparation and separation.

Trade processes were proposed in such a manner as to ensure comprehensive servicing of clients, including organization of connection (ensured internally through DS). Entirely new processes were proposed for electricity purchase and risk management. TOP of clients was separated and strengthened. Transfer of mass clients to non-face channels should lead to very considerable reduction of trade offices.

Supporting processes – **services –** were defined. Personnel services were proposed as a business unit with the ownership of shared employees sold to the processes and with the assurance of the development of their working portfolio. IT were proposed as comprehensive services on the basis of functional and secure applications, development independently, with everything separated and prepared for the possible change of approach of the owner (outsourcing). Legal services were transferred on the basis of performances (possibility of external assurance). Logistics was centralized with just-in-time delivery, consignment, self-service for office appliances and for DS. Considerable reduction of warehouse space was carried out (warehouses transferred from three-level to single-level units). The formerly fragmented transport to regions was centralized, professional transport was partially liquidated, leasing of cars was expanded. In facility management there was centralization of management and provision of spaces on the basis of leasing, shared workplaces and support of homeworking were introduced, recreational facilities and apartments were specified with the aim of their separation.

4.4 Organizational Structure

Types of places were preliminary assessed on the basis of HAY methodology; summarizing the functional positions with the requirement for universality and removal of the knowledge monopoly were defined for them.

Considerable reduction of the scope of vertical management was designed. On the basis of definition of processes, a flat, process-oriented, two-level organizational structure was defined:

- Staff consisting of sections, which can then be divided into departments

- Main business directions (trade, distribution, services) are concentrated into divisions, performance-managed units

Areas prepared for separation were also integrated into independent divisions. All proposed organizational units can be classified into non-organizational units – on the basis of teams.

The target status of employees was proposed:

- Staff – very considerably reduced, temporarily insufficient capacities will be resolved on the basis of shared employees

- Distribution – factual reduction will take place during the application of performance-based management

- Trade – very considerable reduction is proposed, in this stage very radical, it should be specified in the implementation project

- Services – very considerable reduction

A three-element motivation system was proposed – the tariff derived from job assessment, performance motivation based on assessment of professional performance and indexes, and personal assessment taking into consideration knowledge growth and employees´ personal development. Personal assessment is assigned on the basis of carrying out processes for employee assessment.

4.5 Proposal for Implementation Projects

The implementation was proposed in 2 stages:

Stage A: **Implementation of new management system**, which fulfills the basic objective required from the project – to create a dynamic company management system making possible permanent increase in process performance and consisting of the following steps:

- Implementation of organizational changes (setting of the motivation system, definition of jurisdiction, labor contracts, discussions of contracts and occupation of functional positions, modification of the wage system, assessment of employees)

- Implementation of CO changes (internal trade, calculation and balance, planning , setting of the CO system)

- Implementation of strategic management on the BSC basis

- Implementation of process documentation

- Taking over of processes (jurisdiction, assets, operating documentation, lay-out)

- Setting in motion changes leading to changes in company culture (in particular, the new management system and teamwork)

It was recommended to implement this stage in one continuous project with completion in June 2002 at the latest.

Stage B: **Implementation of process changes** was classified according to individual groups of processes. For all processes, first of all it is always necessary to produce a detailed implementation project which includes:

- Detailed design of processes (including detailed lay-out and sources)

- Knowledge maps (subsequently centralized plan of requalification)

- Requirements for IT

- Requirements for other sources, including financial sources

- Time Schedule

The implementation of changes should run in individual stages with completion no later than at the end of 2003.

The social consequences of the project were taken into consideration. One-off change of the management system, including reorganization, was proposed, i.e. immediate reduction of target jobs with the possibility to keep further employees on in the form of job-sharing. This will balance out the pressure resulting from the change in performance management (department managers will not have to fire these job-sharing but can smoothly change requirements for their capacities), together with the pressure on newly utilizing these employees (re-qualification) and seeking further business opportunities.

5.   Learning from the Project

It was clear, given the experience of firms that had already implemented such project, that change would hurt. Participants in the project know during its first two stages that it is better to endure pain a while, to concentrate all their strength during the period of changes and to sacrifice a piece of their existing certainty and comfort than to lose the most important certainty, i.e. a job. It all depends on one factor – how the company manages to become more efficient, to move on and develop further 'business activities so that the result will correspond to the involvement of each employee.

The further development was not as straightforward as expected according to the proposed implementation projects. There were changes in the Board of Directors, the target owner entered the company far earlier than even the biggest optimists expected.

6. Current Situation

It was revealed that there are not 3 or 4 years to prepare the transformation of the company, as was stated before the project started last year. Suddenly, ZSE has only one year to complete the internal transformation and consolidation with other enterprises in the E.ON group. In 2004, when energy market liberalization starts, there will not be time to deal with its own problems – it will have to direct its concerted energy outwards – to clients and ensuring of their loyalty.

Therefore, the implementation projects were redefined and newly timed. Great attention is paid at present to ready solutions and know-how from advanced consolidation projects of E.ON (e.g. JME and in Hungary).

7. Conclusion

Were the 2 completed stages a contribution? the answer is resounding yes. Thanks to the methodological approach and contextual knowledge of advisors from IDS Scheer, ZSE was very well prepared for the unexpectedly rapid entrance of the strategic partner. The transformation started, after harmonization with the global strategy of the E.ON group, continues apace. ZSE is not the only target firm to which type solutions have been transferred, but thanks to its own project preparation it has a range of best practices in many areas which can be offered to other members of the corporation.

And above all, the firm has prepared people – both at the management level and in process teams - who have theoretical knowledge, as well as personal experience from the implementation of process management.

Increasing Process Efficiency at Siemens AG Austria

Maria Beham
Topic Manager, Information Management, Siemens AG Austria

Kurt Broinger
Business Process Framework Executive, Siemens AG Austria

Walter Obrowsky
Project Manager, ARIS Corporate Service, Siemens AG Austria

Gabriele Kaltenbrunner
Product Consultant, IDS Scheer Austria GmbH

Peter Nattermann
Senior Manager, Product Consulting, IDS Scheer AG

Florian Schober
Project Manager, IDS Scheer Schweiz AG

Summary

Siemens AG Austria has subjected its process and IT landscape to progressive change: verification and redesign of all processes relevant for the value chain, definition of future process standards, introduction of SAP R/3 as corporate IT standard, training and coaching.

The aim is to provide comprehensive know-how and documented empirical knowledge for all project phases, both in terms of processes and in terms of the system as such.

The use of the ARIS process management tool and method ensures both

- *Comprehensive documentation in a corporate information system as a comprehensive knowledge base for Siemens co-workers to enable an entrepreneurial process acceleration and*

- *Definition of process standards for the evaluation and benchmarking of processes as well as for the analysis of changes in the operations structure and organizational setup or in the IT landscape to realize sustainable increase of process efficiency*

Key Words

Process Documentation, Integrated Process Architecture, Business Process Standardization, SAP Implementation, Process Harmonization

1. Project Background

1.1 General Information about Siemens AG Austria

Siemens has been active in Austria since 1879. Apart from manufacturing plants, the company comprises a comprehensive sales organization in all of Austria's provinces as well as a number of subsidiaries and holdings. The Siemens Group in Austria is one of the most successful high-tech enterprises as well as the largest private industrial employer in the country. Austria has assumed the regional responsibility for Slovakia, Slovenia, Croatia, Bosnia-Herzegovina, the Union of Serbia and Montenegro, and Romania.

Siemens AG Austria is active in the fields of

1. Information and Communication

2. Research & Development

3. Medical Solutions

4. Automation & Control

5. Procurement and Logistics

6. Power

7. Transportation

1.2 Motivation for the Project

1.2.1 e.p@ss – Electronic Processes at Siemens Standard

e.p@ss is one of the largest change and IT implementation projects in Europe. With a project runtime of only about two years, Siemens AG Austria has subjected its process and IT landscape to progressive change: verification and redesign of all processes relevant for the value chain, definition of future process standards, introduction of SAP R/3 as corporate IT standard, and training and coaching for approximately 3000 users.

The main focus of this effort was on business processes and process owners. All areas and all levels were involved in this large-scale interdivisional cooperation scheme. 35 teams consisting of about 500 internal and external project team members have contributed to this major redesign of business processes.

For the first time ever, e.p@ss provides comprehensive know-how and documented empirical knowledge for all project phases, both in terms of processes and in terms of the system as such.

1.2.2 Process Documentation

The ARIS process management tool was used to provide database-based mapping of the processes defined during the course of the e.p@ss project. This ensured not only comprehensive documentation in a corporate information system, but also the evaluation and benchmarking of processes as well as the analysis of changes in the operations structure and organizational setup or in the IT landscape.

Werner von Siemens, the founder of our company, was chosen as godfather when it came to finding a name for our integrated corporate information system. In this context, the name WERNER stands for the visionary entrepreneurial spirit of this great mastermind in the history of technology.

2. Goals

In the AS-IS situation Siemens AG Austria was faced with process documentation and process-related information that had been administrated and maintained decentralized which brought up the following problems:

- Redundancy which means a high degree (personnel, cost, time) of consolidated maintenance
- Local and not related knowledge
- Local storage that causes access problems

For Siemens AG Austria it was crucial to subsume the decentralized information as:

- Business organizational procedures kept in organization plans
- Business process descriptions maintained in "business blue-prints"
- Information about IT systems in use

And this in a corporate information system for verification and redesign of all processes relevant for the value chain and to offer comprehensive process documentation including process relevant information as documents in use, supporting IT systems, or executing roles.

This comprehensive process documentation is focused on two major targets:

- Defining process standards for ongoing evaluation and optimization

- Creating a comprehensive knowledge base for Siemens co-workers to enable an entrepreneurial process acceleration

The process standard is the basis for introduction of SAP R/3 as corporate IT standard, for training and coaching, for ongoing evaluation and benchmarking of processes as well as the analysis of changes in the operations structure and organizational setup or in the IT landscape.

Siemens AG Austria was looking for a tool as well as for a method that supports the tool-based integration of this individually kept information to provide Siemens co-workers and management with this information online.

2.1 Keeping Process and Process Information Centralized

The target was to develop an enterprise information system that is able to administrate and document relevant information areas as

- Management, support, and business processes
- Documents (e.g. SAP user documentation, risk management documentation, circulars) kept in a document management system that has to be integrated in the solution
- Roles and organizational charts
- IT systems

One of the aims was to subsume and maintain all this decentralized stored information in one common knowledge base. Therefore ARIS Toolset is used by implementing an adequate process architecture.

2.2 Defining Process Standards

Up to this point, processes have been designed as department-specific processes which made evaluation and benchmarking between Siemens business types difficult. Therefore the goal was to define process standards on an interdivisional scale. Based on these "generic processes" provided in the system the business units can document their as-is processes.

2.3 Providing a Knowledge Base to all Siemens AG Austria Co-Workers

Target groups are Siemens AG Austria co-workers and Siemens AG Austria management which means that not just administration but also documentation had to be guaranteed. The demand for easy and permanent access, easy understanding, and the possibility to involve co-workers in a process improvement cycle consequently led to ARIS Web Publisher to provide online documentation.

As it is crucial for Siemens to motivate the co-workers living and even accelerating "their" processes the ARIS Web Publisher has to

- Provide information in a form that covers different information needs of several target groups

- Enhance change management processes

- Adapt to Siemens corporate design

In order to publish only released processes in the Intranet, a release cycle had to be implemented additionally. This release cycle represents an electronic workflow within which the process owner can approve the processes before they are published in the Intranet.

3. Project Description

To reach these defined project goals three major phases had to be realized:

3.1 Framework for Integrated Comprehensive Process Know-How

The process architecture, set up in ARIS Toolset, has to fulfill the definition of standard processes ("generic processes") as well as specific processes according to Siemens business types.

The ARIS Y model was chosen to represent these requirements perfectly:

- Business types are described in product/service trees by their main process steps

- The generic processes describe the processes relevant for the value chain

The modeling of business type-specific processes (through a combination of generic processes and business type models) guarantees standardization and comparison of processes by using milestones.

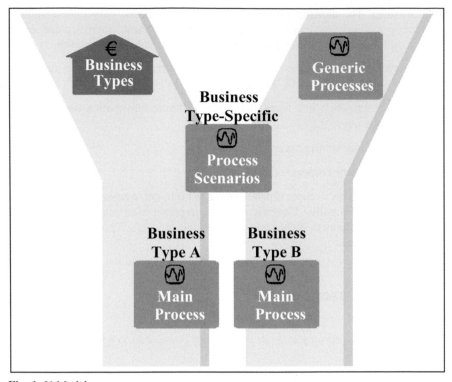

Fig. 1. Y-Model

To design business processes as well as documents, IT systems and roles, an integrated process architecture has been developed in ARIS based on existing business blueprints. Existing information was brought together in workshops with IDS Scheer consultants and Siemens AG Austria project members to create a concept that allows on the one hand a detailed approach by using levels and on the other hand provides information according to views. The process architecture is designed according to two dimensions:

- Level dimension

- View dimension

The level concept meets different information needs, as the levels support the design of the processes to different degrees of detail. The deepest levels of detail include the document level to be able to integrate documents administrated in a document management system.

The process architecture consists of the following levels:

- Level 0: Enterprise Models

- Level 1: Business Models

- Level 2: Overview Models

- Level 3: Main Models

- Level 4: Detail Models

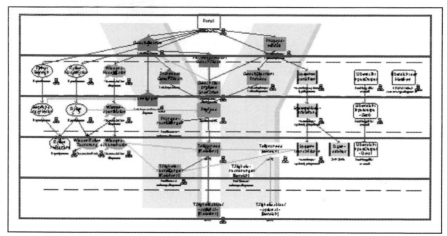

Fig. 2. Process Architecture in ARIS Toolset with Highlighted Level Concept

The view concept has to assure the integration of process-relevant information and thus offers a topic-specific entry like roles, organizational charts or documents. With this view concept the navigation via the view dimension is available, e.g. co-workers are led from their roles to processes executed by themselves.

Views that have been integrated and will be discussed in the following section are (from left to right):

- Management and process roles

- Organizational charts

- Documents and process-related knowledge

- Siemens business types that lead to processes

- Business processes

- IT systems

204

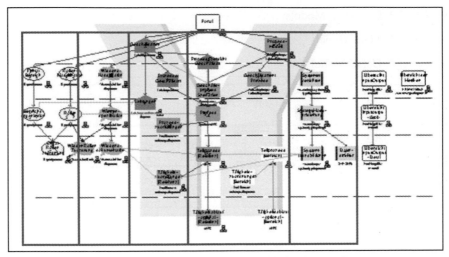

Fig. 3. Process Architecture in ARIS Toolset with Highlighted View-Concept

3.1.1 Integrating Process Information – Organizational Structure

The organizational structure of the company, actually stored and maintained in a non-database supported tool, caused both paper flood and restrictions concerning timely and easy access to organizational charts for Siemens co-workers.

Responsibility for designing and maintaining the organizational structure has been transferred to ARIS to overcome these inconveniences with the integration in the process architecture according to methodology and conventions.

The transformation from the old system in use to ARIS required clear definitions to fulfill the needs of adequate information representation which are:

- Hierarchical design of organizational structure
- Representation of different types of organizational units (as supporting units, managing units, affiliated companies)
- Including managing roles
- Including release documents for updating organizational charts
- Short and long descriptions of organizational units

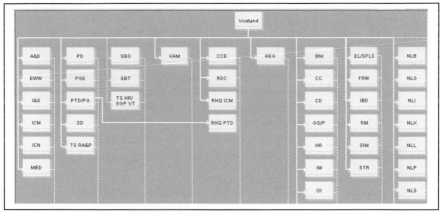

Fig. 4. Siemens Organizational Structure in ARIS

Organizational information consists both of organizational unit charts and organizational role charts. Roles that have been referred to Siemens co-workers contain name and communication information that are originally stored in the Siemens Corporate Directory (SCD). The information from co-workers in the SCD, identified with a unique GID, is used in ARIS. The link between ARIS and SCD is realized by using the GID as an attribute in ARIS. The access to SCD guarantees on the one hand consistent and up-to-date information in the Siemens process architecture and on the other hand reduces maintenance.

The connection of roles and organizational units enables the integration of organizational and process view in a way that every co-worker can follow from organizational units to connected roles and all the way to executed processes. This means that specific process information can be found according to executing process roles.

The target of organizational and process integration is to analyze influences and interdependencies of organizational changes and processes.

3.1.2 Integrating Process Information – Documents

Another important element was to integrate the documents stored and maintained in a document management system into the processes. This means that on the one hand documents are linked to processes with the use of object types "documented knowledge" with different symbols for mandatory documents (documents that have to be used) and other documents. Thus the user is informed about documents in use in certain process steps.

On the other hand, the document view was designed to give an overview of the document structure. Therefore the ARIS object type "knowledge category" is used. The link between modeled documents and the storage in the document management system is managed by ARIS attributes and external links.

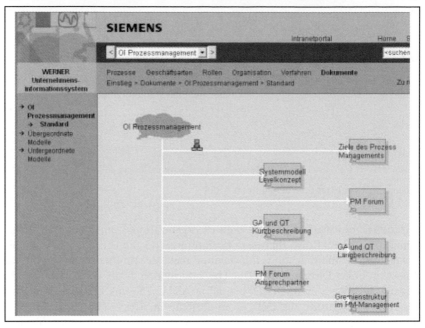

Fig. 5. Documents Structured in an ARIS Knowledge Structure Diagram

3.1.3 Integrating Process Information – IT Systems

IT systems and application types used at Siemens AG Austria are described and administrated in a centralized database called "SISSI". This information, also available online in the Siemens Intranet, has to be integrated into the process description.

The integration is based on a data export from SISSI into the ARIS database. This guarantees an update list of application systems which are reused for process description. The process description in the Siemens Intranet (in "WERNER") offers not only information on supporting application systems in processes but also the link to the web application of SISSI.

IT planning will draw further benefit from this integration as it is the basis for analyzing influences in changes in IT systems and their impact on processes as well as process changes and their impact on the existing IT landscape.

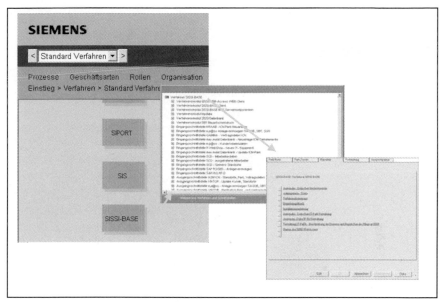

Fig. 6. Integration of Process Information – IT Systems

3.1.4 Integrating Process Information – Milestones

Up to this point, processes have been designed as department-specific processes which made evaluation and benchmarking between Siemens business types difficult. Therefore the goal was to define process standards on an interdivisional scale.

As Siemens business is based on standardization of business types, a standard process definition could be realized by generic processes for these business types. Corporate milestones are used to standardize and to compare the processes.

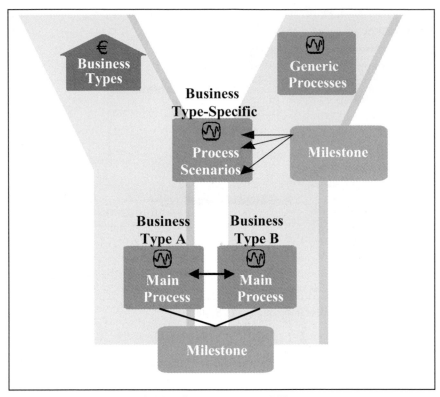

Fig. 7. Comparison of Interdivisional Processes Using Milestones

3.2 Online Documented Empirical Knowledge Base According to Siemens Corporate Design

The framework for integrated and comprehensive documentation of Siemens process know-how in ARIS has to be adapted in an Intranet information system called WERNER, that has to be

- Easily accessible and easy to understand

- Adapted to an online handling of the change management process and

- Integrated in Siemens Corporate Design

The ARIS Web Publisher was used to provide the basis and was extended for numerous functionalities to meet the above defined requirements.

Siemens takes online process documentation as the guarantee to ensure a permanent distribution of process know-how and to provide co-workers with the latest process news. For the acceptance of this medium it was clear that information offered to co-workers had to be transferred into a framework that was both easy to understand and to manage. Some results deriving from these efforts are described below.

According to the view dimension of the process architecture the corporate information system "WERNER" was designed in colors referring to each view, e.g. roles are represented by brown, processes by green, knowledge by light blue. This enables an easy orientation to different views.

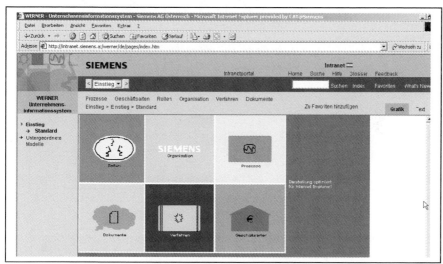

Fig. 8. WERNER Home – Graphical Representation by Colors

For a vertical navigation within the process architecture, which means top down as well as bottom up, ARIS navigation has been extended and is offered as navigation to models that are on one hierarchical level higher or lower. This enables the navigation from the current open model to an overview (one level higher) or to detail (one level below).

Graphical business process documentation was considered to be incomplete for comprehensive understanding of processes. Therefore process models are offered both in graphical and textual form:

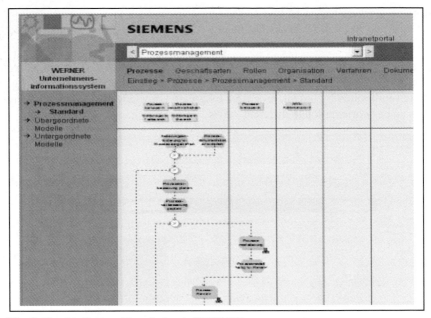

Fig. 9. Graphic Process Description in WERNER

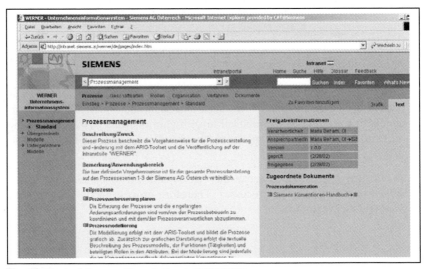

Fig. 10. Textual Process Description in WERNER

Besides graphical and textual information for models ARIS offers information for objects. The user can choose either model or object information. To increase usability the object information is shown in an additional frame.

As not all co-workers are familiar with ARIS terminology, model types and object types have been renamed. Functions are used as "activities", EEPC's are known as "processes", value added chain diagrams are used as "process overviews", and function allocation diagrams are named as "activity descriptions".

Of course the information system WERNER offers all functionalities known and used in www, such as

- Search functions for model search and object search
- "What's new" section for updated information
- Favorites for adding and administrating pages often used

The benefit of this system is not only the access to business process information for all Siemens co-workers but also the opportunity to organize and enhance change management initiatives.

For Siemens AG Austria co-workers this means the opportunity to actively participate in accelerating and improving "their" processes. This is realized by feedback that is sent directly to the process managers indicating automatically in the reference the name of the model that has to be improved.

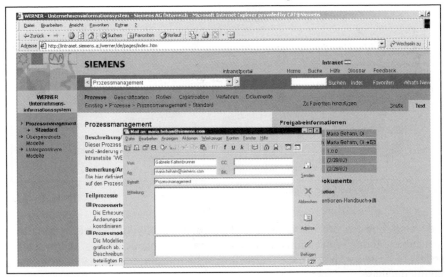

Fig. 11. Feedback for Participation in Change Management Processes

212

3.3 Web-Based Change Management

Continuous improvement with ongoing verification and redesign of business process models is one of the main objectives of this project.

To implement a controlled and continuous online change management cycle, the following requirements had to be fulfilled:

3.3.1 Automated Change Management Cycle

From the modeling up to the online release for co-workers, the process should go through a release cycle that is standardized and executed automatically.

The release cycle is set up on a database management system including three databases

- Development database for modeling and formal reviews

- Staging database for web-based quality review

- Production database for Intranet publication

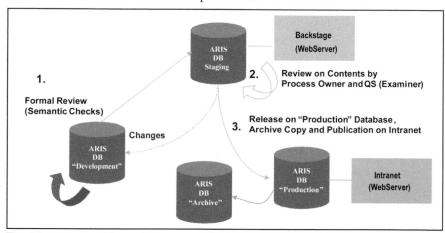

Fig. 12. Automated Change Management Cycle

After modeling the process models will be automatically checked according to Siemens modeling conventions using macro-based semantic checks. All process models indicated with a release flag will then be transferred automatically to the staging database.

The process models from the staging database are prepublished on a backstage web server. The "what's new" category on this web server shows all models that have to be reviewed by process owners and examiners from quality assurance.

If the models can be released they continue the change management cycle by setting the release flag "online" which means directly onto the web server. This information will be saved in ARIS so that all models marked will be transferred to the production database and published on the Siemens Intranet. A copy will be stored in the archive database.

Models that have been rejected from release will be redesigned and have to go through this release cycle again.

3.3.2 Company-Wide Involvement in the Change Management Cycle

The change management cycle includes all persons in charge of the process life cycle who participate directly in the relevant cycle steps.

This is especially important for the release phase where process managers for the release are informed "in time" about processes that have to be released.

But the co-worker involvement is also essential for continuous improvement. On the Siemens Intranet all co-workers support the change management cycle with remarks, improvements that will be directly sent to process managers. Thus processes are kept in the change management cycle to initiate, discuss and verify improvements for "living" processes.

3.3.3 Online Handling of the Change Management Cycle for Process Managers

The realization to release processes "online" was very important as the process representation in ARIS differs from the process documentation in the Intranet. The reason is therefore to release correct process models according both to content and graphical design.

Online means that the process owner and quality assurance members, who are in general not ARIS modelers, do not have access to ARIS. The models that have to be reviewed are offered in the staging web category "what's new" and can be released by setting a release flag.

214

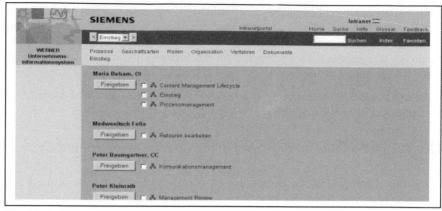

Fig. 13. Online Release of Process Models

4. Results

The implementation of a tool-based process documentation and the realization of process information integration meet the requirements which are defined as:

- Comprehensive business process documentation (including relevant process information) according to common methodology and conventions

- Up-to-date and online availability of process information for all co-workers in the Siemens Intranet according to Siemens Corporate Design

- Quality assurance of processes with defined release cycles including comprehensive release management

- Integrative solution for company-wide process-based knowledge management

- Resource-optimized long-term usability of the enterprise information system guaranteed by an automated update and initiated by changes of the process definition

Besides the realization of these main targets the process documentation covers the documentation needs for process-oriented ERP implementation and migration.

Furthermore the process documentation realizes

- Process-based quality management according to QM standards for process documentation and information

- Change management on the basis of a continuous online improvement from bottom-up feedback mechanisms to process managers

Standardized process documentation together with the use of generic processes enables analysis, verification, and redesign of as-is processes to define internal best practices.

5. Outlook

With this innovative project and the results achieved Siemens is considered as a visionary company. Thus IDS Scheer values this process standardization and documentation project as a reference for customers executing comparable projects.

The relevance of process standardization to succeed in a continuously changing economy is not only proved by the interest of other Siemens groups. It also serves as key element for business process excellence: the continuous change and adaptation of business processes based on a real time measurement of the process performance. Based on the process documentation this measurement will enable managers to control their processes and initiate necessary adaptations of these standard processes.

Therefore Siemens AG Austria expects further benefits for upcoming projects in the field of business process management:

"Due to corporate process management and process documentation with ARIS, Siemens AG Austria is in a position to realize sustainable increase of process efficiency. Based on these results Siemens AG Austria expects additional efficiency arising from process simulation and process optimization." (Ulrich Bleicher, CIO, Siemens AG Austria)

Learning Management Processes and Application Architecture for Learning Environments and Virtual Corporate Universities

Wolfgang Kraemer
CEO, imc information multimedia communication AG

Peter Sprenger
Senior Consultant, imc information multimedia communication AG

Summary

The creation of virtual (corporate) universities not only supports university training and the development of human resources within companies. Rather, it is developing into a strategic concept for putting the paradigm of lifelong learning into practice. In the future, virtual universities will be institutions of knowledge logistics and thus be of great importance to both universities and companies. Virtual universities can procure external knowledge through so-called knowledge suppliers as well as support universities and companies in processing their own knowledge. Members of staff are provided with the necessary knowledge through multimedia in order to support their specific aims, tasks and roles. Linked with this are new areas of responsibility, such as knowledge editing, knowledge services and the coaching of learning.

Key Words

Corporate Universities, Learning Management, Learning Process Engineering, Learnway, L-Reference-Model, Learning Management System (LMS) CLIX, E-Learning, Education Brokerage

1. From Information Society to Knowledge Society

The knowledge conveyed within the framework of university and corporate training and continuing education is subject to ever more rapid changes. In many specialized fields, it is assumed that subject-matter knowledge is completely renewed every six to ten years, with the trend pointing to ever shorter cycles. This is making it more and more difficult to be keep pace with new developments. In some sectors, the innovation cycles are already so short that traditional training schemes are no longer suitable, since the time needed to implement the scheme would exceed the innovation cycle. It is no longer sufficient to complete a course of training and then draw on the acquired knowledge for the remainder of one's professional life. Traditional full-time studies only partly meet the needs of today's society. Learning is thus undergoing a shift from learning on a "just-in-case" basis to learning-on-demand (lifelong learning).

For the knowledge gurus in society, it has become imperative to keep abreast of new developments, trends and knowledge advancements on a continuous basis throughout their professional life. This also entails new challenges for corporations in the fields of in-house training and human resources development.

Globally operating companies must ensure their employees have state-of-the-art knowledge in all areas in order to make sure that corporate strategies are uniformly implemented all over the world. Only a carefully directed information and knowledge transfer, which must also be individually tailored to the employees' needs, can guarantee innovation, speed and profitability (cf. Müller 1999).

This knowledge transfer can succeed with the help of knowledge management concepts which systematically tap the existing knowledge within the organization and make it available on a target group-specific basis. This in recent years much propagated approach has led to greater problem awareness in dealing with knowledge as a resource. With the introduction of in-company knowledge management responsibility functions, such as chief knowledge officers, and the development of knowledge management-specific information systems, it seems this topic has firmly established itself in the corporate environment.

Another aspect is the question as to what knowledge is currently not available in companies that will be needed in the future, and how these knowledge deficits can be overcome. This is a classical task of continuing education or corporate human resources development. The New Media assume a special role in this context, especially from the point of view of organizing these human resources development tasks as efficiently as possible. Leveraging them will make it possible to overcome the former chasm between education and career, working and learning. E-learning is one of the "breakthrough" strategies in corporate e-business and human resources concepts. "In future, we will no longer be able to so strictly separate what is part of our everyday work and what is uncoupled learning. An intermingling is taking place. The imparting of knowledge will be integrated in day-to-day work by means of Internet technologies. This gives us the opportunity to really speak of a 'learning' organization" (cf. Scheer 1999, p. 111 [authors' translation]).

Against this background, more and more companies have started to build up their own (virtual) corporate universities and online academies for their executives and employees. In Germany, for example, this includes companies such as Daimler-Chrysler, Deutsche Lufthansa, Bertelsmann, Deutsche Bank, Metallgesellschaft, Merck and SAP. They form learning alliances with business schools like Harvard, Insead or IMD on the basis of long-term learning alliances (cf. Kraemer & Müller 1999).

Small and medium-sized enterprises are also increasingly investing in e-learning. Companies such as Festo or Kaeser Kompressoren are among the pioneers in the use of e-learning. There is a general trend towards networked Internet-based e-learning solutions for the SME sector in which the activities are coordinated under one roof in order to keep down the investment costs for the individual SMEs.

Jürgen Weber, CEO of Deutsche Lufthansa AG, commented on the challenge of realizing lifelong learning for employees within the company framework as follows: "Among all planned investments, I consider the factor education to be one of the most important" (Weber [no year] [authors' translation]).

Differing institutional organization structures make it possible to depict individual and organizational learning for different target groups, business models and learning resources e.g. virtual universities, online academies or virtual corporate universities. In this context, the term "virtual world of learning and knowledge" has established itself as a generic term for these different manifestations.

E-learning is one of the most important application domains in e-business and, as Fig. 1 and the following remarks testify, the market predictions are accordingly optimistic:

- "...education is a prime candidate for becoming the ultimate electronic commerce application" (Cf. Hämäläinen et.al. 1996, p. 58)

- "Bill Gates, Jeff Bezos and Scott McNealy, to name just a few high-tech bigwigs, have all said that distance learning will be the next big thing online" (Cf. Vesely 1999)

- "Learning with new media will reach a market share of up to 20% in the next four years" (cf. Zinow 1999, p 118 [authors' translation])

220

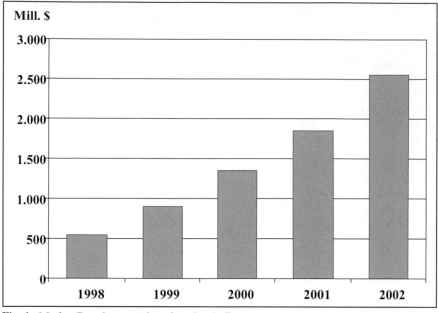

Fig. 1. Market Development for e-learning in Europe
(cf. in this context survey by Datamonitor 1998 p. 1; latest research studies from 2002, e.g. by Berlecon Research, show similar results only for the German market even in a pessimistic scenario)

E-Learning strategies are often implemented by leveraging web-based e-learning solutions, with employees accessing via the Internet course materials offered by private-sector content providers or freely available learning resources, for example from the university environment. Alternatively or as a complement to these, intranet-based e-learning solutions are being built up within companies that allow access to a learning content offer defined by the company's central education management.

This way, lifelong learning that is integrated in day-to-day work is made possible and the way paved from the information society to the knowledge society. The following sections describe the organizational and technical environment required to realize this shift, focusing in particular on so-called virtual corporate universities.

2. Characteristics of Virtual (Corporate) Universities

Not only in corporations, but also for the internal development of universities, the integrative leverage of multimedia as well as their internal and external networking in university education are increasingly being considered a catalyst (cf.

Hultzsch, 1996). Studies reveal that nowadays practically no academic institution still exists that is not concerned with how it can secure a stable competitive position in the education market of the future (Cf. Kraemer et.al., 1998d). The list of globally available tele-based and multimedia-enabled education offers is growing by the day, while at German colleges and universities the online instruction and learning resources are very heterogeneous. This is because terms like telelearning, teleteaching, virtual classroom, virtual university etc. are often used in different contexts, sometimes as synonyms, and without a clear definitional line being drawn between them. The spectrum ranges from presenting information about an academic department on the world wide web so that students can communicate with the professor by e-mail, via making exercises and solutions available on the Internet, through to the full tele-based management of a course of studies on the Net. However, it is significant that the leverage of multimedia applications in the academic realm is by no means standard practice. The use of electronic learning media also differs considerably from department to department. However, a clear trend towards using multimedia can be recognized. "In the next 10 years, under the impact of the penetration of digital media and their internal and external networking, university education will in all likelihood undergo a change more radical than anything that has happened in the past 100 years. The computer, the digital medium, will become the standard educational tool" (cf. Rüttgers, 1997, p. 11 [authors' translation]).

However, even in university education of the future, the new media will not be able to replace "classical" classroom instruction altogether: critics object that the social aspect of education is neglected with many of the new forms of learning, since although subject-matter knowledge can be conveyed, it is difficult to effectively teach so-called soft-skills. Thus, for example, Keil-Slawik notes "Education first and foremost takes place in social institutions, not in virtual ones. These social institutions - presence-based as well as distance learning environments - can be largely and extensively complemented by multimedia; but multimedia can't replace them, since education is a social and not a technical problem" (Keil-Slawik, 1997, p. 41 [authors' translation]). University education in the future will thus be characterized by a combination of face-to-face instruction and the use of multimedia learning solutions. However, due to their specific advantages, the emphasis is likely to increasingly shift to the new forms of learning.

The concrete activities of the respective education and training institutions for implementing e-learning solutions in their teaching are generally carried out on various different levels.

- On the **content level,** existing courses are complemented by virtual offerings or new course materials are even developed especially for the Internet.

- On the **technical level,** new production concepts are developed. They encompass the way multimedia learning units are developed, from "chunking" through to graphic design. Increasingly, modular software (keyword: componentware) and e-commerce concepts are being adapted and applied to the education setting.

222

- On the **organizational level,** new university or continuing education establishment structures are defined, which, for example, lead to the establishment of strategic alliances and cooperations (Kraemer & Milius, 1997).

- On the **pedagogical level,** questions of instructional design and didactic organization of the education products are dealt with.

- On the **administrative level,** services, entitlement and pricing concepts are considered, extending to a continuous updating of staff records in the sense of a dynamic qualification profile as an instrument of human resources development. This way, the knowledge acquired by individual staff members in the course of their employment is documented and updated on a continuous basis.

- On the **methodological level,** concepts for knowledge profile analysis, evaluating the quality of instruction and learning offers as well as testing methods are developed.

2.1 Changes in Knowledge Conveyance

Instruction and learning arrangements that are disseminated via communication media such as the Internet are globally accessible. This promotes a whole new exchange of learning units and materials between the academic and corporate worlds. Next to new forms of tele-based studies, tele-home workstations can also be complemented by tele-learning components, ultimately having a positive impact on the know-how transfer between the academic and corporate sectors. By contrast with conventional education and training programs, media-based education products have the objective to directly integrate knowledge in the learner's individual learning and working environment. In such learning alliances, all the players involved, in other words, the consumers and suppliers of the media-based education services, are brought together quasi just-in-time. Leveraging these education products offers corporations the possibility to ensure the timely and cost-effective qualification of their workforce. The qualification measures are carried out as and when they are needed at home or at the office, thus relieving companies of the frequently quoted constraints imposed by the cost of conventional training sessions (travel expenses, opportunity costs etc.)

For the provision and commercialization of media-based education products, it will, however, be necessary to change how the exchange of knowledge at university level is organized (cf. Kraemer et.al., 1998c). Historically, schools, colleges and universities have had the task to supply learning and research content to their respective customers (students) with the aim of providing them with a qualification in the sense of a competence to act. The academic segment in its classical form serves to prepare students for professional life. Continuing education for the subsequent 35 to 40 working years within the framework of gainful or self-employment takes place for the most part on the basis of human resources development programs in the form of training sessions, seminars, congresses, conferences etc., conducted either by in-house or external training establishments. Thus it makes eminent sense for the knowledge generators in the academic sector to act as content brokers and web together with on- and off-the-job training providers as additional, new customers. This webbing virtualizes the classical organization forms of the campus university, extends it into other sectors of private as well as professional learning. For this virtualization of colleges and universities there are four possible scenarios:

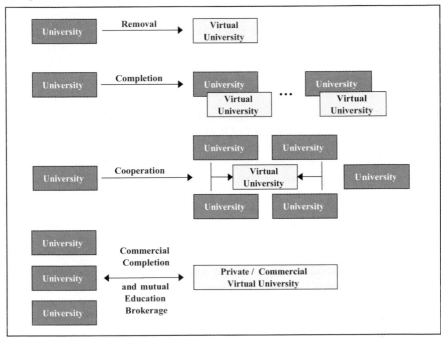

Fig. 2. Leverage Scenarios for Virtual Universities

1. **Replacement** of the traditional, classroom-based university by the virtual university: for example, some universities in the USA work on a for-profit rather than a not-for-profit basis. In this context, the University of Phoenix is already considered as a model for the education market of the 21st century (cf. no author, FAZ 1997, p. 26). This program is geared to interested learners and is offered as a distance learning course on the Internet; a campus is deemed neither necessary nor desirable. Such offers are still regarded by many as cheap "drive thru" education or McUniversity. Other US universities, such as the California Virtual University have in the meantime followed suit and also offer internationally recognized degree courses. Similar education possibilities are also likely to be offered in Germany in the foreseeable future. The first such bases in Europe are currently being built up. German universities therefore face the real danger of losing in the competition against the stronger financial and service-oriented position of the Anglo-American universities. Predictions of what the learning environment of the future will look like even extend to the complete dissolution of classroom-based universities as we know them: "In 30 years from

now, the university campuses will be deserted relics of an outmoded educational tradition. They will become extinct." (Lugger, 1998, p.126). However, before this vision/fiction, in which students can call up the best learning content from the respective learning service providers on the basis of an individual learning strategy, becomes reality, a lot of water still has to flow under the bridge.

2. **Complementing** the classical education offers with multimedia learning content: parallel to brick-and-mortar education, instructors will offer students additional Internet-based education services. Classical education products such as lectures, exercises, books and scripts will be complemented by knowledge conveyance by leveraging a media mix comprising web-based tutorials, university TV and teletutoring.

3. **Cooperation** between classroom-based universities within a virtual study network: the multimedia "processing" of learning content as well as the delivery of tele-based services in virtual learning environments is considered to be highly resource-intensive. It is therefore necessary to coordinate the development aims of comparable media-based learning systems and to save resources by realizing these developments within a network This way, the doubling up of developments can be avoided. The project budgets are relieved of the double expenditure incurred by parallel developments, making it possible to concentrate on the actual tasks in hand. Moreover, the cooperative delivery of education products allows for more design scope than one university department can muster on its own. One real-world example is the inter-university cooperation project "Wirtschaftsinformatik-Online" ("Business Information Systems Online") (WINFO-Line is promoted by the Bertelsmann Foundation and the Heinz Nixdorf Foundation within the framework of the BIG Initiative. Cf. http://www.winfoline.de) (cf. Kraemer et.al., 1998d; Kraemer et.al., 1997; Scheer et.al., 1998; Kraemer, 1999b; Kraemer et.al, 1999), which is described in detail in section 5.1. The participating project partners bring their core competencies and resources into the educational alliance. Core competencies in this setting is understood as courseware that ties in closely with the main fields of research of the respective department. Each project partner develops multimedia education products and services in line with their core competencies. The leverage of information and communication technologies serves communication and coordination between the cooperation partners and the students.

4. **Commercial complementing** and mutual **education brokerage**: this scenario principally aims at the production models of the multimedia learning contents, the organizational form of knowledge conveyance and commercialization aspects of the education products beyond the mission of higher education. A detailed description of this concept is given in section 3 and section 5.2. (cf. Kraemer et.al., 1998a).

69% of corporations are anticipating an increased need for continuing staff training (cf. Hochschulrektorenkonferenz 1996). The reasons for this, however, are not only the globalization and ever-shorter shelf-life of knowledge described above, but also the shift from the Taylorist division of labor to a broader qualification of the workforce (cf. Dürand, 1997, p. 179). Corporations pursue various concrete objectives with their continuing training measures (cf. Klusen, 1975, p. 16):

- To maintain and improve the professional qualifications of the workforce

- To make it easier for staff to adapt to changed technical, economic and social working conditions

- To influence employee's conduct at the workplace in a certain way

- To correct or eliminate employee errors

- To improve on-the-job motivation

As it is becoming more and more difficult for corporations to meet their increased training needs through self-devised programs, they will in future have a stronger presence on the continuing education market as consumers. For learning providers, including universities, this opens up a completely new potential for commercializing their learning content. In this context, multimedia learning technologies are leveraged to optimize learning processes and the logistics of the continuing training measures.

By leveraging Internet- and intranet-based e-learning applications and at the same time building up virtual learning and knowledge environments, corporations, complementary to the established presence-based organization of learning, are organizing the delivery of multimedia learning and knowledge contents. This results in new tasks for human resources development. A comparison of the delivery processes of a university and a (virtual) corporate university illustrates this.

The players at a public university who are involved in the teaching and learning process can be subdivided into supplier and customer groups. Professors and assistants create learning contents within the framework of their research and teaching activities, adapt learning contents of other universities and companies make their practical experience available as best-practice examples. The task of the teaching staff is to develop curricula. Curricula not only assume the function of lesson plans that indicate what learning contents are to be developed, they also determine the content-related structure and the scheduling of a course on the basis of concrete learning objectives. In addition, they encompass didactically prepared course materials and also stipulate the teaching and testing methods to be used. Thus the teaching staff not only function as curricula developers, they also convey the learning contents, tutor and examine the students. The curriculum is reviewed within the framework of evaluation.

The consumers of learning contents are the students, publishing houses, corporate and private-sector education establishments, as well as universities that integrate learning modules from other sources in their own courses and employees in companies who, thanks to the possibilities offered by information and communication technology, can access the course materials of online learning contents offered by individual departments.

The result of these instruction-learning processes, as illustrated in Fig. 3, is not only the provision and the transfer of learning contents, but also the creation of secondary values such as the branding of learning contents and the educators and, hand-in-hand with this, the reputation of the university and its graduates. Furthermore, the management of a public-sector university presupposes a corresponding infrastructure.

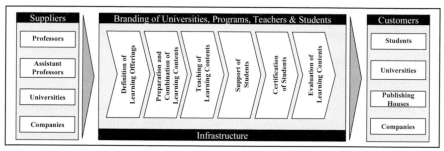

Fig. 3. Delivery Processes and Relationships of a Public-Sector University

The analysis of the delivery processes of a corporate university, as illustrated in Fig. 4, shows that the corporate university neither generates, prepares nor conveys the learning contents, nor does it tutor or examine the learners. Rather, the focus is on the definition, selection, procurement and vending of the learning resources to the respective target groups within the corporation as well as continuously checking the alignment of the learning contents with the corporate strategy.

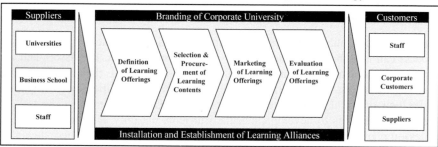

Fig. 4. Delivery Processes in the Corporate University

The generation of learning content in the sense of research, preparation and combination in a curriculum does not take place in a corporate university. What happens here is a definition of strategically relevant topics, which implies an operationalization in concrete learning offers. This leads to a selection and procurement decision with respect to learning contents and the establishment of learning alliances with the respective content suppliers. Learning contents may be procured in-house or be outsourced.

One important criterion of corporate universities is the partnership-based cooperation with international business schools and "Ivy League" universities. With the clear focusing on company-relevant business topics and executive education, these institutions are benefiting from the increasing spread of corporate universities. The business model between corporate universities and these "content providers" is characterized by a clear role distribution. The planning of the curriculum is coordinated by the corporate university, without institutionalizing an extensive university structure with teaching staff and campus. The concrete elaboration of the contents - for example on the basis of case studies - as well as the implementation of the programs and tutoring of the participants is done by the business schools.

The above comparison illustrates the high relevance of learning contents for the building of virtual learning and knowledge environments. The target group-specific delivery of learning and knowledge contents implies incorporating content-editing in human resources development with the following tasks:

- Selection and procurement of suitable media-based learning and knowledge contents (procurement logistics)

- Transformation of "paper-based" contents to multimedia conception worlds (production logistics)

- Enabling employees to use these contents in concrete learning contexts and establishment of an interactive learning coaching on the basis of teletutoring concepts (knowledge distribution)

- Accounting, budgeting, coordination of the learning processes and evaluation of results (knowledge utilization)

One possible editing process is shown in Fig. 5. From this, it becomes clear what steps are necessary to proceed from the first ideas of a learning offer to the concrete use of these learning contents by the workforce.

228

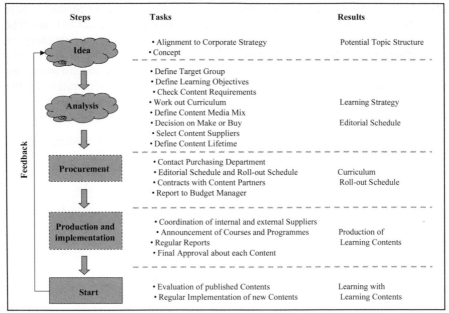

Fig. 5. Example of an Editing Process

In the first step, the potential topic structure for the virtual learning and knowledge environment is defined. This is done by asking what learning contents are likely to be highly relevant within the framework of human resources development. The definition of the topic structure forms the basis for the subsequent analysis phase. Fig. 6 indicates how the contents of the courses and programs might be structured. In this connection, the target groups and learning objectives also have to be defined, i.e. it is determined what contents are to be delivered for what target group. The requirement analysis can be broken down as follows:

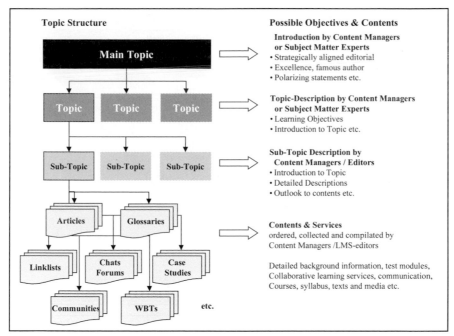

Fig. 6. Topic Structure of a Virtual Learning and Knowledge Environment

Analysis of learning content offers: The market is sounded out for suppliers of media-based contents. These may be external content providers, which includes business schools, universities and the non-corporate learning portal providers described in the previous section. Furthermore, this also includes the companies themselves, which make their "best practice" knowledge accessible to other corporate sectors in the form of best-practice examples (cf. Kraemer, 1999a).

Analysis of learning content requirements: Apart from the contents available on the market, the interests and learning requirements of the potential users must also be taken into account.

This approach answers the questions of what media-based contents are generally available and whether these offers correspond to the current learning requirements of the employees. However, it also means that human resources development can only react to learning requirements with a corresponding delay. It is therefore of particular interest to recognize content-related trends of high relevance for the company as early as possible, in order to be able to make appropriate learning offers available in the introductory phase of a topic. Once all the points of the requirement analysis have been worked through, the editorial schedule ensues, taking into account the defined topics.

230

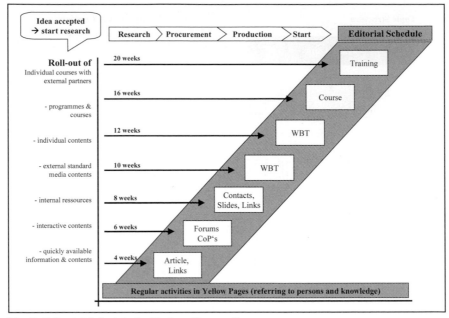

Fig. 7. Editorial Schedule for Various Content Types

Fig. 7 shows the need for a differentiated editorial schedule for the various content types. Thus, for example, more time from start to delivery must be allowed for the development of company-specific learning contents (individual content) than for the integration of already produced contents with a low degree of multimediality and interaction.

The described delivery of learning contents is not a one-off process, as the course materials must be continuously updated and extended.

2.2 Features of Virtual Universities

In order to be able to provide adequate products to meet the concrete demand of companies, suppliers must know what companies' requirements are regarding continuing training programs: these relate to course length, content and organizational form. With regard to course length, companies are generally not interested in long series of seminars; for the most part they prioritize compact training sessions (Hochschulrektorenkonferenz, 1996, p. 34) that enable employees to hone their skills without taking them away from their desk.

Companies' main requirement with respect to learning content is that it corresponds to the concrete requirements of the job (Hochschulrektorenkonferenz, 1996, p.34). When organizing continuing corporate training, companies are increasingly leveraging integrated e-learning solutions and multimedia. The advantages of e-learning for human resources development can, as illustrated in Fig. 8, be characterized as follows:

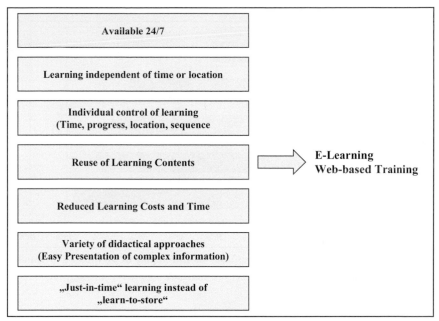

Fig. 8. Advantages of eLearning and Web-Based Training

- The new media not only complement classical knowledge conveyance with additional multimedia elements. Above all, they allow access to knowledge any time, any place. This way, learners can use the online education materials cost-efficiently as and when they need them, independently of traditional time constraints and without having to sacrifice communication and human interaction. This enables companies to realize a homogeneous and rapid distribution of knowledge. Learning communities allow knowledge transfer between all relevant players.

- Learning shifts from being a mostly passive and anonymous consumption in a traditional classroom setting to an individual learning process in which learners can self-direct where, what, when and at what pace they learn. This promotes the development of a learning and work culture that the learners themselves maintain and further develop.

- Beyond making knowledge conveyance independent of time and place, the vision or cyber potentials of interactive multimedia systems open up myriad opportunities for the didactic-pedagogical enrichment, revitalization and redesign of learning and knowledge content. Compared to conventional forms of instruction, such as lectures or seminars, multimedia presentations allow complex subject matter to be illustrated in an understandable way.

232

- In addition, such learning systems accord the learners an effective evaluation of learning results. Teletutors, who can be consulted via e-mail or videoconferencing, guarantee individual learner support.

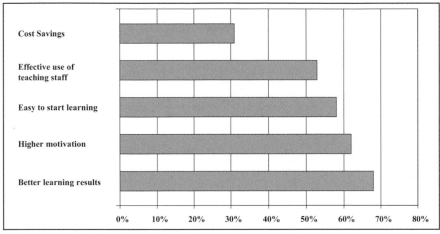

Fig. 9. Expectations of German Companies from the Leveraging of Multimedia in Training and Continuing Training (cf. Dürand, 1997, p. 180) (stated in percent)

The economy is above all hoping to see better learning results from the leveraging of multimedia applications in corporate training and continuing training (cf. Fig. 9). This hope is justified, as studies show that combining various media increases the receptiveness of the human senses (cf. Dürand, 1997), shortening learning time and improving results. The better results in turn have a positive influence on employees' motivation to learn. Another compelling aspect are the cost savings. This is particularly noticeable in the reduction in travel expenses and the opportunity cost of having employees away from their post. The new forms of learning give employees the opportunity to access the corporate training program from their desktop or at home. As a result, companies no longer have to send their staff to training seminars that are generally offered by external training organizations at one central location. This eliminates costs for travel and lodging etc. Learning at the workplace - versus traditional classroom instruction - also accords time savings to companies, because employees do not have to be sent off to a learning center to take a course, but can integrate the learning process in their own work routine, i.e. they can work through a study unit whenever it is convenient.

Fig. 10 in the next section shows the content-related possibilities of corporate universities on the level of the possibilities of a virtual learning platform.

3. E-Learning in Companies: The E-Business of Human Resources Development

3.1 Objectives of Corporate Universities

Corporate universities are oriented towards the strategic challenges the company faces, i.e. their education offer is tailored precisely to the needs of the company. This guarantees a "high degree of implementation in day-to-day work" (Daimler-Chrysler 1998, p. 17). The contents of the programs and courses offered within the framework of the corporate university are determined by the company itself. Thus, the employees acquire and hone precisely those skills and knowledge that they need to perform their job.

According to a survey carried out by the magazine Corporate University Review (cf. Densford, 1998, p. 3), the link between continuing education and the economic objectives of the company is for 84% of the interviewed companies in the USA the main reason for setting up a corporate university.

Second, the consolidation and coordination of all human resources activities and initiatives at corporate level under one umbrella was important for 48% of the interviewed US companies. This means that - as a result of the systematic aggregation and structuring - identifying both deficits and redundancies within the corporate education package, compiling continuing education programs for specific groups of employees as well as integrating additional training modules in the company's overall concept, i.e. administering corporate training, is considerably facilitated. The third objective is the development, dissemination and management of knowledge. Jürgen E. Schrempp, CEO of the DaimlerChrysler Group, says of this:

"We can only belong to the leading companies in the world on a long-term basis if we succeed in transforming the huge potential of ideas, experience and creative energy that is inherent in our company into innovations, new processes, new products and new markets. And if we systematically reinforce and develop core competencies across the board".
(DaimlerChrysler, 1998, p. 5 [authors' translation])

In order to realize this objective, the intellectual capital that already exists within the company has to be documented and made available to every employee. The corporate university is especially suited to this task because it records information about the knowledge level of each individual employee, for example, about the programs and courses a particular employee has completed and the specialized knowledge thus acquired.

The advantage of disseminating "best practice" knowledge is that it allows this knowledge to be meaningfully leveraged elsewhere in the group. On the one hand, these best-practice solutions provide ideas for solving other problems of a similar nature that arise in other areas of the company; on the other hand, they avoid investing time and resources second time round to solve the same problem, although a solution to this problem already exists elsewhere in the company (cf. Daimler-Chrysler, 1998, p. 6).

Furthermore, through the programs and courses offered by the corporate university, contacts are established between employees from different areas of the company. These contacts enable members of the company to broaden their knowledge and horizon beyond the scope of their own experiences and normal perspectives. What's more, they also promote the knowledge transfer within the company (cf. DaimlerChrysler, 1998, p. 11).

With the introduction of a corporate university, along with aspects of human resources development and knowledge management, communication policy objectives are also pursued, because the employees develop a mutual and uniform understanding for the objectives and strategies of the corporation. Under the umbrella of the corporate university, a global planning, coordination and control of group-relevant topics thus takes place.

According to the survey cited above (Densford, 1998, p. 3), companies express little interest in enabling employees to acquire certification and/or academic degrees via the corporate university. Thus, for example, 42% of the interviewed companies offered training that is eligible for academic credit, however, only a few of these companies offered the possibility to actually acquire such certification: "The fact is that a relatively large number of CUs offer training that's eligible for academic credit, but at the same time express little interest in offering certification or degrees, is further indication that their focus is business objectives first." (Densford, 1998, p. 3)

The question as to whether certification is planned in the future or whether a degree from a corporate university might rank as high as a standard degree from a German university elicited the response: "We do not intend to enter into competition with German or international universities and offer degree courses that are equivalent to an MBA or other similarly highly qualified degree." (cf. Müller, 1999, p. 96 [authors' translation])

3.2 Learning Alliances

Apart from differently realized learning scenarios, corporate universities are also distinguished by their concrete education offer. The contents differ, for example, with respect to the importance of theoretical knowledge, the degree of specialization as well as the amount of company-specific knowledge. Apart from contents that can be leveraged within the company, these contents are the result of cooperations with business schools, public and private universities or training organizations, as well as the education departments of other corporations: "As organizations begin taking on the role of educator, the goal of many corporate universities focused on creating unique value-added learning partnerships"(Meister, 1999, p. 91).

With respect to the extent and duration of the cooperation, a large number of different delivery relationships exist between content partners and corporate universities (cf. Töpfer 1999a), ranging from forms of intermittent cooperation, for example if individual university instructors have the task to convey knowledge about a particular topic, through to the definition of comprehensive programs agreed with selected content partners on the basis of long-term contracts.

With the clear focusing on company-relevant business topics and executive continuing education, business schools in particular are benefiting from the increasing proliferation of corporate universities. Their already well-established cooperation with companies, and the access to topics of current practical relevance as well as to corporate data, give them a head start over public-sector universities in terms of time, knowledge and cost (cf. Töpfer, 1999b, p. 37).

The business model between corporate universities and the content partners is characterized by a clear distribution of roles. The planning of the curriculum is coordinated by the corporate university, without institutionalizing an extensive university structure with teaching staff and campus. The concrete elaboration of the contents - for example on the basis of case studies - as well as the implementation of the programs and tutoring of the participants is done by the business schools, as the following statement illustrates:

"Business schools are first and foremost to be seen as knowledge or information brokers in the field of general management for our executive managers, which convey state-of-the-art knowledge. As a corporate group, it is our task to formulate our strategically important topics and design the corresponding contents. Developing the subject-matter, in other words translating these strategic topics into courses or in future also into web-based cases, is the task of the authorized business schools"
(Müller 1999, p. 95 [authors' translation])

4. Learning Platform

Many companies already have a gamut of digital education products for self-directed, auto-didactic learning at their disposal, such as CBTs, WBTs, training videos or materials. Through e-learning shops, these training media are made available to employees centrally and with consistent contents. A shop solution also supports the management of the necessary procurement, distribution and administration processes, through to finance and cost management, if desired. Learners can configure their own learning environment according to their personal preferences.

Through the combination of face-to-face and virtual learning phases (blended learning), it is possible to considerable enhance the quality as well as the efficiency of training and continuing education measures. Knowledge acquisition no longer ends with the handing out of a course credit. With an e-learning community solution, learning processes are integrated in the employees' everyday work. In virtual classrooms or project rooms that are coached and individually organized by teletutors, the course participants meet independently of time and location, discuss problems together, draw up and document solutions, exchange experience and expertise.

With the third development stage, all the relevant business processes are supported within the framework of a comprehensive, integrated education and knowledge management. This focuses not only on the personal interests, skills and career plans of the employees. Just as important are assessment tools with which the efficiency and quality of courseware can be objectively measured as well as subjectively evaluated. An e-learning enterprise solution offers editing tools which allow content experts, such as for example the staff and partners of business schools, to quickly and easily publish learning and knowledge contents in a virtual corporate university.

Fig. 10 presents the application architecture of the CLIX learning platform (Corporate Learning and Information eXchange) of imc information multimedia communication AG.

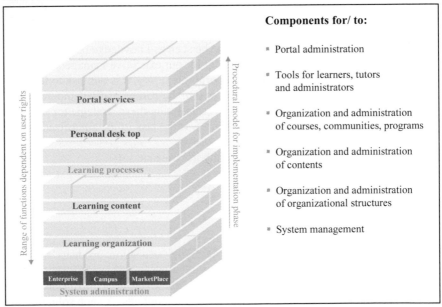

Fig. 10. The Application Architecture for the CLIX Learning Platform (Corporate Learning and Information eXchange) of imc AG (Further Details can be found under http://www.im-c.de/)

4.1 Portal Services

The learners and editors of the Learning Management System (LMS) are able to arrange their individual eLearning portal with the CLIX portal services. Training courses can be promoted with previews of current courses, customers are provided with up-to-date, useful information concerning the learning platform. By structuring the entrance of the learning environment with the portal services it is easier for learners to enter the world of knowledge. This is also where customers can register independently. Login name and password are generated by CLIX automatically and sent to the user by email. Other features of the portal are:

- Students, trainers and administrators can register as a self-service
- Various registration workflows
- Encrypted authentication
- Template-based editing to manage information in different portals
- Integration of advertising banners
- Catalogue preview

4.2 Personal Desktop

Once the learner is registered in the platform he enters the personal desktop, where the learning organization arranges the daily learning as it is needed. Office tools support the organization and planning of learning activities – from the email system right through to the personal course schedule. Discussions with other participants on specialist contents in forums or chats support learners in building up their own knowledge network. There are diverse functionalities for trainers in order to ensure optimum support and individual supervision of students, e.g. overviews displaying the course progress of participants according to courses or modules. The task of the specialist operator consists of controlling the operating processes which are related to the business administration of the product portfolio. CLIX provides tools to manage resources and to edit booking lists. Similarly CLIX makes continuous controlling of training courses possible.

- Quick access to personalized contents
- Catalogues for particular target groups and subject matter
- Libraries for public contents
- Integrated office tools
- Tutor centers for individual supervision
- Rating and review of contents

- User feedback on the training offered

- Knowledge management with communities and directories of subject matter experts

- Resource administration

- Administration of participant, waiting, reservation and cancellation lists

- Data mining and statistical evaluation of course progress, use of contents and economic performance figures

4.3 Learning Processes

On the learning process level the offered training courses are organized. Classroom instruction is combined with multimedia course units, single courses or communities. Al these learning objects can be put together into training programs. The trainings are linked with skill profiles that can be designed individually. Depending on the requirements of the learning organization one can choose from various teaching and learning methods. With the aid of the logic modules in CLIX curricula as complex as needed are created to control the learning process, right through to adaptive course progression.

- Support classroom training, online learning and blended learning

- Administer courses, communities and training programs

- Freely defined skill taxonomies

- Integrated assessment tool with numerous types of questions

- Adaptive course progression through learning logic

- Numerous booking and approval workflows

4.4 Learning Contents

This is where the training organization administers and versions the learning content - the learning objects - regardless of physical file formats and training courses on offer. Re-use of existing learning objects is always possible. There are integrated tools and templates available for authors and editors to create content. Numerous CLIX Content Wizards guide the user through the editing process, from the initial draft right through to publication. Interfaces enable the integration of external content sources such as Business TV or information services. Similarly this is where communication and collaboration instruments that are specific to the course such as forums, chat, bulletin boards or document archives are administered.

- Templates to create and edit learning objects

- Integrated version administration

- Collaborative authoring

- Definition of context related learning object types

- Integration of third party content

- Supports offline CBTs

- Meta data repository to define optional description attributes of contents

- Certification according to international standards for eLearning (SCORM, AICC, IMS, IEEE, DC)

4.5 Learning Organization

CLIX adapts fully to organizational structures and the related operating environment. Individual group and user structures can be created for each client. With the aid of a multi-layer security concept access and administration rights for all CLIX application components can be defined. This means that one can define the user roles as required. User roles can be changed or expanded at any point during the allocated time. This helps CLIX grow continuously in line with learning organizations.

- Client-based system organization

- Representation of individual organizational structures by means of free role definition

- User profiles defined as required

- Free assignment of object related access rights for application components

4.6 System Administration

The components in the system administration are intended for the technical administration of CLIX. A variety of language packages is available. The organization is able to decide the appearance of CLIX by using the CLIX GUI components. There are various encryption methods provided in order to take security aspects into account. A central repository serves to administer the component related processes, functions, data and concepts. Interfaces based on standard technologies make it possible to integrate CLIX into existing IT infrastructures.

- Component repository for branches- and context-specific configuration of processes, data and terminology (CLIX Enterprise, Marketplace, Campus)

- Language packets (German, English, French, Spanish, Italian)
- Complete web-based, graphically tailored user interface
- Standard interfaces to ERP, Content Management and email systems
- Connection to directory services
- Secure transmission of data with LDAP S, SSL, MD 5, DES

5. Introduction and Management of Virtual (Corporate) Universities

The realization of a virtual learning and knowledge environment constitutes an enterprise-wide online education service for qualification offers and the acquisition and exchange of knowledge via the intranet or Internet. The planning and conception implies more than simply the software-technical realization. Rather, it encompasses an overall concept comprising organizational, media-didactic, human resources and operational as well as information technology features.

5.1 Roll-out Consulting as a Key to Success

The introduction of eLearning essentially involves making knowledge and learning processes more efficient by using information technology. This is why eLearning focuses on the competitive role knowledge and learning play in business, educational institutions or universities, and deals with the question of: How to plan the organizational and individual learning processes, to organize and steer them, in order to ensure the performance of an organization and of its employees in the long term. The aim of an eLearning solution is to provide a defined user group with qualifications at low expense and with wide availability of information.

e-Learning solutions support learning processes, where students can individually determine their learning environment, the different stages and times, as well as the speed at which they learn. This promotes the development of a culture of learning and work, which is supported and further developed by the employees themselves. A successful eLearning solution is made up of three components: multimedia and interactive learning content (contents), infrastructure for hardware and software that makes these contents accessible from an organizational aspect and that steers the learning processes (learning platform), as well as services necessary for roll-out and efficient operation of the eLearning solution (services).

What makes eLearning different lies in the term "Learning" itself. The "Learning", which is ultimately the subject and objective of any process design and of IT implementation, is frequently defined only "approximately" and emphasis is placed too often on the technical features instead - the "e" in "eLearning". However the technical potential of a learning platform is not the sole deciding factor in the efficient usage of eLearning. In this respect there is very little difference between the leading systems on the market. What is far more relevant to success is comprehensive roll-out consulting, which illustrates which eLearning application scenarios provide a significant contribution to added value and how functionalities of a learning platform can be adapted into business processes and organizational structures. Successful institutionalization of eLearning therefore requires an overall concept including organizational, personnel, economic, media-specific and didactic issues, and goes far beyond IT aspects such as functionality, design and interfaces, as illustrated in Fig. 11 in the eLearning iceberg.

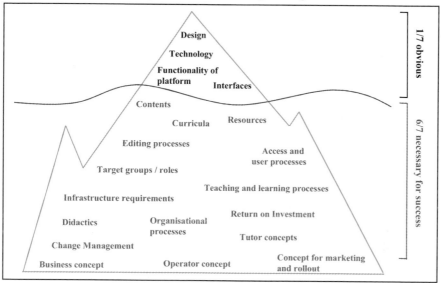

Fig. 11. The eLearning Iceberg

Conception and implementation of an eLearning strategy represents a comprehensive project. Structured methods and procedural models assist significantly in reducing complexity and support a systematic procedure for the introduction of eLearning. The imc Learnway is a Best and Common Practice procedural model that considers all specialist and technical decisions regarding design for the introduction of eLearning in an integrated, process-oriented overall concept. The approximate phases in the Learnway are sketched in Fig. 12. Each phase is associated with a detailed project plan that elucidates possible procedures for introducing (virtual) corporate universities, online academies, employee portals or education markets.

242

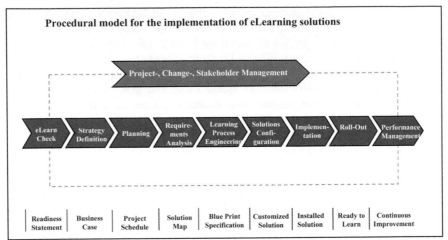

Fig. 12. Procedural Model for the Implementation of eLearning Solutions according to the Consulting Concept of imc information multimedia communication (imc Learn-way)

5.2 eLearn Check

At the start of an eLearning project a careful analysis should always be made taking the initial strategic, organizational and technical circumstances into consideration. From this starting point, not only is it possible to identify first potential problem areas but also to make a rough estimate of the length and costs of the intended project. The eLearnCheck is a systematic, rapid survey of the "eLearning readiness" of a company prior to commencing an eLearning project.

5.3 Strategy Definition

At the start of a project it is seldom possible to fall back on a current, comprehensive and consistent eLearning strategy. If the company has existing internal strategy papers, then there is frequently a lapse of several months between creation of the document and start of the project. The concepts described may frequently be incomplete or no longer conclusive because of other projects realized in the company in the meantime, changes in organizational responsibilities or technological innovations. The first task of strategy definition is to check the existing eLearning strategy and revise it if necessary.

The following aspects need to be taken into account in doing so:

- Interleaving organizational strategy and eLearning strategy

- Structural change with Blended Learning: Online learning and classroom instruction

- Combining Knowledge Management and Learning Management

- Matching course supply and demand

- Procurement strategy for eLearning contents

The updated strategy concept considers the arguments as regards risks and also expense, and potential benefits for all given aspects. Necessary integration is pinpointed. All strategic target dimensions – costs, time and quality – are considered in the Business Case. The Business Case depicts the fundamental feasibility, documents the return on investment and thus serves as a model for management decisions.

5.4 Planning

The draft eLearning strategy should be carried over into operational project objectives and steerable project stages. The total project cycle is run through once in its entirety in theory. The current situation with respect to scheduling, the financial and the personnel situations are analyzed, contact persons are designated for the further project cycle, trends both inside and outside the company are identified, necessary preparatory phases named, any potential difficulties for implementation anticipated and appropriate project stages are defined. The Project Schedule provides a basis for efficient realization of the project. At the same time the project schedule ensures necessary planning security for the customer and also the solution provider with regard to deadlines, costs and personnel needed. These aspects demonstrate that project planning is a project in its own right. Even drafting the plan demands a substantial degree of know-how, in which project management skills, eLearning competence and familiarity with structures and regulations particular to the company have to be combined.

5.5 Requirements Analysis

The eLearning strategy defined at the start of a project is made operational by defining concrete requirements for an eLearning solution. In the practical project work, ideas for an initial draft solution frequently accompany the analysis of solution requirements. The Learning Solution Map therefore already provides a tool to document the results from discussions in the form of a rough concept. The Learning Solution Map depicts the major design areas for an eLearning solution. A further outcome of the Learning Solution Map is the creation of a catalogue of criteria (Request for Proposal) for a learning platform, which can be sent to product vendors for their response. The Learning Solution Map is – when used in this way - a means to a targeted selection of eLearning products.

5.6 Learning Process Engineering

The introduction of a learning platform and the use of Web-based training are not an end in themselves but serve to support economic goals. These goals have one common direction: improvement of learning and knowledge processes in the company. "Improvement" could be interpreted in this context as "Reorganization in order to increase efficiency".

Within the framework of Learning Process Engineering all relevant process chains in learning and knowledge management are examined to make sure they are complete and logically correct. In so doing, potential changes that could be made possible by using new technologies should be exploited in particular. In this way, by using a learning platform, "virtual" course groups can be formed, i.e. groups independent of each other both in terms of time and location - just to give a simple example. Appropriate communication and cooperation processes need to be designed for these virtual learning communities.

The result of Learning Process Engineering is a detailed model of the business processes for the intended eLearning solution, e.g. a corporate university or online academy (Blue Print Specification). In this it is unnecessary to "reinvent the wheel" since the knowledge and the experience from numerous projects introducing eLearning are documented in imc's reference models as shown in Fig. 13), both generally applicable and branch-specific. All important eLearning core business processes are compiled in the outline model - the eLearning process map -. This model consists of over a hundred detailed process models. Models specific to one company can be very quickly derived from these reference models to serve as a foundation for the introduction of eLearning solutions.

The potential benefits of imc eLearning reference models are:

- Discussion basis for strategic planning for eLearning projects

- Basis for selecting and introducing a learning platform

- Fast survey of all relevant processes and the scope of an eLearning solution

- Savings in time, costs and resources in the conception and optimization of eLearning business processes by keeping to Common Practices and Best Practices

- Support for making decisions about the choice of process alternatives

- Efficient learning platform customizing

- Communications tool between project members, in particular staff in charge of IT and HR

- Training tools for administrators, editors and online tutors

The eLearning reference models are illustrated with the ARIS method from IDS Scheer AG. ARIS is recognized worldwide as the leading tool and framework concept for business process modeling. In addition, this phase includes the technical process specification for system integration between the learning platform, ERP standard software systems (e.g. PeopleSoft or SAP), global directory services and office programs (e.g. Lotus Notes, MS Outlook) and integration of the eLearning solution into the existing IT infrastructure.

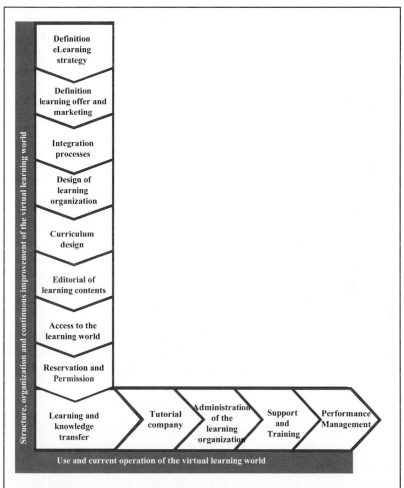

Fig. 13. The L-Reference Model of the Primary Learning Management Business Processes

5.7 Solution Configuration

Customizing entails adapting the software to customers' requirements. This is done by configuring parameter settings with the aid of administration functionalities in the learning platform without changing the source code. This involves for example navigation, client, group, role and authorization, and educational catalogue structure, booking and learning processes, and meta data sets. Starting from the customer's corporate design the virtual learning world is customized. The result is the Customized Solution. In addition components can be adapted, by adding or refining special functionalities desired by the customer. A development process with the specialist concept, DP concept and software design is worked out for these components together with the customer. These components are then implemented according to the customer's requirements.

5.8 Implementation

Existing course contents have to be adapted into the product catalogue of the learning platform in accordance with the structure and categorization determined in the Learning Process Engineering Phase. In this way it is possible to access the contents from different search and start directions via the learning platform. In our experience contents for virtual worlds of learning are provided by various Content Suppliers (external and internal). In the run-up to integration of contents the learning platform needs to be checked to see if the contents match the customers' requirements in terms of form and content. In the next step the contents are officially approved for integration into the learning platform and are then released for users. In addition, the system infrastructure has to be prepared and adjusted with those responsible for IT at the customer's, so that in the next step installation, delivery and final inspection of the learning platform can be carried out (Installed Solution). The entire introduction process of the learning platform must be accompanied by quality assurance measures. All components are subjected to inspections where correct function and interplay with other components are checked.

5.9 Roll-out

In order to identify potential for optimizing the eLearning solution and the accompanying organization, a pilot phase is recommended prior to putting the system into productive use. The functions of the system are subjected to specialist inspection and the effects of introduction on running operation are examined. The relevant staff have to be trained in the technical operation of the learning platform. This involves, in particular, the ongoing adjustment and description of contents as well as management of roles and authorizations. Technical operation requires transferring knowledge about the system architecture, installation, backup and recovery of the learning platform. Production of a multimedia explanation, a so-called guided tour, is recommended for quick familiarization with the functionalities of the learning platform. The company's employees are ready to learn.

5.10 Performance Management

Learning processes, tutoring and operator management of the virtual world of learning are supported using typical platform functionalities such as tracking, monitoring and reporting. At the same time the courses on offer are extended successively. A process of ongoing improvement can be initiated on the basis of evaluation measures for the acceptance, learning efficiency and success of the eLearning offers (Continuous Improvement).

5.11 Change, Project and Stakeholder Management

The availability of a learning platform to all employees make it possible for the company to integrate into one networked structure education and training that were previously in different locations, at different times and organized separately. This is first and foremost a question of an evolutionary and interdisciplinary process of Change Management. The need to involve the relevant stakeholders in this project, from the works council on to the specialist divisions and up to the management, plays a key role in its success. All these people with their various ranges of competence, interests, goals and responsibilities have to be coordinated for the purpose of integrated project management. This project management covers both the drafting and updating of the project plan and also steering of the project meetings and controlling, reporting and communication of the project results.

6. References

(no author) (1997). Eine private Universität im Internet wirbt mit Gewinnen für Aktionäre (A private university woos with profits for ist shareholder in the internet). FAZ – Frankfurter Allgemeine Zeitung, dated 31.10.97, No. 253, p. 26.

DaimlerChrysler AG (Ed.) (1998). Informationsbroschüre zur DaimlerChrysler Corporate University (Information brochure of the DaimlerChrysler Corporate University). Stuttgart, 1998.

Densford, L. (1998). Many CU's under development; aim is to link training to business. Corporate University Review 6 (1998), p. 3.

Dürand, D. (1997) Lernen auf Abruf. (Learning on demand). Wirtschaftswoche No. 42 dated 9.10.97, p. 179.

Hämäläinen, M. et.al. (1996). Electronic Markets for Learning: Education Brokerages on the Internet. Communications of the ACM 39(1996)6, p. 58.

Hochschulrektorenkonferenz (Ed.) (1996. Hochschule und Wirtschaft als Partner in Weiterbildung und Wissenstransfer auf dem europäischen Arbeitsmarkt - Fachtagung der Hochschulrektorenkonferenz in Zusammenarbeit mit der Bundesvereinigung der Deutschen Arbeitgeberverbände, (University and trade as partners in education and knowledge transfer on the european job market – Congress of the committee of university principals in cooperation with the federal consortium of german employer's association). Bonn 1996.

Hultzsch, H. (1996). Telelernen - Die Strategie der deutschen Telekom. (Tele-Learning – German Telekoms new strategy) In Glowalla, U. & Schoop, E. (Eds.): Deutscher Multimedia Kongreß '96 - Perspektiven multimedialer Kommunikation. (German Multimedia Congress 96 – Perspectives of multimedia communication). (pp 91-96) Berlin et al. 1996.

Klusen, N. (1975). Innerbetriebliche Weiterbildung: Methoden und Lösungsformen in der industriellen Praxis. (Corporate Training. Methods and solutions in industrial practice). Berlin 1975, p.16.

Kraemer, W. (1999a). Education Brokerage - Wissensallianzen zwischen Hochschulen und Unternehmen. (Education Brokerage – Knowledge cooperations between universities and companies.) (pp. 18-26) Information Management & Consulting 14 (1999) 1.

Kraemer, W. (1999b). WINFO-Line – Ein interuniversitäres Kooperationsprojekt (WINFO-Line – A inter-university cooperation project) In Bertelsmann Stiftung (Ed.). WINFO-Line: Wirtschaftsinformatik-Online – Annual Report 1997/98. (pp. 9-24) Gütersloh 1999.

Kraemer, W. et.al. (1997) WINFO-LINE - A Virtual University Network: Telelearning Concepts for Distributed Studies in Business Information Systems. Online Educa (Ed.), Berlin 1997

Kraemer, W. et.al. (1998a). Elektronische Bildungsmärkte für ein integriertes Wissens- und Qualifikationsmanagement. (Electronic education markets for an integrated knowledge and qualification management.) In Scheer, A.-W. (Ed.). Neue Märkte, neue Medien, neue Methoden – Roadmap zur agilen Organization. (New markets, new media, new methods – road map to the agile organization). (pp. 571-599). Heidelberg 1998.

Kraemer, W. et.al. (1998c). Virtuelles Lehren und Lernen an deutschen Universitäten - Eine Dokumentation (Virtual education and learning in german universities – a documentation.) In Bertelsmann Stiftung/Heinz Nixdorf Stiftung (Eds.) 2. Edition, Gütersloh 1997.

Kraemer, W. et.al. (1998d). Virtuelle Universität: Fallstudie Wirtschaftsinformatik Online (WINFO-Line) (Virtual University: Case Study Business Information Systems Online (WINFO-Line). Winand, U. & Nathusius, K. (Eds.): Unternehmensnetzwerke und virtuelle Organisationen (Corporate Networks and virtual organization). (pp. 267-280). Stuttgart 1998.

Kraemer, W. et.al. (1999). Projektbericht zu den Arbeitspaketen des Instituts für Wirtschaftsinformatik, Universität des Saarlandes. (Project report of the work of the Institute of Busines Information Systems, Saarland University). In Bertelsmann Stiftung (Ed.). WINFO-Line: Wirtschaftsinformatik-Online – Annual Report 1997/98. (pp. 25-42) Gütersloh 1999.

Kraemer, W. & Müller, M. (1999). Virtuelle Corporate University - Executive Education Architecture und Knowledge Management (Virtual Corporate University – Executive Education Architecture and Knowledge Management.) In Scheer, A.-W. (Ed.). Electronic Business und Knowledge Management - Neue Dimensionen für den Unternehmungserfolg (Electronic Business and Knowledge Management – New dimensions for corporate success). (pp. 491-525). Heidelberg 1999.

Kraemer, W. & Sprenger, P. (2002). E-Learning step by step – Von der Strategie zur Implementierung. (E-Learning step by Stepp – from strategy to implementation.). In: Köllinger, Ph.: eLearning in deutschen Unternehmen. Fallstudien, Konzepte, Implementierung (E-Learning in german companies. Case studies, concepts, and implementation). Düsseldorf 2002.

Kraemer, W.; Sprenger, P.; Scheer, A.-W.: eLearning-Innovationspotenziale erkennen und -Projekte gestalten. (Recognizing e-Learning innovation potentials and managing e-Learning projects). In: Hohenstein, A.; Wilbers, K. (Hrsg.): Handbuch E-Learning. Expertenwissen aus Wissenschaft und Praxis – Strategien, Instrumente, Fallstudien. Köln 2002.

Kraemer, W.; Sprenger, P.; Wachter, C. (2001). Learning Services als Bestandteil einer eHR-Strategie. (Learning Services as part of an eHR-strategy). In: Scheer, A.-W. (Hrsg.): Die eTransformation beginnt! Lessons Learned, Branchenperspektiven, Hybrid Economy, M-Business. (22. Saarbrücker Arbeitstagung 2001 für Industrie, Dienstleistung und Verwaltung. Tagungsband). Heidelberg: 2001, pp 191-226.

Müller, M. (1999). Virtual Corporate University – DaimlerChrysler geht neue Wege in Executive Education und Knowledge Management. (Virtual Corporate University – DaimlerChrysler's new way in Executive Education and Knowledge Management). Information Management & Consulting, 14(1999)3, pp. 94-96.

Rüttgers, J. (1997). Hochschulen für das 21. Jahrhundert, Pressedokumentationen des Bundesministeriums für Bildung, Wissenschaft, Forschung und Technologie, Bonn. (Universities for the 21st century. Press documentation of the secretary of education, research, science and technology of Germany, Bonn). http://www.bmbf.de/deutsch/veroeff/pressedok/pressedok97/pd022697.htm, 1997 p. 11.

Scheer, A.-W. (1999). Noch ist der Kuchen nicht verteilt. (The cake is not yet eaten). Information Management & Consulting 14 (1999)1, p. 111.

Scheer, A.-W. et.al. (1998). Wirtschaftsinformatik-Online (WINFO-Line). (Business Information Systems Online (WINFO-Line) In Reinhard, U. & Schmid, U. (Eds.). who is who in multimedia bildung (who is who in multimedia education) (pp. 224-225). Heidelberg 1998.

Töpfer, A. (1999a). Anforderungen an Corporate Universities und die erfolgreiche Zusammenarbeit mit Universitäten. (Requirements for corporate universities and for the successful cooperation with universities). In IQPC (Ed.). Corporate University, Tagungsband, Frankfurt 1999.

250

Töpfer, A. (1999b): Corporate Universities als Intellectual Capital. Personalwirtschaft 26, Heft 7.

Vesely, R.. (1999). Market Gap and Grown. Business 2.0 4(1999)7, pp. 28-31.

Zinow, R. (1999). Wir investieren ein mittleres Vermögen. (We invest a middle fortune). Information Management & Consulting 14(1999)1, p. 118.

Case Studies
Business Information Systems Online /
Corporate University

Wolfgang Kraemer
CEO, imc information multimedia communication AG

Peter Sprenger
Senior Consultant, imc information multimedia communication AG

Summary

Internet-based e-learning applications are an ideal software instrument for the process-oriented support of knowledge logistics. They give employees the functionality they need to organize and maintain different virtual project teams and supply them with the necessary knowledge. Web-based training, virtual cases and strategic online dialogues are assembled to build new knowledge and education products.

The authors of these case studies present concepts and solutions for the introduction and management of virtual (corporate) universities. They show how universities and companies can manage the change from a presence-based knowledge and learning culture to one that is based on multimedia.

Key Words

Corporate Universities, Learning Management, Learning Process Engineering, Learnway, L-Reference-Model, Learning Management System (LMS) CLIX, E-Learning, Education Brokerage, Winfo-Line, Business Information Systems Online, Leadership Development

1. Case Studies

The following case studies provide an introduction to different aspects of the design and management of virtual (corporate) universities.

2. The Inter-University Cooperation Project "Wirtschaftsinformatik-Online" (Business Information Systems Online)

Wirtschaftsinformatik-Online (WINFO-Line) is promoted by the Bertelsmann Foundation and the Heinz Nixdorf Foundation within the framework of the BIG initiative (Bildungswege in der Informationsgesellschaft - Educational Channels in the Information Society). The business information systems institutes and respective departments at the Saarland, Göttingen, Leipzig and Kassel universities are currently developing a virtual learning environment for the academic subject of Business Information Systems on the world wide web (cf. Kraemer & Milius, 1997). Fig. 1 illustrates the concept and the participating partners of WINFO-Line. The project partners bring their core competencies and resources into the education alliance. Core competencies are understood in this context to be contents of teaching courses that are closely tied in with the main areas of research of the respective departments. Each project partner develops multimedia education products and services in line with their respective core competencies. The leveraging of information and communication technologies serves the communication and coordination between the cooperation partners and the learners. In this setting, the I&C technologies replace the typical attributes of a classroom-based university such as lecture halls or university boards.

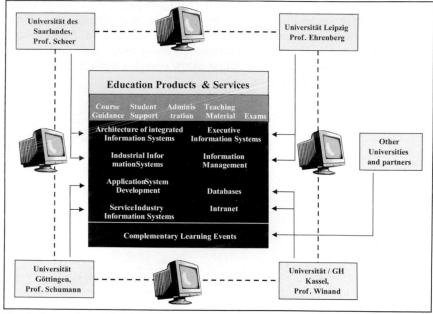

Fig. 1. Conception of the Virtual "Business Information Systems" Field of Study

WINFO-Line proceeds from the approach that the development and introduction of a virtual field of study for Business Information Systems must not perforce lead to an advance change in study courses, but sets out to test how the introduction of multimedia, interactive learning systems can be integrated, what changes are meaningful and how these can be justified.

The students have a free choice of the education products at the WINFO-Line locations Saarbrücken, Leipzig, Göttingen and Kassel. A mutual recognition of the online achievements on the basis of a credit point system is guaranteed. The students thus have the possibility to leverage not only the education products of their home university, but of the other three WINFO-Line project partners as well. Thus the students have a much larger array of courseware at their disposal.

The students' freedom of choice with respect to the leverage of the education products offered in WINFO-Line eliminates the near monopoly power the respective home university has in the past enjoyed. Thus the WINFO-Line project consortium is putting a competitive situation between the different locations to the test. Of interest for the WINFO-Line project team in this setting is the question as to what premises underlie the students' selection of which education products. This allows the team to draw conclusions on the one hand about the learning contents on offer and secondly about the multimedia design of the education products.

Leveraging the WINFO-Line products and services allows students to learn independently of time or place. Whether at home, when travelling or at the office, relevant knowledge can be accessed from almost anywhere in the world. Beyond the decoupling of knowledge conveyance from time and place, the vision or cyber potentials of interactive multimedia systems open up myriad opportunities for the didactic-pedagogical enrichment, revitalization and redesign of learning and knowledge content. Compared to conventional forms of instruction, such as lectures or seminars, multimedia presentations allow complex subject matter to be illustrated in an understandable way.

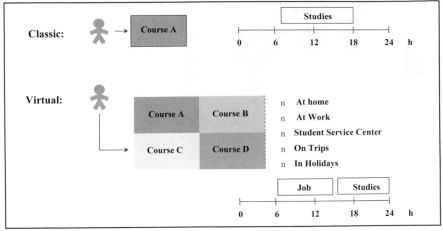

Fig. 2. Time- and Place- Independent Studying

The virtualization of university teaching aims at making access to learning content more flexible for students with the help of the new media and technology, and as a result significantly reducing the length of time needed to complete a course of studies. WINFO-Line distinguishes between two learning scenarios. On the one hand, multimedia courseware can be offered to complement or support traditional classes. Like this, the courseware serves as preparation or deepening of the learning content conveyed in a face-to-face situation. On the other hand, however, it can substitute time- and place-sensitive instruction. This is the case, for example, where multimedia learning systems for self-study completely replace real instruction. However, the two variants are not necessarily mutually exclusive, but can also complement each other. WINFO-Line thus allows students more possibilities to individually plan each semester. For example, it is conceivable that parallel to attending face-to-face courses at their home university, students can in one semester additionally earn credit points from the other WINFO-Line locations, and thus reduce their total study time. Through the increase in the amount of substituting courseware and the subsequent elimination of traditional time constraints for lectures, it is intended, presupposing students' capability for self-organization, to make more efficient use of the available time resources. This aspect also takes into account the fact that more and more students nowadays are forced to supplement state-funded student grants by working part-time to finance their studies. Substituting virtual courseware thus makes learning and working phases more flexible. This is also a way of resolving the conflict of aims between the demand to reduce study times and the improvement of students' financial situation.

The WINFO-LINE education products display the following characteristics:

- Modular structure of the education products

- Each education product is composed of individual learning units. These can be treated independently of each other or be combined: the aim is to eliminate redundancies in the course materials and through knowledge webbing create new, customized instruction

- Uniform structure of the education products

- Each individual learning unit is structured in the same way. The aim is to allow students easy and uniform management of the education products.

The education products and services delivered by WINFO-Line are also used by selected industrial partners in in-house intranets for continuing employee education. This way, it is hoped to establish whether the learning contents and media leveraging for university education differ fundamentally from the needs of corporations or whether the needs of both groups successively converge.

The central idea behind WINFO-Line is that the new media should serve to support learning, but not to make it anonymous and automated. Learning shifts from being a mostly passive and anonymous consumption in a traditional classroom setting to an individual learning process in which learners can self-direct where and at what pace they learn. Receptive learning is thus complemented by active experience and work. It is to be expected that the increasing amount of multimedia-enabled courseware available over the Internet will also lead to an alignment of face-to-face learning at the universities. University staff thus enter into competition for students, who can choose between classroom-based instruction and the courseware available online. The former will in future only be frequented if the students expect attending the courses to bring them added value.

256

2.1 Establishing Electronic Education Markets: Universities as the Providers of Contentware

It is recognizable that through the possibilities offered by information and communication technology, learning contents, separated from the IT realization, take on the characteristics of education or knowledge products. In this context, it has become customary to also speak of contentware (cf. Kraemer & Scheer, 1999). For the compilation and marketing of contentware, it will become necessary to modify the organization of knowledge exchange (cf. Kraemer & Milius, 1997). Companies in the information and communication technology sector will act both as producers and as brokers of multimedia-enabled courseware, for example Deutsche Telekom's Global Learning Initiative, and in this way open up new areas of application and new markets. Education and continuing education institutions will also act as suppliers of contentware, as for example in the case of the private-sector online university imc-university. This leads to growth-generating competition on the education market. Education products and related services will be globally marketable and exportable.

The players in the education market can be subdivided into three groups. On the one hand the consumers of education. This group covers people working in industry, services and administrative functions, unemployed persons who see continuing education as a way of improving their chances on the labor market, self-employed people, students who want to broaden their horizon beyond the scope of knowledge conveyed at universities, but also corporate and non-corporate training institutions as well as universities and colleges that integrate education modules from external sources in their own courseware. The second group are the knowledge providers, who are the suppliers on the education market. This group is composed of universities, colleges and corporations that make their practical experience available in the form of best-practice examples, together with corporate and other training institutes. The third group comprises education brokers who act as brokers between the suppliers and the consumers, as well as assuming the role of mentors and advisers.

The position and role of universities and colleges is still in flux: on the one hand, the possibility exists that universities and colleges buy in multimedia-enabled subjects and courses from other colleges or universities, and thus dispense with building up their own teaching resources; on the other hand, it is conceivable that the universities and colleges themselves assume the role of education brokers, whereby the emphasis here could lie with the choice of education products available on the market and building them into target group-specific curricula. The universities are accorded fairly good chances in this field. Thus, Stanley C. Gabor, for example, concedes: "I would like to suggest that the role of the university in these kinds of activities is very positive because when a company does its own training it is not the same as a university providing the additional dimension of broad thinking and individual development." (Gabor, 1993a, p. 54). The evolution of the education market illustrates what economic potential is available for the providers of media-based education products: „...education is a prime candidate for becoming the ultimate electronic commerce application" (Hämäläinen et.al., 1996, p. 58).

The first step in this direction is to change the way universities and colleges view their role and to develop multimedia courseware within the framework of the virtual university. With this, they will have created the preconditions for becoming competitive on the continuing education market. However, they will only survive if they manage to offer an attractive, market-oriented education program, i.e. one that is geared to the needs of the consumers (Bundesbildungsministerium 1989, p. 79). It is equally important that universities are flexible enough to react quickly and competently to the changing needs of the consumers (Gabor, 1993b, p.15: „The key to continuing studies is its ability to respond broadly and to pursue rapidly.“). For the universities, this means cooperating from the word go, as early as the compilation phase of the knowledge contents, and rethinking their "marketing strategy", which has so far amounted to a near monopoly power in supplying learning content to enrolled students and has not been geared to other candidates for education. A further aim is to link the knowledge providers' core competencies with specialized multimedia services providers, network providers whose infrastructure can be utilized by content and service suppliers, and service providers, who are primarily concerned with vending and delivering products to the final consumers. One possible form of cooperation in this context is a public-private partnership. In order to realize this kind of learning alliance it is necessary to consider the overall increase in knowledge value:

- Content/education providing: Attractive knowledge content is an important success factor in increasing knowledge value. The copyright for high-quality contents generally lies with the educator. The curriculum is worked out by selecting and consolidating the learning content, defining learning goals, selecting teaching methods as well as choosing testing methods. As the availability of multimedia learning content increases, the importance of regulatory, filtering and certification tasks of the educators also grows. The latter is especially relevant, for example, in connection with the mutual recognition of examination achievements in virtual study networks. Thus, educators not only act as curricula developers, they also advise students with selecting multimedia learning contents. Universities, industrial and services companies, corporate, commercial as well as public education and training establishments act as providers of knowledge content. The delivery relationships between these partners may, in turn, differ. For example, universities that already have media-based education services can integrate and consolidate education modules and real-world examples from industrial and services companies into a topic-specific field of knowledge.

- Multimedia production: A simple 1:1 transfer of classical education products such as books or scripts that can be called up via the Internet hardly develops the innovative application potential of multimedia. The development costs for creating and producing multimedia learning contents amount to between 50 and 200 thousand marks per multimedia content hour, depending on the degree of multimediality and the expected professionality, for example with respect to the processing of sound, image, video and animation. One content hour, however, is assumed to be equivalent to one day of face-to-face learning (cf. Kraemer & Zimmermann, 1998, pp. 40-42; Kraemer & Wachter, 1998; Kraemer et.al., 1998b, p. 101). This means that for a one-semester course, at least 30 content hours must be developed. The universities, however, have neither the resources nor the media competencies for realizing this. It therefore seems to make sense that the universities concentrate on specifying the curricula and on the development of multimedia "pre- and intermediate products", and outsource the refining to final products to specialized multimedia producers.

- Network providing: Access to the media-based education products and services presupposes the establishment of a corresponding information and communication infrastructure. These network providers assume the hosting, the upkeep and the maintenance of the technical infrastructure.

- Service providing: Service providers assume the mechanisms of the marketable exchange of services and thus institutionalize an electronic market (On the term electronic markets cf. Schmid 1993) for education products and services. In this electronic market, the exchange relationships between the market partners are illustrated and the interaction processes supported through corresponding services. Apart from vending the education products, service providers also offer tutoring, mentoring and pricing functions. Pricing for knowledge providers and users can be carried out by the service providers on a pay-per-view basis.

The control of all or even parts of this multimedia knowledge value chain opens up the possibility for universities to assume the role of service firms in the education sector. This above all changes the form of the knowledge exchange. The delivery relationships between the universities and students then no longer end with exmatriculation, instead they develop into a lifelong learning alliance. The entire value chain of media-based education products is coordinated in this alliance by education brokers. These learning alliances give rise to completely new tasks and delivery relationships between the players that can be described by means of a customer-supplier scenario as illustrated in Fig. 3.

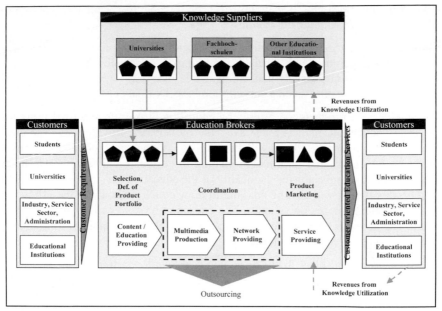

Fig. 3. Education Brokerage

In future, the universities can assume the role of "primary product" developers and suppliers of knowledge content alongside corporate and non-corporate education and training organizations. Here, it is also possible to fall back on the knowledge content that already exists at tertiary level. The precondition, however, is that universities are already aware of the requirements of their potential customers when designing and producing these education modules. This way, a "complementary market" for the knowledge contents of the tertiary sector can be created. The modularity of learning units is a basic requirement in order to enable specialized education products to be assembled and make-or-buy decisions to be taken. Education products on a modular basis have the advantage that they can be reused several times within the framework of similar learning concepts. Therefore it is necessary to define organizational and information technology standards at an early stage with the design and realization of media-based education products, so that education modules from the knowledge providers can be assembled efficiently and tailored to the needs of the respective target group (cf. Kraemer & Zimmermann 1998).

The evaluation, selection and purchasing of education modules is done by education brokers. Since universities currently do not have the capacity for strategic considerations and their realization, the investment decision and the accompanying risk are shifted to the education brokers. With the managerial professionalisation of universities in the direction of service firms and the building up of respective competencies, for example strategic planning, product and customer management, vending, sales etc., it may, however, be possible to anchor the function of education brokerage in the universities.

These education modules are refined and assembled into customized education products in cooperation with specialized multimedia companies. The result is media-based education products that are available over the Internet any time, any where and can be called up on a subscription basis by final consumers.

These education products are offered by education brokers to the final users via electronic education markets made available by network providers. On the electronic education market there will be "hitlists" of the most popular education products, which provide information relating to customer satisfaction and at the same time are an indicator for the quality of the education services on offer. Ultimately, this way it will also be possible to draw conclusions about the efficiency of the suppliers, i.e. the universities. The education brokers will be able to orient themselves towards these evaluation results when selecting suppliers from among the providers of education modules.

The final users can select freely from among the various offers of the education brokers. Successful education services will be in demand, less successful offerings will not survive on the market in the long term. Even the universities will ultimately have to face this competitive situation. This can be used as a yardstick for a market-oriented university ranking that can assist students with their choice of university. Its position on the continuing education market will become a decisive factor for a university's reputation: analyses of customer satisfaction will be carried out that will serve as indicators for the quality of the education programs. The place the university occupies in this ranking will in turn be partly responsible for whether the university manages to engage the loyalty of the best students and professors. Students will only choose those universities with an excellent international reputation. "Universities that are not selected by students must considerably enhance their attractiveness if they want to survive in the long term" (Müller-Böling, 1997, p. 29 [authors' translation]).

A further central point that speaks in favor of universities and colleges assuming an active role in the education markets is the financial aspect. Universities cannot offer their learning content for professional continuing education free of charge, as this would lead to distorted competition. Rather, they must create a pricing system for their continuing education programs that at least strives to cover costs and at the same time provides an incentive to incorporate continuing education as an integral part of their instruction program (Bundesbildungsministerium 1989, p. 77). Such an incentive could consist in income form the vending of contentware flowing directly back to the knowledge providers. Earnings from the vending of the continuing education classes also constitute an additional source of income "in view of the current financial restrictions ... an extremely welcome addition to the basic state financing" (Bundesbildungsministerium, 1989, p. 114 [authors' translation]). This completes the argumentation chain for a refinancing of the universities through the vending of contentware. The financially strong and efficient university of the future is shifting towards becoming an education provider in the international education market.

3. The DaimlerChrysler Corporate University

Deiser explains the need for an inter-subjectively recognized regulative framework for establishing a typology of corporate universities by the fact that many corporations succumb to the temptation "to attach to their in-house or outsourced training departments the grand-sounding label 'university' or 'academy'"(Deiser, no year, p. 41). All the greater, accordingly, are efforts to distinguish, as illustrated in Fig. 4, between the traditional training department and the concept of a corporate university. The shift from training department to corporate university is also in line with the new learning paradigms in the knowledge society. As important key elements for the design, development and management of a corporate university, the loyalty and the commitment of the corporate management, the establishment of a learning alliance with various education partners, the step towards embracing new technologies and the constraint to run the corporate university as an autonomous business unit can be identified. These in-house education academies evolve into strategic nuclear cells of an organization, with the objective of the cost-efficient creation of high-quality learning solutions: "A function or department that is strategically oriented toward integrating the development of people as individuals with their performance as teams and ultimately as an entire organization by linking with suppliers, by conducting wide-ranging research, by facilitating the delivery of content, and by leading the effort to build a superior leadership team" (source not found)

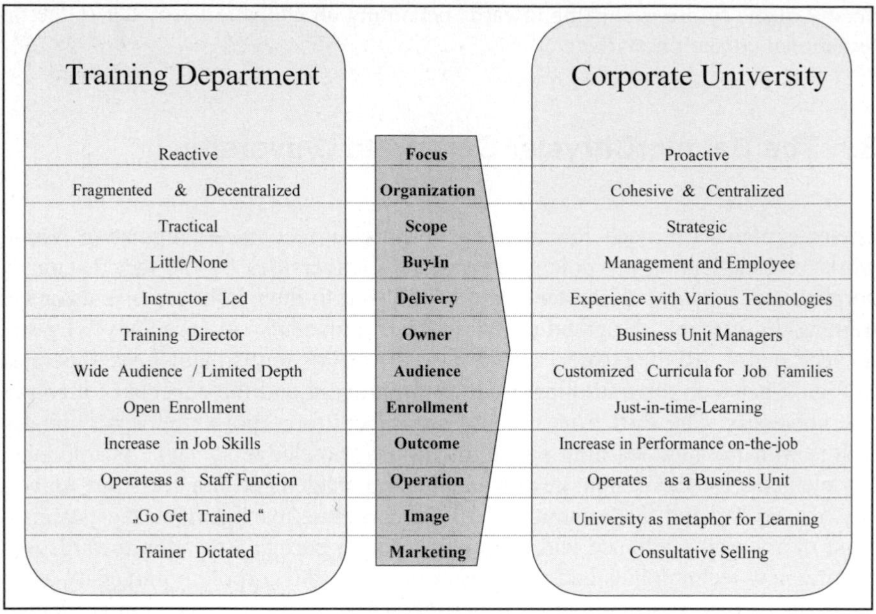

Training Department	Focus	Corporate University
Reactive	**Focus**	Proactive
Fragmented & Decentralized	**Organization**	Cohesive & Centralized
Tractical	**Scope**	Strategic
Little/None	**Buy-In**	Management and Employee
Instructor Led	**Delivery**	Experience with Various Technologies
Training Director	**Owner**	Business Unit Managers
Wide Audience / Limited Depth	**Audience**	Customized Curricula for Job Families
Open Enrollment	**Enrollment**	Just-in-time-Learning
Increase in Job Skills	**Outcome**	Increase in Performance on-the-job
Operates as a Staff Function	**Operation**	Operates as a Business Unit
„Go Get Trained "	**Image**	University as metaphor for Learning
Trainer Dictated	**Marketing**	Consultative Selling

Fig. 4. From Training Center to Corporate University (cf. Meister, 1999, p. 23)

A differentiation between corporate universities can generally be made according to the intensity of the learning activities and how they are linked to the business strategy and processes of the corporation, as well as according to learning scenarios and content (cf. Kraemer 2000).

The DaimlerChrysler Corporate University (DCU) can be classified according to the typology illustrated in Fig. 5.

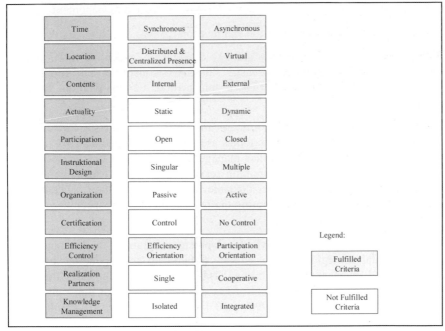

Fig. 5. Typological Features of the DCU

3.1 Objectives, Topics and Target Groups

The DaimlerChrysler Corporate University sees itself as "a strategy-enhancing instrument for the continued global development of the Group and offers best-
practice in executive management development" (DaimlerChrysler 1998, p. 8
[authors' translation]). From this self-image, it is possible to derive the following
objectives that are pursued through the DCU:

- Development of entrepreneurial competencies, or rather, promotion of entrepreneurial understanding

- Widening the deployment spectrum for executive staff by promoting knowledge aimed at extending general management capabilities

- Intensification of the international orientation as well as increased gearing to
  global markets

- Contribution to enhancing the goodwill value through knowledge development
  and dissemination

- Dismantling of organization barriers through international "networking" as well
  as through delegated learning

- Establishment of a global dialogue platform for executive management

- Realization of the corporate vision and mission

With its networked core subjects "strategy dialogues", "executive development" and "innovation and knowledge transfer", the DCU constitutes a learning architecture supported by an intranet-based information, communication, learning, knowledge and content platform.

- **Strategy dialogues** comprise communication sessions within the framework of which "group-relevant, strategic topics are further developed and discussed by the management board and senior management" (DaimlerChrysler 1998, p.14 [authors' translation]). These training sessions are intended to make strategic decisions transparent and understandable, thus increasing their acceptance by senior management and accelerating the realization of the respective plans and measures.

- The objective of the **executive develo**pment program is to promote inter-departmental strategic thinking as well as build up corresponding leadership and general management capabilities. This field thus encompasses the "strategy-oriented further development of key competencies ... [of the] senior management" (DaimlerChrysler 1998, p.10 [authors' translation]). Through programs and training sessions that in part serve to prepare the participants for assuming new managerial functions, but also deal with current group-relevant topics, as well as through best-practice sessions in which current topics, issues, trends and success stories are presented, the knowledge of the Group's senior management is expanded.

- By means of offers from the field of **innovation and knowledge** transfer it is intended to enable all executive members of the Group to continuously apply the existing knowledge about group-relevant issues. The first focus of activities in this context lies on the group-wide extension of "communities of practice". This includes offers of expert forums on strategically relevant Group topics as well as management seminars on the topic of knowledge management.

The education offer of the DCU is geared to the senior executive management of the entire DaimlerChrysler Group, which implies, as shown in Fig. 6, a target group of around 7100 executive staff.

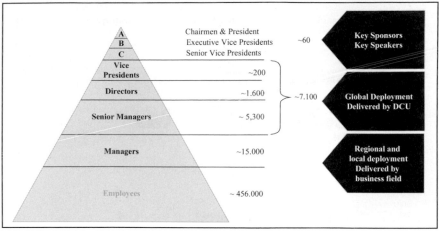

Fig. 6. Target Groups of the DCU (cf. Kraemer & Müller, 1999, p. 522)

3.2 Global Virtual Learning Community

With the face-to-face training sessions of the DCU, approx. 30% of the potential target group is reached per year. The objective of the DaimlerChrysler Online Corporate University ("DCU-Online") is to complement the DCU through online learning information. By leveraging tele-learning and web-based training technologies, digital education products are offered which make it possible to address all executive staff several times a year with respective strategically relevant content and topics. Via the DaimlerChrysler intranet, users of the DCU-Online are supported in their information and learning process 24 hours a day, 7 days a week anywhere in the world. The respective manager can configure an individual learning or communication program and organize it according to his/her personal schedule. In the sense of a "Global Virtual Learning Community", the "DCU-Online" networks the executive staff on a group-wide basis and purposefully promotes an exchange of experience. As described in Fig. 7, face-to-face classes and an intranet-based conveyance of knowledge via the DCU complement and support each other.

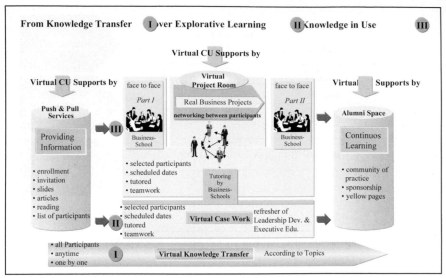

Fig. 7. The DCU-Online in the Context of the DCU (Kraemer & Müller 1999, p. 510)

In the first application scenario the conveyance of knowledge between the DCU-Online participants is supported by synchronous and asynchronous communication (chat, discussion forums, blackboard, e-mail, video conference etc.) "Buddy awareness" refers to the possibility to see at any time which other participants are also online. The information services of the DCU-Online can be subdivided into two groups. Passive information services without a direct reference to a concrete education offer are available to all enrolled DCU-Online participants. Via a glossary, an alphabetical list of all defined key terms is offered. Further information can be called up if the participant has the respective access rights. Via link lists and news, reference is given to topical elements within the intranet and to sources outside the corporate network.

The second group comprises the active information services, so-called "knowledge-push-abo"- services which DCU-Online participants can subscribe to. By defining push objects, every participant determines on what topics information should be delivered. By defining the information logistics, participants can individually determine how much, how often and via what medium information should be sent. Depending on the preferred form of knowledge presentation, various types of media can be selected to receive information on the selected topics.

The second application scenario from Fig. 7 supports the treatment of group-relevant topics at selected times and places. Multimedia-enabled web-based case studies and best-practice results, complemented by additional information and documents from the DCU-Online library for downloading (web-based and computer-based training sessions, business TV reports, video and audio sequences, text files, articles and press releases), are used as preparation for or as a complement to virtual self-study, whereby the participants can support each other and are tutored on a case-to-case basis by tutors from the business schools.

The participants of the DCU-Online not only assume the role of knowledge consumers, but also knowledge deliverers. Demographic profiles and specific knowledge characteristics of the DCU-Online participants are documented in the knowledge maps (Yellow Pages). These profiles are drawn up by the participants themselves when they first enroll. Search functions such as name, position, department, country or field of specialization facilitate the speedy identification of suitable knowledge deliverers. The identification of other in-house knowledge specialists - who, however, do not explicitly belong to the target group of the DCU - and external knowledge deliverers, for example, the teaching staff at the business schools, analysts, trend scouts, consultants, virtual expert networks and communities of practice, is carried out via so-called Blue Pages.

From the combination of DCU face-to-face programs with the DCU-Online intranet-based learning and knowledge platform, the third application scenario from Fig. 7 can be described.

The programs are implemented in the localities of the respective business schools. In virtual learning groups, the knowledge transfer is continued in the staggered, multi-stage programs with the support of teletutors from the business schools. After completion of the programs, the participants are transferred to the DCU-Online's virtual Alumni Space. This ensures the prolongation of the participants' learning activities in the sense of continuous learning. The creation of this informal network pursues the aim to anchor strategically relevant topics in the Group on a continuous and long-term basis.

4. References

(no author) (1998) Europäer entdecken das Online-Training. (Europeans discover Online Training). ComputerZeitung, no year (1998)1/2, p. 1.

(no author) (1997). Eine private Universität im Internet wirbt mit Gewinnen für Aktionäre (A private university woos with profits for ist shareholder in the internet). FAZ – Frankfurter Allgemeine Zeitung, dated 31.10.97, No. 253, p. 26.

Bundesministerium für Bildung und Wissenschaft (Ed.) (1989). Förderung der Zusammenarbeit zwischen Hochschule und Wirtschaft: Abschlußbericht. (Promotion of the cooperation among universities and commerce.) Bad Honnef 1989.

DaimlerChrysler AG (Ed.) (1998). Informationsbroschüre zur DaimlerChrysler Corporate University (Information brochure of the DaimlerChrysler Corporate University). Stuttgart, 1998.

Kraemer, W. (2000). Corporate Universities - Ein Lösungsansatz für die Unterstützung des organisatorischen und individuellen Lernens. (Corporate Universities – A solution for the support of organizational and individual learning). ZfB – Zeitschrift für Betriebswirtschaft Supplement 3/2000, pp. 107-129.

Kraemer, W. et.al. (1998b). Online-Wissensvermittlung für SAP-Projektteams. (Online training for SAP project teams). Information Management & Consulting 13(1998)4, p. 101.

Kraemer, W. et.al. (1998c). Virtuelles Lehren und Lernen an deutschen Universitäten - Eine Dokumentation (Virtual education and learning in german universities – a documentation.) In Bertelsmann Stiftung/Heinz Nixdorf Stiftung (Eds.) 2. Edition, Gütersloh 1997.

Kraemer, W. & Milius, F. (1997) Der Virtuelle Campus: Bildungsdienstleistungen für lernende Organisationen. (Virtual Campus – Education Services for learning organizations). In Scheer, A.-W. (Ed.) Organisationsstrukturen und Informationssysteme auf dem Prüfstand. (Organizational structures and information systems). (pp. 51-81) Heidelberg 1997.

Kraemer, W. & Müller, M. (1999). Virtuelle Corporate University - Executive Education Architecture und Knowledge Management (Virtual Corporate University – Executive Education Architecture and Knowledge Management.) In Scheer, A.-W. (Ed.). Electronic Business und Knowledge Management - Neue Dimensionen für den Unternehmungserfolg (Electronic Business and Knowledge Management – New dimensions for corporate success). (pp. 491-525). Heidelberg 1999.

Kraemer, W. & Scheer, A.-W. (1999). Erschließung neuer Märkte für deutsche Hochschulen durch die Entwicklung medienbasierter Contentware. (Open up new markets for german universities by the development of media-based contentware.). In Küting, K & Langenbucher, G. (Eds.): Internationale Rechnungslegung, Festschrift for Prof. Dr. Claus-Peter Weber on his 60th birthday. (pp. 13-36). Stuttgart 1999.

Kraemer, W. & Sprenger, P. (2002). E-Learning step by step – Von der Strategie zur Implementierung. (E-Learning step by Stepp – from strategy to implementation.). In: Köllinger, Ph.: eLearning in deutschen Unternehmen. Fallstudien, Konzepte, Implementierung (E-Learning in german companies. Case studies, concepts, and implementation). Düsseldorf 2002.

Kraemer, W.; Sprenger, P.; Scheer, A.-W.: eLearning-Innovationspotenziale erkennen und -Projekte gestalten. (Recognizing e-Learning innovation potentials and managing e-Learning projects). In: Hohenstein, A.; Wilbers, K. (Hrsg.): Handbuch E-Learning. Expertenwissen aus Wissenschaft und Praxis – Strategien, Instrumente, Fallstudien. Köln 2002.

Kraemer, W.; Sprenger, P.; Wachter, C. (2001). Learning Services als Bestandteil einer eHR-Strategie. (Learning Services as part of an eHR-strategy). In: Scheer, A.-W. (Hrsg.): Die eTransformation beginnt! Lessons Learned, Branchenperspektiven, Hybrid Economy, M-Business. (22. Saarbrücker Arbeitstagung 2001 für Industrie, Dienstleistung und Verwaltung. Tagungsband). Heidelberg: 2001, pp 191-226.

Kraemer, W. & Wachter, C. (1998). Web-based Training: Konzepte und Best-Practice-Beispiele im SAP-Umfeld (Web-based training: concepts and best-practice examples in the SAP environment.) In imp (Ed.). Effiziente Schulungskonzepte für R/3-

Projektteams und R/3-Endanwender, Tagungsband. (Efficient training concepts for R/3 project teams and R/3 users. Conference Report) Heidelberg 1998.

Kraemer, W. & Zimmermann, V. (1998). Architektur und Komponenten von Internet-basierten Bildungsprodukten (Architecture and components of net-based education products.) In Synergie (Ed.). 4. IT-Trainings-Kongreß, Tagungsband. Bonn 1998.

Meister, J. (1999). Survey of Corporate Universitity Future Directions. New York 1999.

Müller-Böling, D. (1997). Mehr Freiheit für die Universität (More freedom for the university). Die Zeit, issue 21.02.97. p. 29.

Schmid, B. (1993). Elektronische Märkte (Electronic Markets). Wirtschaftsinformatik 35(1993)5, pp. 465-480.

Epilog:
Jazz Improvisation and Management

August-Wilhelm Scheer
Founder and Chairman of the Supervisory Board, IDS Scheer AG

1. Jazz Bands as a Model for Modern Management Teams

Jazz music is based on improvisation. Jazz soloists improvise new melodies on the spot that fit into the prescribed structure of a theme. In extremely short time spans the soloist makes irreversible decisions regarding the pitch of the note he will play, the expression with which he will play it, and its rhythmic placement. At the same time, each note has an immediate effect on the next. The soloist's playing is also influenced by his fellow players.

In a good jazz combo, experts play together, constantly communicating at the same time and place. Each player listens to the others, particularly to the soloist, and responds to the harmonic and melodic development of the solo while the rhythm group's (generally piano, bass and percussion) harmonic and rhythmic figures spur the soloist on. In this way jazz improvisation creates highly intense communication among the players, which in turn leads to great creativity.

In the management world, on the other hand, the concept of improvisation carries negative connotations. When someone says, "We have to improvise," he means that things have not gone as planned, and the team has to scramble. Proper planning, however, requires a stable environment in which to implement the plan, or at least one that can be accurately assessed. On the other hand, planning is problematic in a turbulent environment in which the conditions change quickly. The importance of planning, therefore, is generally de-emphasized in newer books on business management. There are numerous examples of the exact opposite of a planned action happening, yet turning out successful. The Japanese motorcycle company Honda planned its entry into the American market with heavy motorcycles (cf. Mintzberg, 1999). An advance team was sent to the US, but with such a limited budget that they brought along light motorcycles to get around. Domestic names such as Harley Davidson already had a significant presence in the US market, which made it difficult for Honda to break into the same market segment. The team noticed, however, that light bikes could be successful and spontaneously altered the original strategy, garnering Honda a successful entrée into this market segment.

The software firm SAP initially developed the enterprise resource planning (ERP) system R/3 to be a solution for mid-sized companies using the IBM AS 400 platform (cf. Plattner/Scheer/Wendt/Morrow, 2000). The system architecture was changed due to performance problems, which led to the development of a system based on the technical platforms of the client-server architecture with non-specific interfaces such as UNIX and SQL that is now used primarily by large companies around the world.

These examples demonstrate that successful business management is not grounded in doggedly pursuing planning decisions once they have been made, but rather in the alert recognition of new developments and the quick, masterful reaction to them.

The CEO of LEGO Company reportedly introduced his executive board as a jazz combo (cf. Lewin, 1998), in order to show that the band represents the ideal for a modern management team. The way in which creativity comes about in a jazz band is a model for contemporary management behavior.

A team mindset is instrumental in jazz as well as in management. Putting together a team with as diverse a base of core competencies and strong communication using the synergies among the competencies are the key to success.

The relationships between jazz improvisation and management are increasingly the subject of scientific inquiry. A number of interesting examples and insights were reported in a special edition of Organization Science magazine (vol. 9, no. 5, Sept./Oct. 1998). Both jazz musicians and organizational scientists participated in the study. Several examples in this article are taken from that study.

2. At the Edge of Chaos

Modern organizational theory pursues approaches that take into account the dynamics within companies and in markets, and that overcome inflexible organizational principles. This approach is made concrete in the concept of emergent processes. Emergent processes, which can be described as self-developing processes, are driven by employees' ideas, even though these employees may not be entrusted with these tasks. They do not emerge from hard and fast strategies, but rather arise spontaneously in response to the situation. Strategic developments are therefore more often perceived as logically interpretable in hindsight and not as previously planned.

Jazz combos are a source of constant emergent processes. Fig. 1 shows a simple depiction of how connectivity – which can also be interpreted as communication and interaction – and the intensity of control with an organization determine the possibility for flexible, creative behavior (cf. Tomenendal, 2002, and Scholz, 2000). If the organization has many rules, then all work processes are set. If, at the same time, there is little communication between the participants in the organization, so that no informal organization can form outside the constraints of order, then the organization stagnates. It is unable to react quickly to unexpected situations (lower-left section of Fig. 1). If, however, no rules exist, so that during intense interaction everyone talks over everyone else without reaching an outcome, chaos rules (top-right section of the figure). The shaded area represents a corridor of balance between minimal constraint and maximum communication in which an organization is well positioned to react flexibly and creatively. Area II describes a more stable organization that has not yet stagnated, but does not demonstrate spontaneity and flexibility as in the shaded area.

274

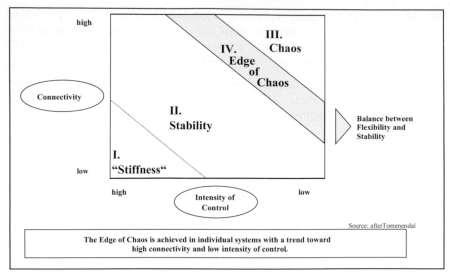

Fig. 1. Balance of Flexibility and Stability

High connectivity among members of the group creates a positive trend because the individual members exhibit relatively wide-ranging core competencies.

The individual musicians in a jazz band are specialists on their respective instruments. Suddenly exchanging instruments among the musicians would not work. Although each one has only a rudimentary understanding of the others' instruments, taken as a whole, they can produce some interesting results. This, of course, requires close communication in order to bring each instrument into the whole. A management group functions the same way. An executive board consists of specialists in law, technology, human resources, production and business activities. As a rule, the problem to be solved requires several of these competencies, which must be brought into the solution process from the group. Similarly, this is only possible with close cooperation. The corridor is therefore reached by a trend toward minimal constraint and maximum connectivity.

Synergies among the various core competencies of the musicians can only blossom when they meet at the same time at the same place. Each player practicing in his own music room without contact with the others would not produce a joint effort. The same is true for assembling the various core competencies of a management team. Developing a corporate strategy by which each member of the board creates a concept for his area and putting it at the other members' disposal is hardly a cooperative strategy. Only when the strategy team comes together in a strategy meeting, the arguments collide with each other, and emotional and heated discussions or even disputes come about, is the atmosphere ripe to create the Edge of Chaos, to advance truly new ideas. Strategy meetings should therefore not be governed by detailed agendas or limited speaking times, but rather include plenty of time for expanding discussions. Results must naturally be summarized in concrete form afterwards.

Challenges set in the corridor can be met ideally by a jazz band. The coordination or need for control within a jazz combo is relatively low. The most important rules are set by the melody of the piece to be played. It is build measure by measure, e.g. in 12-measure sections in the Blues, or 32-measure sections in a typical song. Fig. 2 shows the melody of the well-known "A Night in Tunisia" by Dizzy Gillespie, which is composed in a 32-measure AABA structure. The A-sections consist of eight measures with a set harmonic structure; the B-section, the so-called middle section, also consists of 8 measures. The harmonies of the piece are also shown in Fig. 2. Good jazz improvisers know the harmonic progressions of the standard melodies, i.e. the melodies that jazz musicians play regularly, from memory. During an improvisation the soloist simply follows the structure of the piece; within the harmonic progressions he can devise new melodies on the spot.

One could say that jazz combos produce the greatest creative efforts with minimal constraint.

Fig. 2. Dizzy Gillespie's "A Night in Tunisia"

There is the danger of breaking out of the corridor and lose some creativity. The perception that coordination via a prescribed song structure was too regimented led to the development of free jazz, in which the group improvises practically without a set structure. Because all the musicians in the group did this at once, the interaction was somewhat excessive. Many listeners felt they had erred into chaos. The music was difficult to understand, that is, it was hard to recognize the structure governing the musical events. Because a set structure was not wanted, understanding that structure is necessarily difficult. The participants' communication and the team's ability to play off one another in turn created similarities in repetitive tone colors and collage. Nonetheless this musical direction was short-lived and found its way back to a more structured form. As viewed from the perspective of our model, it had left the top-right section of Fig. 1 and returned to the corridor at the Edge of Chaos.

Leaving the corridor by the lower border means that more and more rules are creeping in or that the constraints are constant but communication is decreasing. This danger appears when a jazz group has been together for a long time and the members know each other inside out. At that point hardly anything unexpected beyond the tried and true happens. Even as fantastic a group as the Oskar Peterson Trio eventually found a successful style to call its own and then simply copied themselves. Recordings from 1985 are essentially no different from recordings made in 1975. Miles Davis, on the other hand, has had multiple effects in developing styles. In the mid-1940s he and Charlie Parker collaborated with others to develop bebop; in the late '40s his famous recording of "Birth Of The Cool" gave birth to cool jazz; in 1959 modal jazz came about with the recording of "Kind of Blue. And later he collaborated with such musicians as Herby Hancock and Chick Corea to create rock jazz.

To prevent a group from stagnating in the repetition of clichés, they must be confronted with new situations in which what they have practiced cannot be applied. It is said that Miles Davis essentially told his musicians not to practice outside of concerts since he was paying them to "practice" on stage; they were not to reel off practiced riffs during concerts but rather be creative and have the courage to try something new. John Coltrane surprised his musicians with completely new harmonic progressions in which they could not use the phrases that had become second nature. A well-known anecdote tells of pianist Tommy Flannigan being confronted by John Coltrane's harmonies in the cult piece "Giant Steps" and having great difficulty assimilating them during a recording session. This recording was released and is considered one of the milestones of jazz. Miles Davis' recording of "Kind of Blue" is another example (cf. Kahn, 2001).

Davis arrived at the recording with only rough sketches of the pieces to be played. The musicians were confronted with a new style of harmonic structure and melodies and had to give their utmost in concentration. This intensity was a source of overwhelming inspiration.

A management team operating in the corridor on the Edge of Chaos also runs the risk of losing the desired balance. Completely disorganized behavior, in which no one accepts the communal need for coordination, leads to contradictory decisions and actions – to chaos. Applying stereotypes ("I already know what he's going to say, so I don't need to listen.") conceals the danger of stagnation. The team can also find new impetus when it is confronted with situations that are out of the ordinary. At a British Airways management seminar, the beds in the hotel were reportedly removed and the participants were forced to sleep in airplane seats (cf. Lewin, 1998), which assuredly led to heated discussion as to how to make the seats more comfortable. It is conceivable that the managers of a software company could be forced to use their own software in a strategy seminar.

Maintaining the balance between flexibility and stagnation is a constant battle.

3. Feel for Time

Jazz is alive in its swing feel. Duke Ellington drove this point home in the title "It Don't Mean a Thing (If It Ain't Got That Swing)." Swing is difficult to describe. It is a rhythmic feeling of tension that never is never resolved during the piece. There are scientific treatises that attempt to explain swing as a conflict between duple meter and triple meter. All attempts at explanation to this point are unsatisfactory, however. The fact remains, you feel it or you don't. While other tensions in music, such as dissonance, are immediately resolved with a consonance, the feeling of swing is maintained throughout the entire piece, making it a source of inspiration for jazz soloists. When agreement rules, when the sense of timing of all the musicians meld together as it were, unexpected explosive and matchless performance can result. One example of this is Ellington's Big Band's 1956 performance at the Newport Jazz Festival. "Diminuendo and Crescendo in Blue" elicited just such an unrepeatable feeling of tension and density, which inspired tenor saxophonist Paul Consalves to play an impromptu solo lasting 28 choruses. The band's bassist at the time, Jimmy Woodie, once told me that the band had arrived the day before from Florida, where they had played the piece for the first time in years. Count Basie's famous drummer Joe Jones was standing near the band at the concert in Newport. He had a newspaper in his hand and kept the beat with it in his other hand. The atmosphere was so dense and ecstatic as to constantly draw out new ideas from the soloists.

Keeping a group in that tension, constantly inspiring them to new ideas, getting them to swing – that is the art of being a top manager. The emotional congruence of the members of a group can be more important than their individual intellectual performance. Opportunities for this emotional congruence must be created. Breaking out of the hectic, day-to-day routine and holding a weekend seminar in an unfamiliar environment and relaxed atmosphere can be helpful. Moderators and drivers (like Joe Jones at the Newport festival) can strengthen the creative processes.

A sense of timing plays a huge role in jazz – in many respects. Anyone who has ever learned to play an instrument knows that it takes a long time to master the instrument. A good example is the story of a woman who was a fan of Benny Goodman's elegant clarinet music and bought her son a clarinet, expecting that the house would be filled with melodious clarinet music from then on (cf. Lewin, 1998). The boy was soon relegated to the garage, however, where he was told to practice in the car . . . with the windows closed. Virtuosity takes time. Managers too must take note of this sentence. The often expect to see the success of a reorganization the next day, ignoring the long learning processes of a new organization.

Innovation does not fall out of the sky. We spent many years doing preliminary research at my research institute before we could develop our software product ARIS. In contrast, many dot.com companies in the last few years believed they could quickly transfer an idea that was working in the US to Germany and build a successful company based on it. They failed miserably.

All the great jazz musicians practiced like mad. It is said that saxophonist John Coltrane left the stage during long percussion solos so he could practice in his dressing room. Charlie Parker too practiced melodies in all keys to the point of obsession, improvising on them. Even the greatest talent is worthless without the diligence and desire to master the dexterity needed.

You cannot only give of yourself, you also have to find fresh input. Musicians such as Miles Davis and Sonny Rollins had long breaks in their careers during which they did not play. Miles Davis retreated into his house for several years (cf. Davis, 2000) to live an introverted life. (There was a dark side to his behavior that was characterized by drugs and sexual escapades.) Sonny Rollins retired to devote himself to the discovery of new worlds of music, spending time on New York City's Williamsburg Bridge playing into the wind to perfect his tone (cf. Wilson, 1991).

Pianist Thelonious Monk lost his license to perform in New York because of a misunderstanding at the beginning of the 1950s. He used this unintentional departure from performing to compose.

Nor is a manager's supply of creativity and dynamism inexhaustible. They must also renew and expand their knowledge via a sabbatical in order to achieve new motivation and creative power.

The soloist's feeling of tension caused by swing is strengthened by other factors. For example, many pieces of music have a so-called break whereby the last few measures of the melody are open for the soloist to jump in with his solo. The best known of these is "A Night in Tunisia," which is cited above (Fig. 2). After the verse and before the improvisation there is an interlude that repeats a rhythmic figure with slightly varied melodies seven times, ending with two eighth notes that prepare the break for the soloist. The soloist has four measures without accompaniment and on the downbeat of the fifth measure must coordinate with the rhythm group as they rejoin the mix. These four measures can be an eternity. Spurred on by the rhythmic phrases, he flies off the end of the ski-jump with the last two eighth notes and has to time his jump so that he lands securely and precisely on the fifth measure. During these four measures, however, his individual feel for timing might beat differently from that of the continuing rhythm. It is not easy to reach an agreement between his own rhythmic perception and the combo's, that is, to find the beat from the previous section – the beat the drummer will resume when the combo enters again. The soloist must fill the four measures and is busy developing ideas and preparing for his landing; he is concentrating on many processes at once that can distract him from the continuing beat.

Managers know this feeling as well. When a company is in crisis, time flows differently. The managers are looking for a quick, efficient decision, find themselves in a situation rife with exceptions, and often think that their environment is marching to the same beat. This, however, is not the case. The environment continues to march at its old pace and is not in the least interested in the company's exceptional situation. Crisis managers look for quick answers to questions in order to have a foundation on which to base the next decision. Time slips through their fingers if liquidity is jeopardized. The environment is unaffected by all that. It is imperative that managers maintain calm in stressful situations and synchronize themselves with the pace of their environment so they do not cause further damage. Being constantly assailed by partners looking for quick answers or decisions can ignite resistance. Reacting too hastily can overinterpret developments. Synchronizing the inner clock with that of the environment is therefore an important factor.

4. Creativity in Improvisation

Improvisation does not imply indiscriminate drivel but rather creating meaningful melodies spontaneously; the soloist must tell a musical story, which naturally is based on a collection of tried and true building blocks. Just as an orator giving a spontaneous talk, a jazz musician must also command a strong vocabulary and rhetorical techniques. He must have a comprehensive knowledge of theory and jazz harmonies, be able to play the melodies of many standard pieces from memory (often in many different keys), as well as know their harmonic progressions. Additionally, he can practice melodic phrases known as patterns, which fit certain combinations of chords. This, however, is only the vocabulary that must be linked spontaneously to create new, meaningful sentences. The chorus must also be fashioned so that the listener understands the intent of the solo. If the musician simply lines up technically impressive tricks one after another like so many exercises, he achieves only randomness. It no longer matters if the fourth chorus is played after the third, or if it could just as easily have been played before the third. The listener would not recognize the construction of the solo.

Perfect solos, as played, for instance, by Chet Baker, Gerry Mulligan, or Miles Davis, are not like that; each chorus builds on the previous ones, and every note has meaning.

Playing more notes per second is no measure of the artistic value of a jazz solo. Musicians such as Chet Baker, Miles Davis, and Gerry Mulligan make an impression by creating melodies using fewer notes.

Managers giving presentations should follow these rules. Less is often more. An onslaught of slides in which umpteen transparencies march across the overhead or beam through the In-Focus projector in a short time makes no impression; clear statements that build logically on one another sell the argument. The higher the manager's position on the ladder, the fewer slides he should use, relying instead on his charisma and personality.

Although intellectual effort, such as adhering to the harmonic development of the piece, is required in improvisation, emotionality also plays a large role. A third component is motor function, which pianists or saxophonists must possess in the form of well trained dexterity. Coordinating these three components, intellect, emotion, and motor function, requires tremendous effort. The emotional side merits particular emphasis. The excitement and tension created by rhythm and swing help the soloist to construct intelligent sentences from the available building blocks of words in the blink of an eye. Much of this happens subconsciously, that is, the soloist immerses himself in the rhythmic and melodic feeling of the piece and lets his heart lead him. He is often surprised himself when he hears a recording of his solo. It is not unlike a centipede, which does not know what a difficult feat of coordination it is for it to walk; it simply walks. If it knew the complexity of the task, it would surely stumble.

Too much intellectual control during a solo can be a hindrance. The soloist holds fast to the practiced patterns and the actual release of spontaneous and unexpected ideas is missing.

Successful entrepreneurs often act based on their gut. Instinct and anxiety are probably indispensable for successful entrepreneurship. Of course, gut feelings are not only inborn but also the result of many-sided experiences, which have become behavior patterns that can be called up spontaneously when the situation demands. Risky decisions, interviews, and forming partnerships with other companies are often decided on gut reactions.

Reacting quickly and coming up with interesting remarks often has to do with humor and wit. Long-winded stories are to be avoided; short anecdotes with a point carry the day. Jazz musicians typically have a feel for wit and humor. The number of jokes about musicians proves it. The shortest one may be:

Three jazz musicians walk past a bar . . . .

Another points up the difficult economic circumstances of jazz musicians:

<u>Question:</u> *How does a jazz musician become a millionaire?*

<u>Answer:</u> *By starting out as a billionaire.*

Humor and wit are not usually abundant commodities at the executive level. Business suits tend to elicit a more formal atmosphere. In this setting a shot of *esprit* and an eye to the punch line could often render affected behavior more personable and communicative.

5.　Jazz as a Learning Process

Jazz is a genre that lives on the continuous learning of the musicians. Each one listens to the others, plays the soloist now, the accompanist then. Because surprising situations are constantly arising, misunderstandings and even mistakes are possible. Jazz is therefore not *musique accomplie*; rather creativity predominates. You cannot be afraid of mistakes if you plan to try new things. Mistakes are part of the learning process; only those who never try something new never make mistakes.

This realization is valid in management as well. Not every idea for a new project is successful. The cancellation of a product is not a failure, but only proves that during product development new discoveries arose that corrected the original assumptions. The courage to open new markets or develop new product ideas must be seen as a positive. Naturally every idea should be analyzed critically, but it should not be killed off from the beginning with overly critical arguments.

In the first hundred years of jazz, changes in style followed closely on each other's heels. We have already mentioned that Miles Davis influenced the development of new musical directions four times during his lifetime.

Being on the crest is only satisfactory in a long career if the style is stable over time. Simply running after each new wave is not enough, since the other artists who created the wave have already established themselves.

In the high-tech world, the ability to open oneself to new waves of technology and help develop them is a requirement for the long-term survival of a company. Companies that led one technological wave only to sleep through the next have disappeared from the market despite their great successes. SAP, on the other hand, has been successful in being on the leading edge of four technological waves with its R/1, R/2, R/3, and mySAP.com products. Digital Equipment, on the other hand, was once the second-largest hardware manufacturer in the world, leading the wave of networked PCs, but overlooking the wave of standardized operating systems, database systems, and networks, only to be bought out by Compaq.

6. Competition and Creativity

The athletic competition among jazz musicians is another driving force for enthusiasm and inspiration in music. To some extent competition is an integral part of a band. Count Basie's band, for instance, employed representatives of various tenor sax schools, whose solos amounted to intense "tenor battles" as to who was the best, that is, the most imaginative and expressive, musician. Students of tenor saxophonist Colman Hawkins represented a sonorous, vibrato-rich style of playing, which Lester Young and his students preferred a more restrained style. In the beginning Hershel Evans and Lester Young were the established combatants; later it was Frank Foster and Frank Wess. The famous Miles Davis Sextet employed polar opposites Cannonball Adderley, a saxophonist associated with the blues, and John Coltrane with his more modern style.

Musicians can kindle each other in jam sessions, inspiring each other to true flights of fancy. They also try to outdo one another in "trading fours," i.e. in playing four measures of a chorus in alternation. In impresario Norman Grantz's Jazz at the Philharmonic concert tours, combos were put together in such a way that the battles became the highlights of these concerts. This competition is not hurtful; rather it serves to provide inspiration. The players absorb other players' ideas, incorporating them into their own improvisations, resulting in a high degree of communication.

Agreeable harmony need not rule the day among members of a management team; competition in this context can improve the team's performance. It may not, however, be harmful; individuals should not desire overmuch to make their mark at the expense of other team members. Conceptual differences of opinion and differing temperaments can, however, increase creativity and promote new strategies. Drivers and preservers within a team can temper overly risky maneuvers while at the same time averting the danger of stagnation.

7. Right and Wrong are Neighbors

Once in a while a wrong note makes its way into an improvisation. A wrong note means that the pitch sounds harsh in the momentary harmonic context. In the rule, the neighboring pitches a half-step above and below the wrong note sound "right" in the harmonic context. If the player is successful in playing the neighboring pitch as soon as he perceives the "wrong" note, the listener hardly notices it as the wrong note becomes nothing more than a passing note and the "correct" note is emphasized.

Similarly, in the aforementioned examples of Honda's introduction in the US market and the development of SAP R/3, the "right" strategy lay adjacent to the "wrong" one.

If the Honda team had retreated from the US following the miscarriage of its original plan to introduce heavy motorcycles to the market, its subsequent market success with light bikes would have been precluded. They were correct in recognizing the US as a foreign market; the right product was only a half-step away from the original one.

The R/3 development team could have given up when they discovered that their original product was not technically appropriate. But in this case as well, the right solution was immediately next to the wrong one. The were correct in developing a new software for decentralized computer systems, but the proprietary AS 400 platform was wrong and the neighboring solution with the UNIX operating system and other neutral standards was the correct choice.

This knowledge means that what appears to be a failure need not necessarily be final, but must be analyzed to determine its causes, and the neighboring variants checked carefully to find the pearl inside the oyster.

There is another possible reaction to playing a wrong note: simply emphasize it all the more, intentionally sustain it, or repeat it several times. Because there is actually no such thing as a wrong note, only unaccustomed sounds in a particularly harmonic context, one can interpret the note as intentional. Harmonic "ouches" are customary in music because they can be resolved subsequently in more pleasing harmonies. Intentionally emphasizing a wrong note in order to resolve it is therefore an acceptable technique. This process is reminiscent of the cynical sentiment, which is therefore to be avoided, "Telling an outright lie and then insisting on its veracity as good as makes it true."

8. Relaunching Old Products

A song that serves as the basis for an improvisation consists of a metrical structure, harmonic structure, and the melody. Variations on metrical structure are relatively limited in jazz. The 32-measure bar form AABA consisting of four 8-measure phrases dominates. Some harmonic progressions are particularly well suited to improvisation. So that the melodies that fit them do not get old, new melodies are often composed to these harmonies. The best known is the blues form, to which untold melodies have been composed, followed by "rhythm changes," based on George Gershwin's "I Got Rhythm." The harmonic progressions in this form are also simple and offer the improviser many opportunities to develop the melody. Many melodies have developed to far beyond the original theme of "I Got Rhythm" that they hardly seem related, for instance Sonny Rollins' "Oleo" or Charlie Parker's "Thriving on a Riff."

Developing new products based on successful existing products is called a relaunch in corporate marketing. In a relaunch, a proven product concept is modernized with a new marketing profile or updated technically. Consumers pick up on what they are accustomed to and have accepted in order to obtain something attractive in the form of new properties or image factors.

9. The Jazz Solo as a Dynamic Process

When a jazz musician starts his solo, he doesn't know the whole construction, let alone the melodic arch he will play. Moreover, he begins with a phrase that may build on the last notes of the previous solo. The next phrase is then influenced by the preceding one and is either the answer to the first measures he played or a development of these measures. As he continues, this process repeats itself while picking up and incorporating impetus from the other players. Basically, a solo is a self-perpetuating development process in which the musical thoughts build on their predecessors and become the basis for those that follow.

Similarly, the history of a company develops from decisions and strategies that build upon one another. Not every decision or strategic direction must be ideal in itself; rather their contribution to the overall development is important. Wrong decisions, after they have been corrected, can have made sense as they contributed to increasing knowledge. A phrase in a solo that in and of itself may demonstrate little intuition can spur the musician on to give his next musical thought more content.

10. Can Improvisation be Learned?

Just as classical composition is taught in conservatories and composition can be learned, so can jazz improvisation be learned. The contradiction of the creative energy of a composer or jazz improviser constitutes nothing more than the expansion of what has already been learned with new sounds. Improvisers can learn just as orators learn the words, grammar, and word combinations that they put together in a spontaneous speech according to their emotional state and intentions. Prepared speeches are generally boring, while an extemporaneous speech delivered with passion can be interesting.

The jazz musician's grammar is the study of jazz harmony. Whereas an orchestral player in a classical orchestra primarily requires the ability to play from the printed page and therefore does not absolutely need a comprehensive knowledge of harmony, this knowledge is of utmost importance to jazz musicians and brings them a step closer to the requirements placed upon composers in the classical world. In addition to the harmonic structure – the grammar – the vocabulary is also important. There are untold snippets of tunes, usually constrained to one to four measures, that can be practiced for individual chords or chord progressions. Learning these melodic bits from memory and stringing them together mechanically in a solo is by no means a successful improvisation. Musical depth, surprising ideas, and emotional involvement are all missing.

An important instrument for a manager is his influence on his team or his customer's decision-makers using rhetoric. Phrases learned in rhetoric classes are often immediately recognized as just that and are rarely convincing, but more often expose the speaker for what he is. Charisma is also the result of the life experience of a personality. In exactly this way the jazz soloist's overall personality determines his musical depth. There is no argument that Louis Armstrong played technically and musically brilliant solos in the 1920s that are still worth listening to today. His trumpet playing in his later years, however, also holds the highs and lows of his life and is worlds apart from his earlier style in the strength of its musical expressivity. The same is true for musicians like Miles Davis or Sonny Rollins. Precisely because the individuality of musical expression is in the foreground of jazz there are unique opportunities for incorporating the musician's individual personality.

Dynamism, aggression and technical brilliance are not the be all and end all of management. Great entrepreneurial personalities radiate social competence, life experience, and autonomy. Living and learning go hand in hand.

11. References

Barrett, F. J. "Creativity and Improvisation in Jazz and Organizations: Implications for Organizational Learning" in Organization Science, vol. 9, no. 5, Sept./Oct., (1998), pp. 605-622.

Davis, M. Autobiography. Heyne Verlag, Munich, 2000.

Kahn, A. Kind of blue: The making of the Miles Davis masterpiece. Granta Books, London, 2001.

Lewin, A. Y. "Jazz Improvisation as a Metaphor for Organization Theory" in Organization Science, vol. 9, no. 5 (1998), p 539.

Mintzberg, H. Strategiesafari. Eine Reise durch die Wildnis des strategischen Managements [Strategy Safari. A trip through the wilds of the strategic management]. Ueberreuter Verlag, Vienna, 1999.

Plattner, H.; Scheer, A.-W.; Wendt, S.; Morrow, D. S. Hasso Plattner im Gespräch: Dem Wandel voraus [A conversation with Hasso Plattner. Ahead of the change]. Galileo Press, Bonn, 2000.

Scheer, A.-W. Unternehmen gründen ist nicht schwer ... [Start-ups are easy, but...]. Springer Verlag, Berlin et al., 2000.

Scholz, C. Strategische Organisation: Multiperspektivität und Virtualität [Strategic organization. Multiperspectivity and virtuality]. 2nd expanded edition. Verlag Moderne Industrie, Landsberg/Lech, 2000.

Tomenendal, M. "Virtuelle Organisation am Rand des Chaos – Eine komplex-dynamische Modellierung organisatorischer Virtualität" ["Virtual organization at the edge of chaos. A complex-dynamic modelling of organizational virtuality"]. Dissertation, Saarbrücken, 2002.

Wilson, P. N. Sonny Rollins. Sein Leben, seine Musik, seine Schallplatten [Sonny Rollins. His life, music, and recordings]. Oreos Verlag, Schaftlach, 1991.

Organization Science, vol. 9, no. 5, 1998.

Appendix: The Authors

Abolhassan, Dr. Ferri
Co-Chairman and CEO,
IDS Scheer AG
Altenkesseler Strasse 17
66115 Saarbrücken
Germany

Beham, Maria
Topic Manager, Information Management,
Siemens AG Österreich
Erdberger Lände 26
A-1030 Wien
Austria

Brady, Ed
IT Director,
American Meter Company
300 Welsh Road
Building One
Horsham, PA 19044-2234
USA

Broinger, Kurt
Business Process Framework Executive,
Siemens AG Österreich
Erdberger Lände 26
A-1030 Wien
Austria

Devečka, Andrej
CEO ZSE Bratislava,
Západoslovenská energetika, a.s.
Culenova 6
816 47 Bratislava
Slovak Republic

Doganov, Dr. Boyan
Director,
Republic of Bulgaria Ministry of Health,
The World Bank Project Management Unit
54a, Vassil Levski Bld.
1000 Sofia
Bulgaria

Ester, Ralf Martin
Managing Director,
IDS Scheer Schweiz AG
Industriestrasse 50a
CH-8044 Wallisellen/Zürich
Switzerland

Exeler, Steffen
Senior Consultant,
IDS Scheer AG
Altenkesseler Strasse 17
66115 Saarbrücken
Germany

Gulledge, Dr. Thomas R.
Professor and Director,
George Mason University
Enterprise Engineering Laboratory,
MS 2E4
Fairfax, VA 22030-4444
USA

Hammer, Dr. Michael
President,
Hammer and Company
One Cambridge Center
Cambridge, MA 02142
USA

Hayes, Philip

President,
Teamworks Partners, Inc.
Washington, DC USA

P.O. Box 22359
Nashville, TN 37202
USA

Jost, Dr. Wolfram

Member of the Executive Board,
IDS Scheer AG

Altenkesseler Strasse 17
66115 Saarbrücken
Germany

Kalenda, Václav

Senior Consultant,
IDS Scheer CZ

Pekarska 7
155 00 Praha 5
Czech Republic

Kaltenbrunner, Gabriele

Product Consultant,
IDS Scheer Austria GmbH

Landstraßer Hauptstraße 71/2
A-1030 Wien
Austria

Kirchmer, Dr. Mathias F.W.

President and CEO IDS Scheer, Inc.,
CEO IDS Scheer Japan,
Member of the Extended Executive
Board,
IDS Scheer AG

1205 Westlakes Drive
Berwyn, PA 19312
USA

Kraemer, Dr. Wolfgang

CEO,
imc information multimedia
communication AG

Altenkesseler Strasse 17
66115 Saarbrücken
Germany

Lotterer, Alexander

Consultant,
IDS Scheer, Inc.

1205 Westlakes Drive
Berwyn, PA 19312
USA

Lovšin, B. Sc., M. Eng. Peter

Work Process Development Department,
Slovenian Railways

Kolodvorska 11
SI - 1000 Ljubljana
Slovenia

Low, Siow Hoon

Senior Manager,
MMI Holdings Ltd

29 Woodlands Industrial Park E1
01-16, Lobby 3, Northtech Building
Singapore 757716
Singapore

Nachev, Prof. Gencho

General Manager,
Republic of Bulgaria Ministry of
Health,
National Health Insurance Fund

54a, Vassil Levski Bld.
1000 Sofia
Bulgaria

Naidoo, Trevor
Consulting Services Manager,
IDS Scheer, Inc.
1205 Westlakes Drive
Berwyn, PA 19312
USA

Nattermann, Dr. Peter
Senior Manager, Product Consulting,
IDS Scheer AG
Altenkesseler Straße 17
D-66115 Saarbrücken
Germany

Obrowsky, Walter
Project Manager, ARIS Coporate
Service,
Siemens AG Österreich
Erdberger Lände 26
A-1030 Wien
Austria

Orbanić, D. Sc. Josip
Manager of Quality and Environment
System,
Slovenian Railways
Kolodvorska 11
SI - 1000 Ljubljana
Solvenia

Pustatičnik, M. Sc. Iztok
Project Manager,
ERA, d.d.
Prešernova 10
SI - 3504 Velenje
Slovenia

Rieger, Christian
Vice President,
IDS-Gintic Pte Ltd
Unit 109, Innovation Ctr, Blk 2
16 Nanyang Drive
Singapore 637722
Singapore

Scharsig, Marc
Director, Consulting Services,
IDS Scheer, Inc.
1205 Westlakes Drive, Suite 270
Berwyn, PA 19312
USA

**Scheer, Prof. Dr. Dr. hc. mult.
August-Wilhelm**
Founder and Chairman of the Supervi-
sory Board,
IDS Scheer AG
Altenkesseler Strasse 17
66115 Saarbrücken
Germany

Schober, Florian
Project Manager,
IDS Scheer Schweiz AG
Industriestraße 50a
CH-8304 Wallisellen
Switzerland

Simon, Georg
Director Product Consulting,
IDS Scheer, Inc.
1205 Westlakes Drive, Suite 270
Berwyn, PA 19312
USA

Sirota, Ján

Product Director,
IDS Scheer SK

Kutlíkova 17
851 02 Bratislava
Slovak Republic

Sobocan, Miro

Managing Director,
IDS Scheer Slovenia d.o.o.

Letaliska cesta 27
SI - 1000 Ljubljana
Slovenia

Sprenger, M.A. Peter

Senior Consultant,
imc information multimedia
communication AG

Altenkesseler Strasse 17
66115 Saarbrücken
Germany

Talsma, PMP Kelly

Project Manager,
Quixtar

5101 Spaulding Plaza
Ada, MI, 49301-9174
USA

Wilms, Sven

Member of the Extened Supervisory
Board,
IDS Scheer AG

Altenkesseler Strasse 17
66115 Saarbrücken
Germany

ARIS Easy Design

The Tool for Newcomers to Business Process Engineering

The Tool for Newcomers to e-Business Engineering

In this era of e-business, ARIS Easy Design is the tool for those professionals just getting started in business process optimization. Key operations take place in specialized departments of a company. The target group for ARIS Easy Design, with its modeling, presentation and reporting functions, are the employees in technical departments and occasional users who can document their (process) knowledge in the form of graphic models. ARIS Easy Design is the ideal solution for enterprise-wide utilization.

Multiple User Levels

ARIS Easy Design is an organizational tool for the design of e-business processes that is easy to use for both beginners and professionals. The target group for ARIS Easy Design, with its modeling, presentation, and reporting functions, are the employees in technical departments and occasional users who document their knowledge in the form of graphic models.

You would like to know more about ARIS Easy Design?

IDS Scheer would like to provide you with ARIS Easy Design Demo CD.

Please fill out the Fax Reply Sheet below and we will get back to you!

IDS SCHEER

FAX REPLY SHEET: + 49(0)681 – 210 12 31

As offered in the book Business Process Change Management – ARIS in Practice I would like to order the Demo CD ARIS Easy Design.

Please send it to:

Company / Organization: _____

Title, First Name, Last Name: _____

Position: _____

Street: _____

ZIP-Code, City: _____

Country: _____

Telephone: _____

Fax: _____

E-Mail: _____

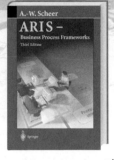